a custom publication

Kirk Perry
English Composition
WR 121
Portland Community College - Cascade

Pearson Learning Solutions

New York Boston San Francisco
London Toronto Sydney Tokyo Singapore Madrid
Mexico City Munich Paris Cape Town Hong Kong Montreal

Senior Vice President, Editorial and Marketing: Patrick F. Boles
Senior Sponsoring Editor: Natalie Danner
Development Editor: Mary Kate Paris
Editorial Assistant: Jill Johnson
Marketing Manager: Brian T. Berkeley
Operations Manager: Eric M. Kenney
Production Manager: Jennifer Berry
Rights Manager: Jillian Santos
Art Director: Renée Sartell
Cover Designers: Kristen Kiley, Blithe Russo, Tess Mattern, and Renée Sartell

Cover Art: "Gigantia Mountains & Sea of Cortes," by R.G.K. Photography, Copyright © Tony Stone Images; "Dime," courtesy of the Shaw Collection; "Open Book On Table Edge w/Pencil," courtesy of PhotoAlto Photography/Veer Incorporated; "Open Book On Table Near Table's Corner," courtesy of Fancy Photography/Veer Incorporated; "Scrabble Pieces and a Die," by G. Herbst, courtesy of PlainPicture Photography/Veer Incorporated; "Binary codes in bowls," by John Still, courtesy of Photographer's Choice/Getty Images; "Close-up of an open book," courtesy of Glowimages/Getty Images; "College Students Sitting At Tables," courtesy of Blend/PunchStock; "Red and blue circles," courtesy of Corbis Images; "Laptop screen showing photograph of landscape," courtesy of Martin Holtcamp/Getty Images; "Apples flying," courtesy of Arne Morgenstern/Getty Images.

Printed in the United States of America.

Please visit our website at *www.pearsoncustom.com.*

Attention bookstores: For permission to return any unsold stock, contact us at *pe-uscustomreturns@pearson.com.*

Pearson Learning Solutions, 501 Boylston Street, Suite 900, Boston, MA 02116
A Pearson Education Company
www.pearsoned.com

1 2 3 4 5 6 7 8 9 10 XXXX 14 13 12 11 10 09

ISBN 10: 0-558-28051-X
ISBN 13: 978-0-558-28051-2

Contents

Narration

Comparison

Definition

Narration

Throughout most of our lives, we read, write, listen to, and tell stories. Our religious and cultural values are often passed on through stories, as is our history. And of course, stories have always entertained us.

Narration is the act of relating a story; the story itself is called a *narrative.* While narrative is a complex form with a variety of purposes, most meaningful narratives, particularly essays, have a point. Fairy tales, religious stories, and historical narratives are all told in order to drive home a point—about behavior, belief, or national identity. To convey that point, the writer of narrative must pay attention to the *conventions* of narration.

Often, the point of a narrative essay is stated or implied in the first paragraph, but sometimes the writer waits until the end. The clarity of that point is dependent on the writer's ability to *show* the reader what happens rather than simply *tell* about the action. A writer can achieve this goal by paying careful attention to organization, detail, and word choice. Organization in a narrative is almost always chronological; the story is told in a specific time sequence. Such organization allows readers to follow the action without becoming confused. Organization is supported by clear, precise details; readers must be able to envision the action in order to understand the story. These details are created by descriptive word choice, or diction. The following narrative, from Maya Angelou's "Graduation," illustrates these features:

> *Amazingly the great day finally dawned and I was out of bed before I knew it. I threw open the back door to see it more clearly, but Momma said, "Sister, come away from that door and put your robe on." I hoped the memory of that morning would never leave me. Sunlight was itself young, and the day had none of the insistence maturity would bring it in a few hours. In my robe and barefoot in the backyard, under cover of going to see about my new beans, I gave myself up to the*

> *gentle warmth and thanked God that no matter what evil I had done in my life He had allowed me to live to see this day. Somewhere in my fatalism I had expected to die, accidentally, and never have the chance to walk up the stairs in the auditorium and gracefully receive my hard-earned diploma. Out of God's merciful bosom I had won reprieve. Bailey came out in his robe and gave me a box wrapped in Christmas paper. He said he had saved his money for months to pay for it. It felt like a box of chocolates, but I knew Bailey wouldn't save money to buy candy when we had all we could want under our noses. He was as proud of the gift as I. It was a soft-leather-bound copy of a collection of poems by Edgar Allan Poe, or, as Bailey and I called him, "Eap." I turned to "Annabel Lee" and we walked up and down the garden rows, the cool dirt between our toes, reciting the beautifully sad lines.*

Notice how Angelou organizes her story in simple chronological order: she goes to the door in the early morning, relishes the sweetness of the day, is joined by her brother, receives his gift, and then recites poetry with him as they walk through the garden. The author also brings readers into the narrative through the use of specific details: the warmth of the day is "gentle," Bailey's present is wrapped in Christmas paper and feels like a box of chocolates, the book is bound in soft leather, and she and her brother feel "the cool dirt between [their] toes." Both organization and detail, supported by precise diction, make the scene real to readers.

While narration may be the primary rhetorical strategy employed in an essay, it may also be used in an essay employing a different strategy. For example, a persuasive essay might use a brief story to support its argument, or a cause-and-effect essay might use a narrative to illustrate a sequence of events. In these cases, narrative is used as an *example*. In fact, one could argue that the narrative "Graduation" is an extended example of the evils of segregation and the resilience of African Americans in the face of discrimination. As the excerpt illustrates, regardless of how it is used, an effective narrative will command the reader's attention.

Description

If you have ever tried to recreate for someone who has not seen it a sunset over the ocean, an unusual animal in a zoo, or a building with unique architectural features, then you know how important description is. When a writer describes something, she or he creates an image with words. In order to do that, the writer must also be a careful observer of the world around him or her. Sometimes writers offer readers *objective* descriptions, recreating for the reader, in precise detail, the image as it might appear to anyone observing it. But sometimes writers create *subjective* descriptions, reproducing the image as it appears to the writer, including the writer's emotional response to the image. A sunset, for example, might be described purely in terms of the colors of the sky, the size of the sun relative to the horizon, and the time required for the sun to sink below the horizon. Subjectively, on the other hand, the sunset might be described as infusing the sky with hopeful illumination, or instilling in the observer a sense of peace, or creating in the observer an awe of nature.

In "Graduation," Angelou describes class valedictorian Henry Reed in objective terms, as "a small, very black boy with hooded eyes, a long, broad nose and an oddly shaped head." She describes the days preceding graduation, however, in subjective terms: "The faded beige of former times had been replaced with strong and sure colors. . . . Clouds that lazed across the sky were objects of great concern to me. Their shiftier shapes might have held a message that in my new happiness and with a little bit of time I'd soon decipher."

Whatever the description, there must be a *purpose* for presenting it, an impression that the writer wants to leave with the reader. That purpose might be simply to create an image in the reader's mind, as Angelou does in her description of the days before her graduation. But description may also be used in conjunction with other rhetorical strategies, for example, to describe an effect. Angelou does this in "Graduation" when she describes her feelings as she listens to the white speaker denigrating her people: "The man's dead words fell like bricks around the auditorium and too many settled in my belly. . . . Every girl in my row had found something new to do with her handkerchief. Some folded the tiny squares into love knots, some into triangles, but most were wadding them, then pressing them flat on their yellow laps." The vivid detail of this description shows the reader how Angelou and her classmates felt rather than simply telling the reader about it. The good writer of description will try to arouse the reader's senses—of sight, smell, touch, taste, hearing, and movement. Unlike narrative, a description rarely involves a time sequence (unless the thing described involves time) and arrangement is spatial rather than chronological. But like narrative, a description must include clear details if it is to be successful. A good description, as the Angelou examples illustrate, will leave the reader with the sense that he or she has experienced the image along with the writer.

Example

If you have ever been asked to explain a theory or concept so that the average person can understand it, then you are aware of the importance of example. Examples are particularly useful in making abstractions concrete. A political scientist might offer the examples of Great Britain and Israel to explain the parliamentary system of government; a psychologist might offer the examples of particular patients to explain certain neuroses; a literary critic might offer the examples of Edith Wharton and Henry James to explain the concept of realism and naturalism. For examples like these to be effective, they must be relevant to the concept being explained. The examples must also be typical and not an exception; the concrete example must truly be representative of the concept.

In "Graduation," Maya Angelou presents the concept of segregation and racial discrimination through the example of Edward Donleavy's speech to the graduates, but within that example, she also provides specific examples of what segregation meant to her and her friends. When Donleavy sings the praises of African American athletes like Olympic star Jesse Owens and world heavyweight champion Joe Louis (known as the "Brown Bomber"), the young Angelou thinks,

> *Owens and the Brown Bomber were great heroes in our world, but what school official in the white-goddom of Little Rock had the right to decide that those two men must be our only heroes? Who decided that for Henry Reed to become a scientist he had to work like George Washington Carver, as a bootblack, to buy a lousy microscope? Bailey was obviously always going to be too small to be an athlete, so which concrete angel glued to what country seat had decided that if my brother wanted to become a lawyer he had to first pay penance for his skin by picking cotton and hoeing corn and studying correspondence books at night for twenty years?*

Angelou's examples of African Americans facing overwhelming obstacles in their quest for success are obvious to the reader. Not all examples are so obvious, however, and thus the writer who uses examples must be careful to explain or analyze how they relate to some concept. It is only when the example is as clearly relevant as Angelou's that the writer can leave it to the reader to figure out the connection.

As with other strategies of development, example requires that the writer use specific details in order to *show* rather than simply *tell.* Thus, Angelou uses names such as Jesse Owens, the Brown Bomber, and George Washington Carver; she also uses details such as the concrete angel glued to the country seat, as well as specific images of hoeing corn and picking cotton. All of these details help make the example clearer and more concrete in readers' minds. Example leaves the reader with a specific impression of the concept being explained; to that end, organization is crucial.

Sometimes a writer will use different examples to illustrate specific features of a concept. One patient, for example, might illustrate the idea that obsessive-compulsive disorder often interferes with an individual's capacity to perform at work, while another patient illustrates the impact of the disorder on family life. Or a writer may move from the least significant example to the most significant, and sometimes even from most to least significant. In Angelou's piece, the less important (to her) example of Henry Reed is presented first, with the more important example of her brother Bailey presented second—and in greater detail.

While example can be used as the primary rhetorical strategy of an essay, often it is used in support of other strategies. Writers of *argument* often use examples to provide *evidence* in support of a position, while writers of *definition* use examples to *clarify* the term being described. Often, a narrative is an extended example: "Graduation" might be considered, in its entirety, an example of the evils of segregation and the resilience of African Americans. Whatever the strategy, it is essential to remember that whether it is used as the primary or secondary strategy, example must always contribute to the specific point that the writer is trying to make.

Comparison and Contrast

One of the easiest ways for us to understand a thing is to consider it alongside something else, emphasizing either similarities, differences, or both. We are always making comparisons: of products, in order to determine which is the best buy; of restaurants, in order to determine which is most appropriate for a given occasion; of candidates for office, in order to determine which will best serve our interests. What these three examples illustrate is that we use comparison and contrast not for its own sake but to support a point. Thus, if you use this strategy in your writing, you should always keep the *point* of your comparison in mind.

Usually, the two subjects under comparison will have something in common; that common feature will constitute the basis for comparison. When you were deciding on a college, for example, you may have considered a large public university, a small private college, or a community college. These kinds of schools are quite different, but they all share at least one common basis for comparison: they are all institutions of higher education. When making comparisons, it is important to maintain the *same basis* for each subject being compared. For example, if you scrutinize the liberal arts *curriculum* of the first two schools, but then focus on the *location* of the third school, you have undermined your comparison by changing the basis. By focusing on the same qualities of each subject, you maintain that basis.

In "Graduation," Maya Angelou uses comparison and contrast briefly when she refers to Mr. Donleavy's speech praising the accomplishments of both white and African American children in the school district. In response to his words, she thinks, "The white kids were going to have a chance to become Galileos and Madame Curies and Edisons and Gaugins, and our boys (the girls weren't even in on it) would try to be Jesse Owenses and Joe Louises." In this case, the basis for comparison is the field in which children might hope to succeed.

Later in the essay, Angelou contrasts her appreciation of "Lift Ev'ry Voice and Sing," known as "the Negro National Anthem," to her response to Patrick Henry's "Give me liberty or give me death" speech:

> *Each child I know had learned ["Lift Ev'ry Voice"] with his ABC's and along with "Jesus Loves Me This I Know." But I personally had never heard it before. Never heard the words, despite the thousand of times I had sung them. Never thought they had anything to do with me. On the other hand, the words of Patrick Henry had made such an impression on me that I had been able to stretch myself tall and trembling and say, "I know not what course others may take, but as for me, give me liberty or give me death."*

Angelou's basis for comparison in this example is the child's misunderstanding of the relevance of famous words.

The Angelou examples represent *comparison* and *contrast* used in support of other rhetorical strategies (e.g., *narrative* and *persuasion*). At times, however, an entire essay can be written using the comparison-and-contrast strategy. In such essays, appropriate organization is essential. Most writers recognize two primary methods of organization for comparison and contrast: point-by-point or subject-by-subject. Consider the educational institutions mentioned earlier, for example: if you were to write an essay on the topic, you might organize your comparison by looking at curriculum, cost, and location of the institutions. For each of these categories, you would consider each school in turn. This is a point-by-point organization. But you might also choose to consider the individual school, focusing on curriculum, cost, and location of each before moving on to a discussion of the next school. This organization is subject-by-subject. In outline form, the two organizations would look like this:

Point-by-Point	**Subject-by-Subject**
Curriculum	Large Public University
large public university	curriculum
small private college	cost
community college	location
Cost	Small Private College
large public university	curriculum
small private college	cost
community college	location
Location	Community College
large public university	curriculum
small private college	cost
community college	location

Occasionally, a writer will combine the two organizing strategies. Regardless of the strategy you choose, establishing a *pattern* for the comparison will make the essay clearer and easier for the reader to understand.

Whether a comparison is used in support of another rhetorical strategy or presented as the primary strategy in an essay, the same guidelines apply: the comparison must have a *point,* it must operate on a common *basis,* and (in the case of an essay) it must be *organized* appropriately.

Classification and Division

When we walk into a supermarket, we see individual items classified into categories: produce, dairy, bakery, and the like. And when we pursue a college major, we find the field of study divided into individual courses. Given the amount of information we must process every day, it would be difficult indeed to negotiate our way through life without classification and division. As a rhetorical strategy, classification and division allows writers to make sense of what might otherwise seem to be random ideas.

While the two strategies share similar principles, classification involves sorting items into categories, moving from the individual to the group, while division breaks a whole into parts, moving from group to individual. Thus, classification emphasizes similarities among items in a group, while division emphasizes differences. Such analyses allow us to understand how parts relate to wholes and how things work. In the supermarket, for example, products that share certain qualities are placed together: cheese, milk, cream, and butter can all be classified as dairy products. As a college major, the broad subject of American history is divided into courses that focus on different time periods: colonial, federal, Civil War, twentieth-century. Both classification and division help people to put information into a coherent order by identifying relationships either between parts and the whole or among parts.

For classification and division to be successful, the same *principle* must be used throughout the analysis. Think about how confusing it would be if the supermarket manager classified some products by *purpose*, some by *price*, and some by *brand*! There would be one aisle for dairy products, another for products over three dollars, and another for Kraft products. This failure to employ a uniform principle would result in some dairy products being in the dairy aisle, some in the over-three-dollar aisle, and some in the Kraft aisle. Shoppers would have an extremely difficult time finding their way around the store. Similarly, an essay dividing heads of state might use the categories of monarch, prime minister, and president. To also introduce male and female as categories would confuse the reader; no coherent order would emerge, because some of the categories are based on title and some on gender.

Maya Angelou uses classification and division to a limited extent in "Graduation." When she divides the general category academic honors, she uses a principle commonly used in elementary schools: "No absences, no tardiness, and my academic work was among the best of the year." And when she divides academic work into categories, she uses a performance principle more appropriate to a twelve year old: "I could say the preamble to the Constitution even faster than Bailey. . . . I had memorized the presidents of the United States from Washington to Roosevelt in chronological as well as alphabetical order."

In addition to ensuring that the same principle is used in classifying and dividing, it is also important to keep the *level* of the subclasses *parallel* and the treatment *equal.* Monarch, prime minister, and president, for example, are all parallel titles—each is a general category for a head of state. To introduce Ronald Reagan as a parallel category would not make sense; he represents a further subcategory, individual heads of state. Finally, the identification of categories should account for every significant item in the group: to neglect to include presidents as a class of heads of state would make for an incomplete treatment of the subject.

When Angelou classifies the opportunities open to children in the South in the 1940s, she creates two parallel classes: white children and African American children. She then creates several subclasses for each of the primary classes, treating each subclass equally: "The white kids were going to have a chance to become Galileos and Madame Curies and Edisons and Gaugins, and our boys (the girls weren't even in on it) would try to be Jesse Owenses and Joe Louises." The subclasses for white children include a variety of exalted occupations, including inventors, scientists, and painters; the subclasses for African American children are only two, both of them athletic: runners and boxers. That Angelou uses names of famous people keeps her classes equal; had she written, "inventors and women scientists and Gaugins," she would not have been treating the classes equally. And her limiting the classes open to African American children to only two accounts for what at that time constituted almost the only options open to those children.

As with other rhetorical strategies, classification and division must have a purpose. Dividing heads of state into subclasses allows a student of political science to examine different governmental systems; dividing a college major into separate courses allows a student to understand relationships among courses; classifying supermarket products into categories allows shoppers to find easily what they are looking for. Angelou's use of classification and division allows her readers to understand the mind of a twelve year old and to appreciate the limited options open to African American children as compared to white children in the 1940s. What matters is not whether the purpose is simple or profound; what matters is that there is a purpose.

Definition

Definition of terms and concepts is essential to the clear understanding of any subject. If the reader is to share common ground with the writer, then the writer has the responsibility to clarify his or her meaning to the reader. In some cases, definitions are *formal*: short, dictionary-like explanations of a term. If you were asked to define *psychoanalytic criticism*, for example, you might offer a brief definition: it is a school of criticism that relies on Freud's theories of personality development in analyzing literary works. Frequently, however, definitions are *extended*, requiring a paragraph, an essay, or even an entire book to clarify the meaning of a term or concept. If you were expected to apply psychoanalytic criticism to a novel, for example, you would need to explain the intricacies of the school, and this would require an extended definition. In this case, your entire essay might constitute an extended definition, with the novel serving as an example of this particular school of literary criticism.

Maya Angelou provides a brief definition of "A & M (agricultural and mechanical schools)" in "Graduation": they were schools "which trained Negro youths to be carpenters, farmers, handymen, masons, maids, cooks and baby nurses." When she is wallowing in the self-loathing brought on by Donleavy's speech, she engages in an extended definition of humanity, especially for African Americans:

> *It was awful to be a Negro and have no control over my life. It was brutal to be young and already trained to sit quietly and listen to charges brought against my color with no chance of defense. We should all be dead. I thought I should like to see us all dead, one on top of the other. A pyramid of flesh with the whitefolks on the bottom, as the broad base, then the Indians with their silly tomahawks and teepees and wigwams and treaties, the Negroes with their mops and recipes and cotton sacks and spirituals sticking out of their mouths. The Dutch children should all stumble in their wooden shoes and*

> *break their necks. The French should choke to death on the Louisiana Purchase (1803) while silkworms ate all the Chinese with their stupid pigtails. As a species, we were an abomination. All of us.*

Both formal and extended definitions comprise three parts: *term*, *class*, and *differentiation*. The *term* is that which is being defined, psychoanalytic criticism, for example. The *class* identifies the general category in which the term is found—in this case, a school of literary criticism. *Differentiation* distinguishes the term from other terms in the same class, such as feminist criticism, formalist criticism, and Marxist criticism. If the definition is to be effective, all three parts must be clear, complete, and detailed. Depending on the audience, the language used in the definition can be either technical or general. An audience unfamiliar with Freud's theories, for example, would need to have the terms *id*, *ego*, and *superego* explained in lay terms, while an audience familiar with his work would be able to understand a technical explanation that assumed knowledge of these key terms. Although Angelou's extended definition of humanity is metaphorical rather than literal, it is still possible to identify term (races), class (humanity), and differentiation (whites, Indians, Negroes, Dutch, French, and Chinese).

Writers employing this rhetorical strategy must be careful to avoid what is known as *circular definition*, in which the term is simply restated in different words. For example, "Organic food is food that is grown organically" is a circular definition. The definition does *nothing* to help the reader understand the concept!

Using definition as a strategy can be interesting because it almost always involves other rhetorical strategies. Example is frequently used in defining terms: a song by the Mighty Mighty Bosstones, for example, might be used to help define *ska music*. Comparison and contrast might be used in the same definition, contrasting ska to heavy metal music. A definition of contemporary music in general might involve division and classification, dividing it into ska, rap, reggae, and other categories. In addition, a definition might use metaphor or analogy, comparing the term imaginatively to something else, or negation, stating what the term is not.

Angelou employs some of these strategies in "Graduation." She uses examples of African American working tools (mops, recipes, and cotton sacks) to help define her race. She contrasts the aspirations of white children and African American children to help define opportunity. And finally, she defines the human species by dividing it into different races.

Definition may be used for its own purpose, or it may support another purpose—*persuasion*, for example. Regardless of purpose, however, a good definition must be detailed, complete, and presented in such a way that the audience can understand it.

Process Analysis

Whenever we follow instructions in putting something together (a bicycle, for example) or try to explain why something happens (leaves changing color in autumn, for example), we engage in *process analysis*. Process analysis breaks a process down into logical steps; for example, in putting the bicycle together, it is necessary to construct the entire handlebar unit before attaching it to the frame of the bike. Such an analysis has a purpose, as does any good process analysis. A *directive process analysis* (constructing the bicycle) tells readers *how to do something*, while an *informative process analysis* (leaves turning color) *explains a phenomenon*. If either type of process analysis is to be effective, the steps must be delineated in clear detail. (Anyone who has tried to put a bicycle together using inadequate instructions can attest to the need for clear detail!)

In "Graduation," Maya Angelou recounts the usual process followed during an assembly at the Lafayette County Training School:

> *The school band struck up a march and all classes filed in as had been rehearsed. We stood in front of our seats, as assigned, and on a signal from the choir director, we sat. No sooner had this been accomplished than the band started to play the national anthem. We rose again and sang the song, after which we recited the pledge of allegiance.*

The significance of clearly delineated steps becomes clear in this piece immediately following the recitation of the pledge of allegiance, when the next step in the process is changed:

> *We remained standing for a brief minute before the choir director and the principal signaled to us, rather desperately I thought, to take our seats. The command was so unusual that our carefully rehearsed and smooth-running machine was thrown off. For a full minute we fumbled for our chairs and*

> *bumped into each other awkwardly. Habits change or solidify under pressure, so in our state of nervous tension we had been ready to follow our usual assembly pattern: the American national anthem, then the pledge of allegiance, then the song every Black person I knew called the Negro National Anthem. All done in the same key, with the same passion and most often standing on the same foot.*

The significance of a well-defined process is illustrated in this passage when Angelou and her classmates become convinced that this disruption signals "worse things to come," which of course is precisely what happens when the white politician Edward Donleavy addresses the assembly.

The process outlined by Angelou is a chronological one, but processes can be simultaneous or cyclical as well. An example of a simultaneous process might be the signs of autumn: leaves turn color, daylight becomes shorter, and temperatures drop. Autumn itself, of course, is part of the cyclical process of changing seasons. Understanding a process allows us to see an object or an event in a new way, sometimes helping us understand how something happens and sometimes helping us understand why it happens.

When using process analysis as a strategy, it is important to appreciate the audience. Angelou, for example, knows that her readership extends beyond African Americans who grew up in the rural South, so she explains the song that follows the pledge of allegiance. In recreating the sequence accurately, she allows her audience to understand the unease felt by the graduates when the process is disrupted. If Angelou knew that her audience was unfamiliar with American patriotic rituals, she would also have to define the term *pledge of allegiance*. The concept of a national anthem is a fairly universal one, but many countries do not feature a pledge of allegiance to the flag. Similarly, a biologist explaining the signs of autumn would have to define terms such as "photosynthesis" for a general audience.

As evidenced in Maya Angelou's "Graduation," process analysis need not constitute the primary rhetorical strategy for an essay. Essays outlining scientific or mechanical processes often use this as a primary strategy, but essays featuring narration, description, definition, and other rhetorical strategies may also employ process analysis. Regardless of whether the strategy is primary or secondary, following the guidelines above will ensure that the process analysis is effective.

Cause and Effect

Whenever you try to answer the question "why?" you are engaging in cause-and-effect analysis. Sometimes the analysis is simple: If a car won't start on a winter morning, chances are the battery is too weak to get a cold engine moving. But often the analysis is complex: In 1991, when war broke out in the Balkans after the fall of the Soviet Union, the causes ranged from economics, to religion, to nationalism, to ideology. Cause and effect can be used in support of another rhetorical strategy, for example, *persuasion*. Or it can be used as the primary rhetorical strategy in an essay. Whether the strategy is used as a primary or supporting strategy, or whether it focuses primarily on causes or effects, the features of the strategy remain the same.

One of those features is the identification of causes as either *immediate* or *remote*. In the case of the Balkans, for example, one of the immediate causes of the fighting was ethnic divisions among inhabitants of the area. These divisions became apparent shortly after the end of Soviet domination of the region, and thus were easily recognizable as a cause of the conflict. But the situation cannot be understood fully without considering remote causes, some of which go back to the redrawing of national boundaries following World War I. Since this cause is found in the history of a conflict that occurred over sixty years earlier, it is not so obvious as the more immediate causes. Nonetheless, remote causes are sometimes even more significant than immediate causes in explaining an effect.

Maya Angelou analyzes both immediate and remote causes in "Graduation." The immediate cause, for example, of the graduates' discomfort at the beginning of the graduation ceremony is a change in the order of the program:

> *We remained standing for a brief minute [after singing the national anthem] before the choir director and the principal signaled to us, rather desperately I thought, to take our seats. The command was so unusual that our carefully rehearsed and smooth-running machine was thrown off.*

The effect of this change in the program is profound: "Finding my seat at last, I was overcome with a presentiment of worse things to come. Something unrehearsed, unplanned, was going to happen, and we were going to be made to look bad." Later, valedictorian Henry Reed's leading the graduates in singing the Negro National Anthem constitutes the immediate cause for renewed pride: "We were on top again. As always, again. We survived. . . . I was no longer simply a member of the proud graduating class of 1940; I was a proud member of the wonderful, beautiful Negro race."

Throughout "Graduation," however, Angelou also implies remote causes for the emotions she feels throughout the ceremony. When she contemplates how "awful" it is "to be a Negro and have no control over my life," she is referring to the seventy-five years of segregation that followed the end of the Civil War. When she listens to Donleavy recount the great improvements to be made to the white schools, she is referring to the deep-seated inequality foisted on African Americans in the South. And later, when she sings the praises of "Black known and unknown poets" whose tales and songs have sustained her race, she is referring to the ongoing struggle of African Americans to achieve freedom and dignity. The imposition of segregation after the Civil War, the inequality built into the Southern social fabric, and the simmering rebellion within the African American community—all of these constitute remote causes for the young Angelou's reactions on her graduation night.

Another feature of cause-and-effect analysis is the distinction between *primary* and *contributory* causes. While the primary cause of the lengthy Balkan war can be found in the tensions within the region itself, a contributory cause might be the rest of the world's failure to intervene early in the conflict. Similarly, the primary cause of Angelou's dismay during the graduation ceremony is the denigrating speech delivered by Edward Donleavy. A contributory cause is the reaction of the leaders of the African American community: the principal's normally powerful voice nearly fades into silence when he introduces Donleavy, and when the speaker's driver takes the principal's seat on the dais, confusion ensues and no one objects. The identification of immediate and remote, primary and contributory, causes enriches the analysis of complex issues.

By now it should be clear that cause-and-effect analysis normally includes multiple causes; it often includes multiple effects as well. Consider once again the Balkan war example: It has been determined that the conflict was the result of many causes. One of those causes, however, was itself responsible for more than just the Balkan war. The armistice that ended World War I not only set the stage for later conflict in the Balkans, but also resulted in conditions in Germany that led to the rise of Nazism under Adolf Hitler. In fact, an effect of a given cause often becomes the cause of yet another effect. The terms imposed on Germany after World War I, for example, resulted in humiliation and economic turmoil in that country. In turn, the national humiliation and deplorable economic conditions resulted in public unrest, which in turn resulted in the rise of the National Socialist, or Nazi Party. The rise of Nazism contributed to the outbreak of World War II in Europe.

In "Graduation," Donleavy's speech causes the young Angelou to ponder the injustices heaped on her people, which apprehension, in turn, causes her not to hear her name when she is called to the stage to receive her diploma. The change in the program caused by Donleavy's appearance causes the graduates to lose their composure, which results in valedictorian Henry Reed's decision to change the program yet again and sing the Negro National Anthem, which causes the graduates to regain not only their composure but their pride. These multiple causes and multiple effects make cause-and-effect analysis more complicated than other rhetorical strategies such as *description* or *comparison and contrast.*

The key to handling this complex strategy effectively lies in recognizing legitimate causes and effects. For a cause to be credible, it must be both *necessary* and *sufficient* to produce an effect. To illustrate this requirement, consider the simple example of the car that fails to start. In determining the cause of the problem, a mechanic checks under the hood. If all other parts of the engine are working, then a weak or dead battery is both a necessary and sufficient cause of the car's failure to start. Checking the engine, the mechanic is looking for connections or relationships to determine the cause of the problem. A car's failure to start is a mechanical or an electrical problem; therefore, the causes probably lie in the mechanical or electrical operations of the car. In a more complex problem such as determining the causes of the Balkan war, a historian will also look for connections and relationships, in this case economic conditions, nationalism, religious conflicts, and the history of the region. The mechanic and the historian are experts in their respective fields, so they are likely to avoid a common fallacy found in cause-and-effect analysis. Called *post-hoc reasoning,* this fallacy proceeds from the assumption that simply because a phenomenon or an event precedes another, the first is the cause of the second. If, for example, the owner of the car had lent it to a friend the day before, there is no reason why she should blame her friend for the problem; the two events may be merely *coincidental.*

In "Graduation," the arrival of an unanticipated speaker would not in itself constitute a necessary and sufficient cause for the turmoil that follows. It is Edward Donleavy's position as a white politician, as well as his treatment of both the dignitaries on the dais and the audience in the hall, that make his appearance a necessary and sufficient cause. Earlier in the essay, Angelou describes her youthful conviction that God would punish her evil deeds by somehow not allowing her to participate in graduation. Had she attributed the turmoil caused by Donleavy's speech to her own evil deeds, she would have been falling into a *post-hoc* fallacy.

Another common problem found in cause-and-effect analysis involves *oversimplification.* This problem usually results from a failure to appreciate the complexity of causes and effects. For example, an uninformed writer might attribute the rise of Nazism solely to the economic conditions in Germany during the 1930s, ignoring the simmering anti-Semitism in the country, the disputes over territory along the borders with Austria and France, the inefficiency of the government, and a number of other causes. When analyzing the causes of a particular event or phenomenon, it is necessary to consider a variety of causes—immediate *and* remote, primary *and* contributing.

An essay employing cause-and-effect analysis can be organized by first describing the effect and then analyzing the causes that led to it, or by analyzing the causes first and then concluding with the effect. The writer should make this choice based on what he or she wants to emphasize in the analysis. For example, a writer who wants to emphasize the *history* of the Balkan war might elaborate on the various causes before discussing the war itself, while a writer who wants to emphasize possible *solutions* to the conflict might begin by focusing on the conflict, and then analyzing the causes that led to it. As in essays employing other strategies, the approach taken by the writer should reflect both the topic and the purpose of the essay.

Argument: Traditional Model

Argument and Persuasion

A century and a half ago, many prominent Americans were engaged in a heated debate over slavery. Abolitionists (opponents of slavery) cited the Declaration of Independence, claiming that "all men are created equal" and decrying an institution that allowed one person to be the property of another. Slaveholders pointed to the Bible, claiming that the Old Testament identified certain races as "sons of Cain," destined to be enslaved throughout history. Eventually the slavery issue was settled by the Civil War, but prior to and during that conflict, speakers and writers engaged in **argument** about the legitimacy of slavery. Put simply, argument refers to the presentation of a claim (e.g., that slavery should be abolished) and evidence (e.g., citations from the Declaration, stories of mistreated slaves) to support it. Those engaged in argument seek to persuade their audience to accept a certain position or take a certain action. While argument and persuasion are not precisely synonymous, their purposes are similar. **Persuasion** seeks to sway an audience, often employing appeals to emotion; **argument** seeks to justify a position, always employing appeals to reason and sometimes appeals to emotion as well. As in the case of the abolition debate, the most effective arguments involve appeals to both reason and emotion. In this chapter, we will discuss three models of argument: **Rogerian**, based on the work of psychologist Carl Rogers; **Toulmin**, based on the work of philosphopher Stephen Toulmin; and **Aristotelian** or **classical**, based on the work of the Greek philosopher Aristotle.

Although slavery has not been an issue since 1865, race has remained one of the most debated topics in American culture. During the immediate post-Civil War period, questions revolved around basic civil rights for freed slaves; in the late nineteenth and early twentieth century, arguments about segregation and equal protection under the law predominated. The mid-twentieth century saw the emergence of a powerful Civil Rights movement aimed at finally guaranteeing integration, voting rights, and equal opportunity in employment and education. By the latter decades of the twentieth century, the gains achieved by the Civil Rights movement resulted in a backlash aimed specifically at affirmative action programs designed to level the playing field for African Americans in hiring, promotion, and access to higher education. In the 1970s and 1980s several high-profile cases claiming what came to be known as "reverse discrimination" found their way to the Supreme Court, often resulting in decisions that constrained affirmative action and equal opportunity programs. Such a case was *Taxman v. Board of Education of the Township of Piscataway*, in which Sharon Taxman, a white teacher, claimed reverse discrimination after having been laid off from her job in 1989. In order to maintain a racially diverse faculty in a school system with a 30 percent African American population, the Piscataway school board had chosen to retain Debra Williams, an African American teacher whose qualifications they judged equivalent to Taxman's and who had been hired on the same day as Taxman. During the period in which the case was being heard by various appellate courts, United States Supreme Court decisions had begun to reflect an increasingly narrow and conservative interpretation of civil rights law; by the time the Court agreed to hear the Taxman case, civil rights groups were fearful that a decision might further erode the gains made through affirmative action programs. This concern led to one of the most unusual situations in the history of Supreme Court cases: Civil rights groups that were not party to the suit consented to contribute to an out-of-court settlement in favor of Taxman. Response to the settlement was immediate and vocal, with conservative and liberal organizations alike speculating on its impact on affirmative action. In an essay published in *The New York Times Magazine*, two former justice department officials argued for the continuing necessity of affirmative action, particularly in countering unintentional discrimination. In "Not Color Blind: Just Blind," former Attorney General Nicholas deB. Katzenbach and former Assistant Attorney General Burke Marshall present a carefully reasoned, strongly supported argument that will be used to illustrate features of Rogerian, Toulmin, and Aristotelian models throughout this chapter.

Evidence

Both argument and persuasion share one crucial quality: Their claims must be supported by evidence. That evidence may take the form of reasoning, appeals to authority, reference to statistics or facts, or appeals to the audience's needs or values. Regardless of the nature of the supporting evidence, for an argument to be legitimate, that support must be presented. This is what differentiates argument from mere **statement of opinion**. In contemporary society, statement of opinion is often mistaken for argument. If you listen to talk radio or watch tabloid television, you hear endless unsubstantiated opinions presented as if they were full-blown arguments. The reason such programs do little other than reinforce existing beliefs shared by their audiences is precisely that no argument is taking place. The key to to convincing an impartial or unsympathetic audience of the legitimacy of a claim lies not in stating the claim but in supporting it with evidence. This chapter will explore the various kinds of support used to justify claims made in arguments.

Inductive and Deductive Reasoning

In constructing arguments based on rational rather than emotional appeals, it is necessary to understand the distinction between the two primary types of reasoning. **Inductive reasoning** involves moving from specific evidence to a general conclusion, while **deductive reasoning** moves from a general statement to specific conclusions. Katzenbach and Marshall use inductive reasoning in concluding that African Americans still suffer from discrimination on the basis of race:

Evidence:	African Americans are less likely to be hired by white bosses.
	African Americans are less likely to be promoted in their jobs. African Americans are less likely to be admitted to colleges and universities.
Conclusion:	African Americans suffer from discrimination.

A deductive approach, on the other hand, involves presenting a **syllogism**. A syllogism comprises three parts: the **major premise** (a general statement about a category or class); the **minor premise** (a specific statement about one member of that category or class); and the **conclusion** (derived about the specific member). If presented in the form of a syllogism, the argument made by opponents of affirmative action looks like this:

Major premise:	Discrimination on the basis of race is always unjust.
Minor premise:	Affirmative action discriminates on the basis of race.
Conclusion:	Affirmative action is unjust.

As you are probably aware from looking at this syllogism, it is necessary for the major premise to be valid in all cases if the conclusion is to be viable. Katzenbach and Marshall, in fact, argue implicitly that the major premise is not valid, stating, "For racial bias to be a problem, it must be accompanied by power" (para. 27). Therefore, according to their reasoning, discrimination is not *always* unjust, rendering the syllogism invalid and the argument unpersuasive.

Audience

All models of argument emphasize **audience**. Because the most basic goal of argument is to convince the audience of the legitimacy of a claim, the arguer must be aware of the knowledge, values, and needs of the audience. Katzenbach and Marshall's essay was published in *The New York Times Magazine*, the Sunday magazine of one of the most respected newspapers in the world. Readers of the *Times* are considered to be generally well educated and largely centrist or liberal in their political beliefs. Thus the authors can assume a certain familiarity with issues, understanding of legal and constitutional concepts, and acceptance of affirmative action. Their task in making an argument is to appeal to common **beliefs** and **values** of their audience. By focusing on the history of affirmative action, the distinction between policies that discriminate against individuals and those that seek to "create a reasonably integrated work force" (para. 14) and student body, Katzenbach and Marshall underscore their audience's assumed belief in integration as a key feature of their system of values. By acknowledging that discrimination in the late twentieth century is often inadvertent, they may also appeal to opponents of affirmative action who do not want to be characterized as racist.

Acknowledging/Rebutting Opposition

Acknowledgment of opposing arguments is an essential component of any audience-based model of argument. Acknowledging the opposition enhances the arguer's credibility and strengthens the argument as well. Regardless of the nature of the rebuttal, it is essential to the strength and validity of the argument that opposing views be aired and dealt with.

Katzenbach and Marshall acknowledge their opposition by clearly and objectively articulating the opposing view. Critics of affirmative action, they state, "affirm the goal of an integrated society and do not contend that we have yet achieved it. Critics simply argue that it is morally and constitutionally wrong to seek its achievement through race-based programs that give a 'preference' to African-Americans. . . ." Critics claim that affirmative action "denies 'equal opportunity' to whites and is antithetical to awarding jobs or promotions or college admissions on the basis of 'merit'" (para. 8). This summary avoids a negative characterization of their opponents; indeed, it acknowledges not only the good intentions of affirmative action critics, but points to a shared belief in integration as well.

The authors are careful, however, to offer a firm rebuttal of the opposing view. In this essay they take aim at the critics' position that affirmative action is "a system for favoring a less-qualified African-American over a better-qualified white—a system of 'preference' rather than 'merit'" (para. 14). In response, Katzenbach and Marshall make three points: First, they argue that critics misrepresent the goal of affirmative action by characterizing it as pitting individuals against one another for the same position. The actual goal, according to the authors, is to achieve an overall balance in the workplace or student body. Second, they argue that critics misrepresent "merit" as a clearly defined, measurable term. The authors assert that often merit is based on subjective judgment and specific circumstances, and cannot be defined in the same way for each situation. Third, they argue that critics misrepresent the treatment of African Americans under affirmative action by using the term 'preference.' The authors argue that such a term assumes that without affirmative action, the playing field would be level, while evidence suggests otherwise (paras. 15–17). This pattern of opposing view followed by rebuttal lends strength to Katzenbach and Marshall's argument.

The Rogerian Model of Argument

In preparing an argument it is important to consider various approaches to argument and persuasion. Two of the more common approaches used today are the **Rogerian** and the **Toulmin** models. While this chapter focuses primarily on the Toulmin model, the Rogerian model is worth studying for its emphasis on common ground. This model was developed based on psychologist Carl Rogers's work on conflict. Noting that adversarial arguments often result in opponents becoming entrenched in their own positions, Rogers suggests an approach that seeks common ground in order to negotiate a mutually acceptable position. "Not Color Blind: Just Blind" employs the Rogerian model to the extent that Katzenbach and Marshall acknowledge their opposition and assert its validity, and then find a common ground from which all sides can view the issue. Finally, they present evidence to establish their position as the most reasonable. An outline of their argument on college admissions from a Rogerian perspective might look something like this:

A. **Acknowledge opposing position** that racial considerations in admissions do not result in each applicant's being judged solely on merit (i.e., some minority students may be admitted over equally qualified non-minority students).

B. **Find common ground**, namely that both sides are interested in eliminating racial inequities.

C. **Present evidence** that even without affirmative action, academic merit is only one of many factors considered in accepting students, that merit itself is subjective and difficult to define, and that without affirmative action, African American students are less likely to apply to or be admitted to college.

Arguers who use the Rogerian approach truly seek to persuade their audience rather than to win an argument. Although their essay includes features of the Rogerian model, Katzenbach and Marshall clearly want to win their argument with critics of affirmative action. An analysis of the essay from a Toulmin perspective demonstrates the effectiveness of that model.

The Toulmin Model of Argument

In 1958, philosopher Stephen Toulmin published *The Uses of Argument*, a book that challenged traditional logic-based argument models. Toulmin based his model on the adversarial process of a courtroom, in which each position is challenged openly and judged by a third party. Toulmin's model emphasizes the audience of an argument, and charges the arguer with not only providing support for his or her position, but acknowledging and rebutting the opposition as well. In this regard, Toulmin's model resembles that of Carl Rogers. The key to the Toulmin approach, and the feature that distinguishes it from the Rogerian, is a strong link between the thesis and the evidence supporting that thesis. The primary components of the Toulmin model are **claim** (thesis), **grounds** (evidence or emotional appeal), and **warrant** (assumption linking claim to grounds).

Claims

In arguing for the retention of racial considerations in college and university admissions, Katzenbach and Marshall seek to persuade their audience in several ways. In addressing those who argue for purely merit-based admissions, they acknowledge the value of merit but question its definition and the extent to which it is used in college admissions. They also seek to convince those who call racial considerations a form of racism that the policy is intended solely to level the playing field for students who have been denied opportunities in elementary and secondary school and who would otherwise be denied admission to college. In addition, they seek to convince those who agree with them that the very existence of affirmative action is in jeopardy, and pressure must be exerted to ensure its survival.

The purpose of an argument is embedded in the claim, the point that the arguer wants to make. The thesis of an argument, whether stated or implied, presents the claim. Claims can be divided into three primary categories: **claims of fact**, **claims of value**, and **claims of policy**. The type of claim depends on the purpose of the argument; in turn, the structure and development of the argument depends largely on the type of claim being presented.

Claims of fact are assertions about the existence of a certain condition. In the argument about racial considerations, proponents and opponents alike attempt to establish certain facts about such policies in order to frame their arguments. The competing claims of fact as outlined in Katzenbach and Marshall include the following:

Claim 1: Affirmative action sometimes results in an African American applicant being admitted to a college over a white applicant with better test scores.

Claim 2: Test scores are only one of many criteria considered in college admissions decisions.

In each case, the claim must be supported by data, hard evidence that establishes the existence of the condition stated in the claim. Katzenbach and Marshall acknowledge that in some instances, racial considerations result in the acceptance of an African American student with a lower test score over a white student with a higher score. But they also offer evidence that college admission is based on a number of factors, including "geography, financial ability, relationship to graduates or relationship to people important in other ways to the institution," as well as "musical or athletic talent" (para. 21).

Claims of value are statements of judgment regarding the worth of something. Katzenbach and Marshall make the following claim of value regarding diversity:

Claim: A diverse student body is desirable in preparing students for work in an integrated society.

Often based on tastes or moral beliefs, claims of value must be supported by establishing criteria by which the judgments are made. In this case, Katzenbach and Marshall indicate that even opponents of affirmative action agree that diversity is a desirable goal, implicit in the general acceptance of civil rights legislation in the latter half of the twentieth century.

Claims of policy are calls to action. One of Katzenbach and Marshall's goals is to offset what they consider the erosion of affirmative action policies. The following claim of policy reflects that goal:

Claim: Affirmative action must be preserved.

Claims of policy must be supported by reasons for taking a specific action. Reasons for reaffirming the value of affirmative action, according to Katzenbach and Marshall, include the continued existence of unintentional discrimination, the need for a racially diverse student body and work force, and simple justice as articulated in the United States Consitution.

In order for a claim to be effective, the terms of the claim must be clearly defined. For example, implicit in Katzenbach and Marshall's argument is the contention that if and when American society is truly "color blind," then affirmative action in college admissions will no longer be necessary.

Grounds

Grounds, also called *support* or *supporting evidence*, comprise everything the arguer offers to justify a claim. Grounds may include **facts**, **data**, **statistics**, **opinions of experts or affected individuals**, **examples**, and **appeals to emotion**. The nature of the grounds normally depends on the type of claim being presented.

Facts offered in support of a claim should be irrefutable. The number of African American students enrolling in California public colleges and universities dropped after race could no longer be considered in admissions decisions. This fact is used to support Katzenbach and Marshall's argument in favor of such consideration.

Data and *statistics* offer numerical evidence to support a claim. Although Katzenbach and Marshall do not offer statistical evidence for the fact noted above, such evidence is available. These statistics, however, can be interpreted in a number of ways: Opponents of race consideration, for example, might argue that the reduction in numbers of African American college students reflected the qualifications of applicants rather than the need for race considerations.

The *opinion of experts* is valuable not only to support a particular interpretation of statistics but also to lend credibility to a claim. The opinion of someone with recognized expertise in a community is far more valuable than that of an uninformed person. Of course, Katzenbach and Marshall are themselves highly qualified to comment on civil rights legislation, but they also cite President John F. Kennedy and civil rights activist Martin Luther King, Jr. in support of their argument. The *opinion of affected individuals* is also effective. In a *Washington Post* article on the Taxman case, for example, Debra Williams's tearful response to the settlement is reported, highlighting the impact of the case on African Americans who rely on the protection of affirmative action policies.

Examples provide support for claims if they can be used in such a way that the audience draws generalizations from them. The primary example cited in Katzenbach and Marshall's essay, the Taxman v. Piscataway case, illustrates their concerns for the future of affirmative action.

Appeals to emotion differ from other grounds in that they do not rely on logic. Instead, appeals to emotion attempt to forge a link between the arguer and the audience by focusing on the needs of the audience or the values shared with the audience. Katzenbach and Marshall do not employ emotional appeals in their essay, but their argument could be supported by reference to individual African American applicants whose industriousness, determination, and potential are ignored because their scores on standardized tests do not meet a college's requirements for admission.

Warrants

Perhaps the least familiar of the three components of the Toulmin model, the *warrant* is nonetheless crucial to the success of an argument. Put simply, the warrant is the assumption or belief, shared by the arguer and the audience, that underlies the entire argument. A warrant can be considered a guarantee for the argument or, as Toulmin himself referred to it, a bridge between the claim and the grounds. Katzenbach and Marshall's argument, including the warrant, might look like this:

Claim:	Affirmative action policies are still necessary.
Grounds:	Racial inequality remains a problem in American culture; the playing field is not yet level, largely because of unconscious racism.
Warrant:	Racial discrimination cannot be tolerated in American society.

If the audience shares the authors' assumptions about equality and humanity, then their claim and grounds will be convincing.

Implicit and Explicit Warrants: Backing

Warrants such as those just illustrated are *implicit*; that is, they are obvious to any reasonable person in this culture. Occasionally, however, it is necessary to make the warrant *explicit.* Consider, for example, the 1954 Supreme Court decision in *Brown v. Board of Education of Topeka, Kansas.* The claim represented in that decision is related to Katzenbach and Marshall's: Segregation is unconstitutional. The grounds are also similar: Segregation results in poorer facilities for black students. In 1954, however, it was necessary that the warrant be spelled out: Separate facilities are inherently unequal. At the time, such an assumption was not common; thus the Court had to make the warrant clear. Whether the warrant is explicit or implicit, if it effectively links the grounds to the claim, then the argument will itself be effective.

If the warrant is not explicit, that is, if it is not necessarily shared by the audience, then it must be supported by *backing.* Just as the grounds support the claim, the backing supports the warrant. As with other evidence, backing can take several different forms. Chief Justice Earl Warren, for example, in offering backing for the warrant on which the *Brown* decision was based, cited the fact that during the time of the 1896 *Plessy v. Ferguson* decision, when the Court ruled that separate facilities were not inherently unequal, public education did not serve the purpose it did in 1954. Calling late nineteenth-century education "rudimentary," Warren noted that rural schools often combined several grades, that often the school year was a mere three months long, and that compulsory attendance was not enforced. In 1954, on the other hand, education was "the very foundation of good citizenship" as well as a necessary component to success in the workplace. Warren also cited the opinion of experts in his warrant, noting that psychologists in the 1950s agreed that segregation implied inferiority and therefore impeded black children's motivation. This backing for the Court's argument was necessary precisely because assumptions about the role of education and the effects of segregation had changed substantially between 1896 and 1954.

Qualifiers

Another significant feature of the Toulmin model is the *qualifier.* Consider the absolute nature of the following claim: *Each admissions decision* based on racial considerations addresses a previous educational inequity. To render this claim invalid, a single example of an upper-middle class African American student who has benefited from such a policy would suffice. Katzenbach and Marshall, however, contend that race-based considerations should not be considered in terms of individuals. Thus they attach a qualifier to the claim, that might be worded as follows:

Qualified claim: Race-based considerations in admissions decisions focus not on individual inequities but rather on achieving a diverse, integrated student body representative of the culture at large.

As illustrated in this example, amending claims to include qualifiers can facilitate an argument by heading off opposing claims before they are made.

The Logic of Argument (Aristotelian Argument)

The Rogerian and Toulmin approaches to argument are particularly effective in dealing with contemporary issues; however, both models owe a significant debt to the ancient Greek philosopher Aristotle, who developed one of the earliest analyses of argument in Western thought. Aristotle's *Rhetoric* identifies three means by which an arguer attempts to persuade an audience:

1. *Logos*—rational appeals
2. *Ethos*—emphasis on the integrity of the arguer
3. *Pathos*—emotional appeals

As these terms indicate, traditional Aristotelian argument focuses not only on appeals to reason but to emotion and to integrity or credibility as well.

Logos

Considered the most important category of proof by rhetoricians from Aristotle to the present, *logos* appeals to the rational mind. *Logos* refers to the internal consistency of the argument, as well as to its reliance on reason and common sense. The *logos* of an argument favoring racial considerations in college and university admissions policies is illustrated in Katzenbach and Marshall's carefully constructed reasoning and use of supporting evidence.

Categories of Logical Proof

Logical proof in an argument can be presented in a number of ways. The nature of the claim, the type of grounds, and the nature of the warrant all determine the type of proof or line of reasoning employed to support the warrant. This section focuses on six specific lines of reasoning: **argument from generalization**, **argument from definition**, **argument from cause**, **argument from sign**, **argument from analogy**, and **argument from parallel case**.

Argument from generalization is also known as *inductive reasoning* (as described earlier in this chapter). Generalization involves offering a series of examples that when taken together support a position. For example, when Katzenbach and Marshall itemize the specific types of obstacles faced by African American workers and students, it is reasonable to conclude that those workers and students are victims of discrimination. The resulting argument would look like this:

Argument:	African Americans suffer from discrimination.
Support:	African Americans are less likely to be hired by white bosses.
	African Americans are less likely to be promoted in their jobs. African Americans are less likely to be admitted to colleges and universities.

Argument from definition calls on the arguer to establish a common understanding of key terms with the audience. If such an understanding does not exist, then the argument cannot proceed. Chief Justice Earl Warren, in writing the decision in *Brown v. Board of Education*, found it necessary to define public education in order to make his case. Claiming that public education in the 1950s was designed to prepare students for citizenship, he then made the case that separate facilities placed unconstitutional burdens on African Americans relegated to those facilities. Taken as an argument itself, Warren's definition can be outlined as follows:

Argument: Segregated schools are by definition unequal.

Support: Segregated schools do not offer African American children the opportunity to learn good citizenship, one of the primary functions of public education.

Argument from cause posits that a specific action results in a specific effect. In presenting a causation argument, it is necessary to link the cause to the effect; the audience must be convinced that the situation presented is not coincidence. Katzenbach and Marshall, in arguing that race-based consideration is necessary in college admissions decisions, establish the relationship between the abandonment of such policies and lower numbers of African American students enrolled in college. Their argument from cause would look like this:

Argument: Race-based consideration must be retained in order to increase the number of African American students enrolling in college.

Support: Eliminating race-based consideration, while retaining other non-merit-based considerations, has resulted in fewer African American applicants applying to or being admitted to college.

Argument from sign focuses on symptoms or indicators of a particular condition. Some of the most obvious signs with which we are familiar are symptoms of disease: stuffy nose, a cough, and a fever are signs of a cold. Although there is not always a causal relationship between the sign and the condition indicated, argument from sign can nevertheless be effective. One might argue, for example, that racially intolerant attitudes are a sign of a campus that is homogeneous, or lacking in diversity. The lack of diversity may not have caused the intolerant attitudes; nonetheless, the attitudes signify a homogeneous campus community. The argument from sign would look like this:

Argument: Racially intolerant attitudes are a sign of a homogeneous campus.

Support: On campuses lacking in diversity, racially intolerant attitudes are more prevalent than on diverse campuses.

Argument from analogy uses an object or situation to represent an unrelated object or situation. The power of the analogy normally rests in the imagery it suggests, but at times rational connections between the two things strengthen the analogy. In taped conversations with President Nixon about the Watergate cover-up, White House Counsel John Dean referred to the growing scandal as a cancer eating at the presidency. Such an analogy is powerful in its imagery, but there is little real resemblance between a cancer-ridden body and the office of the presidency. An argument from analogy that calls on more rational connections would read as follows:

Argument: Like a field planted year after year with only one crop, a homogeneous campus community yields little growth.

Support: Lack of diversity makes the campus atmosphere less productive, just as overplanting a single crop year after year makes the soil less productive.

Argument from parallel case is used regularly in courts of law. Whenever attorneys cite a precedent, they are arguing from parallel case. Based on comparisons between objects or conditions with shared characteristics, argument from parallel case asks the audience to believe that what happened in one situation can be expected to happen in another. A faulty argument from parallel case was made by the defendants in *Brown v. Board of Education*. The defense cited the 1896 *Plessy v. Ferguson* case in which separate facilities were not deemed inherently unequal. As noted previously, however, the Warren Court rejected that argument, citing changing circumstances. In this case, the defense position that conditions in 1954 replicated those in 1896 was declared faulty. Several years after the *Brown* case, however, plaintiffs from Little Rock, Arkansas made a valid argument from parallel case, which would read as follows:

Argument: Segregated public schools in Little Rock, Arkansas in 1960 were inherently unequal.

Support: The Supreme Court ruled in 1954 that segregated public schools in Topeka, Kansas were inherently unequal.

Avoiding Logical Fallacies

As the example from *Brown v. Board of Education* indicates, not all arguments, even if they follow a specific model, are valid. In addition to falling prey to such errors as failing to acknowledge changing times, arguers can also fall into what are known as **logical fallacies**. Such fallacies occur when the arguer is not careful in matching the grounds to the claim, or when the warrant is either irrelevant to the claim and support or is based on insubstantial backing. Logical fallacies include the following:

***Post hoc* reasoning** assumes that simply because a phenomenon or an event precedes another, the first is the cause of the second. If a white student is denied admission to a public university which uses racial considerations in admission decisions, the admissions policy is not necessarily the cause for denial. Any number of other causes, from the student's test scores to her intended major program of study, might have contributed to the decision.

Non sequitur (Latin for "it does not follow") is illustrated in Katzenbach and Marshall's rejection of the association of merit with standardized test scores. Because one student's score on a standardized test is lower than another student's score, it does not follow that the second student is better qualified.

Either/or assumes the possibility of only two diametrically opposed outcomes. To argue that colleges either maintain high admission standards or foster racial diversity is to ignore other possibilities, for example that considering a number of criteria, including both standardized test scores and race, might result in a diverse institution with high standards.

Hasty generalization is also called jumping to conclusions. Just because integration of Central High School in Little Rock, Arkansas resulted in Federal intervention, there was no reason to assume that all integration programs would require National Guard troops. Some communities were better prepared to abide by the *Brown v. Board of Education* decision than others.

Begging the question involves assuming that a conclusion is valid and using that conclusion as part of the argument. Some opponents of affirmative action point to lower African American enrollment statistics following the abandonment of race-based considerations in admissions decisions as evidence that affirmative action resulted in unqualified students being admitted to college. Such a conclusion begs the question of what consitutes appropriate qualifications for admission.

Ad hominem (Latin for "to the man") is an attack made on a person's character rather than on the position the person has taken. To discredit an opponent of affirmative action because he is in the midst of a messy divorce is to avoid the issue at hand.

Appeal to faulty authority involves attributing expertise on an issue to someone whose expertise lies in a different area. Supporting affirmative action because a prominent show-business celebrity supports it is an example of this fallacy.

Red herring is a term for intentional diversion of attention away from an issue. Segregationist leaders in Arkansas in the early 1960s called up the specter of communism when confronted with civil rights activists demanding integrated schools, appealing to Cold War fears.

False analogy ignores the fact that two analogous things or situations are not alike in all respects. Many American historians now consider the analogy of America as a melting pot to be essentially false. While the many nationalities that make up this country do, like the ingredients in a melting pot, exist in harmony, they do not necessarily blend and become indistinguishable from one another.

Obviously, maintaining the integrity of a logical argument is often a challenge. The legitimacy of the argument depends on sound reasoning and avoidance of logical fallacies.

Ethos

Ethos is often equal in importance to logos in an argument because it establishes the credibility and sincerity of the author. Ethos establishes a relationship between the arguer and the audience that supports the rational appeal of the argument. If the arguer is deemed to have integrity, expertise, and a fair-minded approach, the argument is enhanced. For example, Katzenbach and Marshall's combined *ethos* is established both within and without "Not Color Blind." Within the essay the authors establish their credibility by demonstrating their understanding of the history of civil rights legislation and their reasonableness in acknowledging the opposition. A brief look at their biographies also establishes their *ethos*. Both have degrees from prestigious institutions, both have held high-ranking positions in the United States Justice Department, and both have written extensively on legal issues. These credentials lend credibility to their position. The establishment of credentials refers to a form of ethical proof called **argument from authority.**

Argument from authority is used to support the logical argument by calling on the opinions of experts in the field. Because it is possible to find experts to support any number of positions in a given argument, establishing the credibility of the expert is essential. As discussed in the section on grounds, the expert should possess appropriate credentials and be respected in the field. Of course it is also essential that the authority's expertise be relevant to the topic at hand. Arguments against public school segregation after 1954 exemplify argument from authority:

Argument: Segregated schools are inherently unequal.

Support: The United States Supreme Court decided this point in 1954.

For an argument to have sound ethical appeal, it is necessary for the arguer to establish his or her own integrity, as well as the integrity of authorities cited in support of the claim.

Pathos

Pathos is perhaps the most familiar type of proof found in everyday arguments. Appealing strictly to the emotions of the audience, *pathos* can strengthen an otherwise sound rational argument by engaging the audience on a more personal level. A purely emotional argument is rarely convincing; however, expanding the appeal of an argument beyond *logos* and *ethos* can enhance it. Emotional appeals, if legitimately related to the claim, will strengthen a rational argument. The reason for this is simple: Human beings make decisions based on emotion as well as on reason. Indeed, sometimes emotional concerns outweigh rational concerns. Katzenbach and Marshall choose not to employ emotional appeals in "Not Color Blind," perhaps because they wish to avoid being labeled as overly sentimental in their observations on race. An effective example of *pathos* can be found, however, in Maya Angelou's "Graduation," a chapter from her memoir *I Know Why the Caged Bird Sings*. Angelou herself is the product of a segregated school system, and in "Graduation" she evokes her feelings as she listens to the insulting, condescending address of Edward Donleavy, the white speaker at her eighth grade graduation:

> Graduation, the hush-hush magic time of frills and gifts and congratulations and diplomas, was finished for me before my name was called. The accomplishment was nothing. The meticulous maps, drawn in three colors of ink, learning and spelling decasyllabic words, memorizing the whole of *The Rape of Lucrece*—it was for nothing. Donleavy had exposed us.

The demoralization of a young girl whose hopes had only recently included heading "for the freedom of open fields" supports the implicit argument against segregation that permeates Angelou's piece. By presenting her audience not with statistics and principles but rather with the image of a young girl's disillusionment, she provides a personal touch that brings the issue into clearer focus.

Language and *Pathos*

"Graduation" also illustrates the significance of language in *pathos*. When considering the meaning of words, it is important to distinguish between *denotation*, the dictionary definition of the word, and *connotation*, the implied meaning or emotional overtones of the word. The word *group*, for example, is rather neutral in both denotation and connotation; it refers to a number of people with some common purpose. Change the word to *gang*, however, and while the dictionary meaning may remain essentially the same, the sinister implications of the word, the sense of danger or violence, cannot be ignored. Thus a newspaper account referring to a *group* of civil rights activists creates a different image than one referring to a *gang* of activists. Angelou uses connotation when she asks why her brother has to "pay penance for his skin" in order to study law. Her reference to penance calls up religious images of sinning against God, thereby heightening the impact of this condemnation of segregation. Similarly, when she describes the uncomfortably deferential demeanor of the principal and the teachers during Donleavy's speech, she writes, "the ancient tragedy was being replayed." Tragedy is often considered the highest form of drama; ancient tragedy, particularly Greek tragedy, is considered the model for everything that has followed. The implication Angelou makes, then, is that this is much more than simply an uncomfortable moment for these school officials; the scene has universal implications.

Emotional Proof

Arguments from emotion fall into two categories: **motivational appeals** and **appeals to values**. Each appeal can strengthen a rational argument.

Motivational appeals rely on an understanding of people's needs and desires. In addition to basic biological needs such as food and shelter, people also have needs for safety, for belonging, for self-expression, and so on. In "Not Color Blind" Katzenbach and Marshall tap into their audience's motivations for providing the best possible educational experience for the next generation. They assert that, "a diverse student body contributes to educational excellence and to the preparation of students to live in an integrated society" (para. 23), tapping into their readers' need to think of themselves as responsible, forward-thinking people with the best interests of their children at heart. Their appeal might be presented as follows:

Argument: You should share our commitment to a diverse student body.

Appeal: Responsible, forward-thinking people are committed to diversity in the student body, and you want to be considered a responsible, forward-thinking person.

Appeals to values rely on commonly held beliefs about what is good or desirable. (Appeals to values are similar to claims of value in the Toulmin model.) Political campaigns throughout the past twenty-five years, for example, have focused on terms such as "family values," which, while vague and often ill-defined, nonetheless resonate with many voters. By calling upon a value shared by the audience, an arguer can strengthen a rational argument. One of the values shared by Katzenbach and Marshall's primary audience involves the concept of merit which is invoked in the authors' claim that "those African-Americans who can qualify for the institutional admissions pool would probably not be as successful as they are without superior motivation and determination—qualities most Americans would associate with merit" (para. 24). If their readers agree that motivation and determination are consistent with American values, then it becomes difficult for them to reject the authors' position on race-based considerations in college admissions. The argument can be outlined as follows:

Argument:	Race-based considerations result in the admission of determined, motivated African American students.
Appeal:	Determination and motivation are qualities that are valued in American society.

These lines of argument can be employed in any number of combinations. Most successful arguments will balance *logos*, *ethos*, and *pathos* in such a way that audiences are convinced not only by reason, but by authority and emotion as well.

Reading and Writing Arguments

Now that you have a clearer understanding of the nature of argument, you are better equipped to analyze written arguments and to compose your own arguments. Referring to the above discussion of the components of an effective argument, you should be able to use the following advice to read argumentative texts with a critical eye.

Reading Arguments Critically

A critical reader creates a dialogue with a text by making observations, asking questions, considering the author's ideas, analyzing the author's perspective in relation to those of others, forging connections with other pieces—in short, the critical reader *responds* to what the writer is saying. Responding effectively to an argument normally involves three activities: **understanding the topic**, **evaluating the evidence**, and **considering alternative perspectives**.

Understanding the Topic

Although well-written arguments will provide you with enough information to understand the topic at hand, the writer is still presenting the material from his or her own perspective. Therefore, in order to read and understand another's argument effectively, you must first take stock of your own knowledge of the topic. This activity involves considering what you already know about the topic and what your perspective is on the topic, as well as recalling what else you may have read about the topic. If you discover that your knowledge is quite limited, you may want to investigate the topic further by talking to other informed students or professors, reading about the topic in newspapers or magazines, or researching the topic on the Web. When you begin reading the argument itself, try to identify background information presented within it. Katzenbach and Marshall, for example, explain the basic facts of *Taxman v. Board of Education of the Township of Piscataway* early in their essay, and follow with a brief history of affirmative action. In this way the authors familiarize their readers with the context of their argument.

Understanding the topic also includes identifying the claim, the grounds, and the warrant of the argument. Not all arguments are presented according to the Toulmin model, but it is possible to apply the model to most arguments. Thus the first thing to do after establishing your understanding of the piece is to highlight the author's statement of the claim. While many arguments feature clear statements of claim, some do not. Chief Justice Warren, for example, states the claim clearly in the *Brown* decision: "Separate educational facilities are inherently unequal." In "Not Color Blind," on the other hand, the claim is not stated explicity, but can be inferred from Katzenbach and Marshall's argument. The claim might be stated as such: "Affirmative action and other race-based considerations are still necessary in order to achieve an integrated work force and student body."

Recognizing the grounds, or support for the claim, is the next step in reading an argument critically. The discussion of supporting evidence in the previous chapter identifies several kinds of support found in Katzenbach and Marshall's essay: the fact that the playing field is not even, for example, or that affirmative action policies are intended to achieve balance rather than to favor one individual over another. Chief Justice Warren cites the changing nature of public education between 1896 and 1954, decisions in recent cases involving segregated educational facilities, and the opinions of psychologists on the effects of inferior education.

Identifying the warrant is usually a more difficult task that involves interpretation. Among Katzenbach and Marshall's warrants are assumptions that racial discrimination is unconstitutional and ethically wrong, and that a diverse work force and student body are desirable goals.

In order to facilitate your dialogue with the text, it is important to do more than simply read and identify elements passively. Underline or highlight claims and grounds; summarize them in the margins of the text; make note of questions you have regarding your understanding of certain items. If the selection includes terms that you do not understand, look them up. Often understanding one key term can turn an incomprehensible paragraph into a model of clear prose.

Evaluating the Evidence

Sometimes readers take one of two contradictory approaches to a text. The first approach assumes that a published piece must be right and accepted without question. The second, usually occurring when reading something expressing a contrary position, simply dismisses the argument without considering its merits. Neither approach is conducive to critical reading. In the first case, while publication lends a certain credibility to an argument, it is possible to find published arguments featuring opposing views on almost any topic. In the second case, it is necessary to understand that most published arguments are presented in the interests of continuing a dialogue on the issue. To dismiss the argument out of hand is to cut off conversation. The critical reader assumes neither that the author is unquestionably right nor unquestionably wrong. Instead, the critical reader evaluates the evidence presented by the author in support of the claim. This is precisely what Chief Justice Warren does in the *Brown* decision. Part of the evidence presented to the Court was a precedent, the 1896 *Plessy v. Ferguson* case, in which separate facilities were ruled not a unanimous Court) notes that the nature and purposes of public education differ profoundly in 1896 and 1954 and that psychologists have in the meantime identified the negative impact of unequal treatment. Thus the *Plessy* case is not deemed a legitimate precedent, and it is rejected as grounds. While it may not be easy to determine the legitimacy of grounds or warrants in the arguments you read, you can measure them against the grounds you offer for your own position as well as those offered by people making opposing claims.

It is worth noting that you can reject the grounds and warrant in an argument without rejecting the claim itself. Many of us have been in the position of agreeing with a certain claim but bemoaning the fact that the grounds are insufficient to support it. You may support capital punishment, for example, but find unconvincing the argument that asks how you would feel if your mother or brother were murdered. Your judgment of the legitimacy of argument will not reflect your position on the issue, only your evaluation of the evidence. It is always wise to distinguish between your agreement with a claim and your evaluation of the legitimacy of the grounds.

Considering Alternative Perspectives

Because a published argument is usually designed to further dialogue on a certain issue, you should consider reading alternative arguments in order to assess the effectiveness of the original argument you have read. It is only after considering an issue from multiple perspectives that you can consider yourself truly capable of taking a position on that issue. For Chief Justice Warren, of course, it was necessary to consider alternative arguments; his job (and the job of his fellow justices) was to examine the grounds for a number of different claims regarding segregated schools. After reading "Not Color Blind," you might consider alternative perspectives on affirmative action. In the past two decades affirmative action has come under fire not only from white conservatives but from African American activists as well. While writers such as Henry Louis Gates and Orlando Patterson have written extensively about the value of affirmative action, it has been criticized by writers such as Shelby Steele and judges such as Clarence Thomas. Perhaps the most valuable result of reading alternative perspectives on an issue is the realization that few issues lend themselves to only two opposing positions. More often than not, a number of positions between the two extremes exist as well, and they can enlighten readers to the complexity of most arguments.

Once you have established an understanding of the topic, evaluated the evidence, and considered alternative perspectives, you should be prepared to respond to the argument. If that response is to take the form of a formal essay, then the following guidelines will be helpful.

Writing Arguments

Writing argumentative essays is not entirely different from writing other types of essays. Indeed, argumentative essays often employ narrative, definition, cause-and-effect, and other rhetorical strategies. The writing process itself is similar as well: You will engage in prewriting, composing, revising, and editing—just as you do in all of your formal writing. Argumentative essays, however, involve a more refined process of writing. Just as in reading arguments, in writing them you must understand the topic, evaluate the evidence, and consider alternative perspectives. In writing arguments, you engage in the same specific activities associated with reading arguments critically:

> **Understanding the topic**: Research the issue thoroughly and develop your own claim.
>
> **Evaluating the evidence**: Determine what evidence supports your claim and decide on an organizational strategy.
>
> **Considering alternative perspectives**: Identify the most convincing arguments in opposition to your claim and address them.

Understanding the Topic

If you are to write a convincing argument on any topic, you must be familiar with the issues involved. While you may be able to engage in informal debate about an issue, it is unlikely that you can compose a well-supported argumentative essay without doing some formal research. Reading newspapers, magazines, and public documents; consulting reputable Web sites; interviewing well-informed individuals; and attending relevant meetings of groups or organizations will help you to familiarize yourself with the multiple perspectives from which the issue can be considered. Just as the Warren Court had to review a number of precedents before handing down the decision in *Brown v. Board of Education*, you must become familiar with the background of your topic before writing your argument. It is even conceivable that you may change your position on the issue after researching it. Regardless of whether your research alters or solidifies your position, however, your task once you have completed your preliminary review of the issue is to develop a claim, or thesis, that you think is defensible.

For the purposes of this discussion, consider the following scenario: A toxic waste site has been proposed for an area adjacent to your town. After investigating the impact such facilities have had on other communities, you either oppose or support the proposal. This example not only taps into a heated current debate, but it also involves issues of health, the environment, and economics, thus offering the opportunity to support the claim (whether in opposition to or in support of the facility) from a number of different perspectives. One possible thesis on this topic is the following:

Thesis: Because of its impact on the economy, public health, and the environment, a toxic waste site should not be built in this community.

Whether or not you open your essay with the explicitly stated claim is a decision that can wait until later; it is normally best to concentrate on developing the argument itself before considering how to present it to your audience.

At this point, however, it is important to remember that failure to understand your audience will likely undermine an otherwise strong argument. As mentioned earlier in the chapter, it is essential to recognize the needs and values of the audience as you compose your argument; remember, the most basic goal of argument is to convince the audience of the legitimacy of a claim. Thus the advice offered previously is worth repeating: Some audiences will be entirely sympathetic to your position, some antithetic, and many will fall somewhere between those two extremes. Your task in making an argument is to appeal to the **beliefs** and **values** of your audience. Identifying common beliefs and values will facilitate your task. For example, most members of a community will be sensitive to the economic impact of a toxic waste site; a facility providing both jobs and tax dollars is an attractive prospect. You will be more persuasive, then, if you address economic concerns. Perhaps you might balance the economic advantages of a waste site with the increased costs of health care, loss of work due to illness, and decline of property values in order to appeal to those whose position stems from their sense of economic values.

Evaluating the Evidence

The evidence you choose to ground your argument depends not only on the nature of the claim itself but also on the needs and values of your audience. For example, if your community has demonstrated environmental awareness through recycling programs and conservation of land, then the environmental argument will be particularly appealing to them. If the community normally considers economic issues of primary importance, then the economic impact of the site should be emphasized. Katzenbach and Marshall's audience, the readership of the *New York Times Magazine*, values reasoned argument and intellecutally challenging discussion; thus the authors avoid overt emotional appeals. The nature and presentation of your evidence will also depend on your audience.

Suppose you have determined from your research and your knowledge of the people in the community that while economic issues are important to them, their primary concerns involve health and the environment. The following evidence, then, would be appropriate:

Evidence: Toxic waste sites have been known to pollute the environment.

Increases in serious illnesses, including cancer, have been associated with toxic waste sites.

Communities in which toxic waste sites have been built have experienced a decline in property values and a loss of businesses.

In order to convince your audience of the legitimacy of this evidence, you will have to provide information such as examples of communities in which toxic waste sites have been built, the opinion of experts on the relationship between the sites and disease, and analyses of the economic impact of the sites. The strength of your argument will depend in large part on how effectively you present this material. Pages of statistics with little narrative to break them up, for example, will likely confuse or bore all but the most technical audiences. Failure to make your warrant clear will also result in an unconvincing argument. While it is hardly necessary to state explicitly that the community values health, the environment, and a sound economic base, it will be necessary to establish the relative value of each of these features to a community. If you evaluate your evidence as conscientiously as you would that of an argument you were reading, your argument should be sound.

Considering Alternative Perspectives

When reading an argument, you consider alternative perspectives in order to evaluate the argument's effectiveness and to gauge your response to it. When writing an argument, you consider the opposition in order to strengthen your presentation. If you have conducted thorough research prior to making your claim, you should be aware of the alternative perspectives that might challenge your position. Because of the significance of precedent in supporting a legal argument, for example, Chief Justice Warren addresses the *Plessy v. Ferguson* case explicitly in his argument, rebutting *Plessy's* claim by discussing the altered nature of public schools. You may have discovered evidence that toxic waste sites bring needed tax revenues and jobs to the communities in which they are situated. If you are to argue successfully against the site, then you must address this evidence. Pointing to a decline in property values and a loss of other small businesses could effectively counter the impact of this evidence:

Opposing view: Toxic waste sites are an economic boon to communities because they generate tax revenues and increase employment.

Rebuttal: While the sites do provide taxes and jobs, their positive economic impact is mitigated by a decline in property values and a loss of other businesses.

What happens, however, if you do not have sufficient evidence to refute the economic claim? In this case, it will probably be necessary to revise your evidence to emphasize only health and environment, and to acknowledge that while toxic waste sites do have some positive economic impact, their overall negative impact is more significant:

Opposing view: Toxic waste sites are an economic boon to communities because they generate tax revenues and increase employment.

Acknowledgment/ Rebuttal: While such facilities are economically valuable to a community, their negative impact on environment and health outweighs any economic benefits.

Whether you acknowledge alternative perspectives or rebut them, including them in your argument reveals not only that you are well versed in the subject, but also that you are fair minded.

Composing the Paper

Once you have a clear idea of your position and the evidence you will use to support it, you can determine how to present your argument to your audience. At this stage you can rely on what you have learned about writing essays in general, using a few tips related specifically to argumentative writing.

Introduction/Statement of Thesis

A variety of options exist for introducing an argument. You may want to begin with an anecdote, a brief story designed to engage your audience. You may want to begin with a statement of your thesis, establishing from the first sentence that you take this issue seriously. You may choose to use your introduction to establish the background of the issue and save your thesis until the essay's conclusion, after presenting evidence in favor of your position. These decisions will depend in large part on your audience. If your audience includes families in the community, for example, a well-chosen anecdote might drive home to them the real impact the facility would have on their lives. If the audience is less personally involved in the issue, however, you might choose simply to state your position. And if you want to persuade your audience without their necessarily being aware of it, you can wait until the end to state your claim, bringing the audience to your conclusion through your presentation.

Your introduction also depends on the nature of the subject and the argument itself. It might be necessary, for example, to define terms in your introduction, or to provide background information that is not familiar to your audience. If the subject is particularly controversial, it will be necessary to acknowledge the legitimacy of various alternative perspectives before beginning the argument. Deciding how to introduce the argument is not simply a stylistic decision. The effectiveness of the argument itself will be influenced by the way in which it is introduced.

Organization of Evidence

Since it is the evidence that ultimately convinces most audiences, the decision on how to organize that evidence is a crucial one. As in determining how to introduce the argument, audience considerations are important in selecting an organizing strategy. An unfriendly audience needs to be led step-by-step to your conclusion. In that case, you might want to begin with the least significant item of evidence and move to the most significant. This strategy assumes that if you can convince your audience to agree with you in small increments, then the audience will have no choice but to accept your claim at the end. Of course, the decision on how significant any piece of evidence is rests with the audience. A community overwhelmingly concerned with a high unemployment rate, for example, may consider the economic implications of a toxic waste site far more significant than any long-term environmental impact. Moving from the environmental to the health and then to the economic evidence might be the most effective organizational strategy for this audience.

If your evidence includes something especially compelling, you will want to reverse this organization and start with the strongest piece of evidence. Suppose your evidence includes a report from a prestigious university indicating that the groundwater within several miles of every toxic waste site built in the past decade has become contaminated. This evidence might be so powerful that you want to present it to your audience first, placing the rest of your evidence in a supporting role to this, the star witness. The advantage of such an organizational strategy is that you all but convince your audience with your first piece of evidence, making it easier for them to accept your other, less compelling evidence.

What do you do if the opposite is true? If there is a particularly strong opposing claim, you wish to deal with that claim first. If you delay your rebuttal until you have presented your own evidence, you have already lost your audience. It is possible that your audience will read your entire argument distracted by their curiosity about how you will deal with the opposition. Thus it is sometimes wise to present the opposing argument first, acknowledging its legitimacy, and then refuting its claims before moving on to your own evidence. The advantage of this approach is that you clear your readers' minds of distraction at the same time that you present yourself as a fair-minded person.

If you keep in mind both the audience and the nature of your evidence as you determine your organizational strategy, you should be able to construct a solid foundation on which to base your claim.

Conclusion

A conventional conclusion to an argumentative paper will sum up the evidence and reinforce the thesis. If you have chosen to save your thesis for the end of the paper, however, that thesis will be stated explicitly for the first time in the conclusion. Other alternatives include returning to an anecdote used in the introduction, perhaps by completing the story based on the evidence you have amassed. You may also wish to issue a call to action in your conclusion. If you believe that your audience has been convinced, for example, that the toxic waste site should not be built in the community, you may conclude with a call to become active in the movement opposing the site. Whether you sum up, state the thesis for the first time, complete an anecdote, or issue a call to action, you want to make sure that your conclusion leaves your audience thinking seriously about your position—if not convinced that it is the right position.

Revision and Editing

The guidelines for revising a written argument are essentially the same as those for any other kind of paper: making sure that the thesis is clear, whether explicitly stated or implied; making sure that the organization is coherent and the evidence sound; and making sure that the conclusion is consistent and forceful. In particular, in revising an argumentative paper you should ask yourself the following questions:

1. Is your thesis clear, your position evident?
2. Is the audience provided with sufficient background on the topic?

3. Are all relevant terms defined?
4. Is the relevance of each item of evidence to the thesis made clear?
5. Are all underlying assumptions identified?
6. Are opposing views acknowledged and satisfactorily rebutted?
7. Is the organization of evidence effective?
8. Is the conclusion forceful and consistent with the thesis and evidence?

When you are ready to edit your paper, remember the discussion of *ethos* earlier in this chapter. The effectiveness of your argument depends in part on the audience's perception of you as author. One of the surest and easiest ways to undermine your effectiveness is to ignore mechanical, grammatical, spelling, and format issues. At best your audience will be distracted by errors; at worst they will question the credibility of a writer either unwilling or unable to conform to the most basic conventions of standard written English. While it is obviously the argument itself that convinces the audience, a carefully edited paper will tell your audience that you not only care about your topic, but that you are a competent writer as well.

Narration

An American Childhood

Annie Dillard

Annie Dillard (1945–) was born in Pittsburgh, Pennsylvania. She received a B.A. (1967) and an M.A. (1968) from Hollins College and then embarked on a career as a writer and teacher. Dillard has worked as a columnist for The Living Wilderness *and a contributing editor for* Harper's, *and taught at Western Washington University and Wesleyan University in Connecticut. Fascinated with the intricacies of the natural world and blessed with an introspective, poetic mind, Dillard has developed a reputation for exploring the relationships between humans and nature, physically and spiritually. She has been compared to Henry David Thoreau, and her work has been compared to his* Walden. *An accomplished writer, Dillard has published nonfiction, poetry, literary criticism, essays, autobiographies, and a novel. Her published work includes* Pilgrim at Tinker Creek *(1974), observations about nature for which she received the Pulitzer Prize;* Tickets for a Prayer Wheel *(1974), a volume of poetry;* Living By Fiction *(1982), a collection of literary criticism;* Teaching a Stone to Talk *(1982), a collection of essays;* An American Childhood *(1987), an account of her youth in Pittsburgh;* The Writing Life, *(1989), reflections on the process of writing; and* The Living, *(1992), a novel. As you read this essay, discover how the environment in which Dillard lived as a young girl helped shape this learned, curious writer.*

Excerpt from *An American Childhood.* Published by HarperCollins Publishers, Inc.

1 One Sunday afternoon Mother wandered through our kitchen, where Father was making a sandwich and listening to the ball game. The Pirates were playing the New York Giants at Forbes Field. In those days, the Giants had a utility infielder named Wayne Terwilliger. Just as Mother passed through, the radio announcer cried—with undue drama—"Terwilliger bunts one!" 1

"Terwilliger bunts one?" Mother cried back, stopped short. She turned. "Is that English?"

"The player's name is Terwilliger," Father said. "He bunted."

"That's marvelous," Mother said. "'Terwilliger bunts one.' No wonder you listen to baseball. 'Terwilliger bunts one.'"

5 For the next seven or eight years, Mother made this surprising string of syllables her own. Testing a microphone, she repeated, "Terwilliger bunts one"; testing a pen or a typewriter, she wrote it. If, as happened surprisingly often in the course of various improvised gags, she pretended to whisper something else in my ear, she actually whispered, "Terwilliger bunts one." Whenever someone used a French phrase, or a Latin one, she answered solemnly, "Terwilliger bunts one." If Mother had had, like Andrew Carnegie, the opportunity to cook up a motto for a coat of arms, hers would have read simply and tellingly, "Terwilliger bunts one." (Carnegie's was "Death to Privilege.") 5

She served us with other words and phrases. On a Florida trip, she repeated tremulously, "That . . . is a royal poinciana." I don't remember the tree; I remember the thrill in her voice. She pronounced it carefully, and spelled it. She also liked to say "portulaca."

The drama of the words "Tamiami Trail" stirred her, we learned on the same Florida trip. People built Tampa on one coast, and they built Miami on another. Then—the height of visionary ambition and folly—they piled a slow, tremendous road through the terrible Everglades to connect them. To build the road, men stood sunk in muck to their armpits. They fought off cottonmouth moccasins and six-foot alligators. They slept in boats, wet. They blasted muck with dynamite, cut jungle with machetes; they laid logs, dragged drilling machines, hauled dredges, heaped limestone. The road took fourteen years to build up by the shovelful, a Panama Canal in reverse, and cost hundreds of lives from tropical, mosquito-carried diseases. Then, capping it all, some genius thought of the word Tamiami: they called the road from Tampa to Miami, this very road under our spinning wheels, the

Tamiami Trail. Some called it Alligator Alley. Anyone could drive over this road without a thought.

Hearing this, moved, I thought all the suffering of road building was worth it (it wasn't my suffering), now that we had this new thing to hang these new words on—Alligator Alley for those who liked things cute, and, for connoisseurs like Mother, for lovers of the human drama in all its boldness and terror, the Tamiami Trail.

Back home, Mother cut clips from reels of talk, as it were, and played them back at leisure. She noticed that many Pittsburghers confuse "leave" and "let." One kind relative brightened our morning by mentioning why she'd brought her son to visit: "He wanted to come with me, so I left him." Mother filled in Amy and me on locutions we missed. "I can't do it on Friday," her pretty sister told a crowded dinner party, "because Friday's the day I lay in the stores."

10 (All unconsciously, though, we ourselves used some pure Pittsburghisms. We said "tele pole," pronounced "telly pole," for that splintery sidewalk post I loved to climb. We said "slippy"—the sidewalks are "slippy." We said, "That's all the farther I could go." And we said, as Pittsburghers do say, "This glass needs washed," or "The dog needs walked"—a usage our father eschewed; he knew it was not standard English, nor even comprehensible English, but he never let on.) 10

"Spell 'poinsettia,'" Mother would throw out at me, smiling with pleasure. "Spell 'sherbet.'" The idea was not to make us whizzes, but, quite the contrary, to remind us—and I, especially, needed reminding—that we didn't know it all just yet.

"There's a deer standing in the front hall," she told me one quiet evening in the country.

"Really?"

"No. I just wanted to tell you something once without your saying, 'I know.'"

15 Supermarkets in the middle 1950s began luring, or bothering, customers by giving out Top Value Stamps or Green Stamps. When, shopping with Mother, we got to the head of the checkout line, the checker, always a young man, asked, "Save stamps?"

"No," Mother replied genially, week after week, "I build model airplanes." I believe she originated this line. It took me years to determine where the joke lay.

Anyone who met her verbal challenges she adored. She had surgery on one of her eyes. On the operating table, just before she conked out, she appealed feelingly to the surgeon, saying, as she had been planning to say for weeks, "Will I be able to play the piano?" "Not on me," the surgeon said. "You won't pull that old one on me."

It was, indeed, an old one. The surgeon was supposed to answer, "Yes, my dear, brave woman, you will be able to play the piano after this operation," to which Mother intended to reply, "Oh, good, I've always wanted to play the piano." This pat scenario bored her; she loved having it interrupted. It must have galled her that usually her acquaintances were so predictably unalert; it must have galled her that, for the length of her life, she could surprise everyone so continually, so easily, when she had been the same all along. At any rate, she loved anyone who, as she put it, saw it coming, and called her on it.

She regarded the instructions on bureaucratic forms as straight lines. "Do you advocate the overthrow of the United States government by force or violence?" After some thought she wrote, "Force." She regarded children, even babies, as straight men. When Molly learned to crawl, Mother delighted in buying her gowns with drawstrings at the bottom, like Swee'pea's, because, as she explained energetically, you could easily step on the drawstring without the baby's noticing, so that she crawled and crawled and crawled and never got anywhere except into a small ball at the gown's top.

20 When we children were young, she mothered us tenderly and dependably; as we got older, she resumed her career of anarchism. She collared us into her gags. If she answered the phone on a wrong number, she told the caller, "Just a minute," and dragged the receiver to Amy or me, saying, "Here, take this, your name is Cecile," or, worse, just, "It's for you." You had to think on your feet. But did you want to perform well as Cecile, or did you want to take pity on the wretched caller?

During a family trip to the Highland Park Zoo, Mother and I were alone for a minute. She approached a young couple holding hands on a bench by the seals, and addressed the young man in dripping tones: "Where have you been? Still got those baby-blue eyes; always did slay me. And this"—a swift nod at the dumbstruck young woman, who had removed her hand from the man's—"must be the one you were telling me about. She's not so bad, really, as you used to make out. But listen, you know how I miss you, you know where to reach me, same old place. And there's Ann over there—see how she's grown? See the blue eyes?"

And off she sashayed, taking me firmly by the hand, and leading us around briskly past the monkey house and away. She cocked an ear back, and both of us heard the desperate man begin, in a high-pitched wail, "I swear, I never saw her before in my life . . . "

On a long, sloping beach by the ocean, she lay stretched out sunning with Father and friends, until the conversation gradually grew tedious, when without forethought she gave a little push with her heel and rolled away. People were stunned. She rolled deadpan and apparently effortlessly, arms and legs extended and tidy, down the beach to the distant water's edge, where she lay at ease just as she had been, but half in the surf, and well out of earshot.

She dearly loved to fluster people by throwing out a game's rules at whim—when she was getting bored, losing in a dull sort of way, and when everybody else was taking it too seriously. If you turned your back, she moved the checkers around on the board. When you got them all straightened out, she denied she'd touched them; the next time you turned your back, she lined them up on the rug or hid them under your chair. In a betting rummy game called Michigan, she routinely played out of turn, or called out a card she didn't hold, or counted backward, simply to amuse herself by causing an uproar and watching the rest of us do double takes and have fits. (Much later, when serious suitors came to call, Mother subjected them to this fast card game as a trial by ordeal; she used it as an intelligence test and a measure of spirit. If the poor man could stay a round without breaking down or running out, he got to marry one of us, if he still wanted to.)

She excelled at bridge, playing fast and boldly, but when the stakes were low and the hands dull, she bid slams for the devilment of it, or raised her opponents' suit to bug them, or showed her hand, or tossed her cards in a handful behind her back in a characteristic swift motion accompanied by a vibrantly innocent look. It drove our stolid father crazy. The hand was over before it began, and the guests were appalled. How do you score it, who deals now, what do you do with a crazy person who is having so much fun? Or they were down seven, and the guests were appalled. "Pam!" "Dammit, Pam!" He groaned. What ails such people? What on earth possesses them? He rubbed his face.

She was an unstoppable force; she never let go. When we moved across town, she persuaded the U.S. Post Office to let her keep her old address—forever—because she'd had stationery printed. I don't know how she did it. Every new post office worker, over decades, needed to learn that although the Doaks' mail is addressed to here, it is delivered to there.

Mother's energy and intelligence suited her for a greater role in a larger arena—mayor of New York, say—than the one she had. She followed American politics closely; she had been known to vote for Democrats. She saw how things should be run, but she had nothing to run but our household. Even there, small minds bugged her; she was smarter than the people who designed the things she had to use all day for the length of her life.

"Look," she said. "Whoever designed this corkscrew never used one. Why would anyone sell it without trying it out?" So she invented a better one. She showed me a drawing of it. The spirit of American enterprise never faded in Mother. If capitalizing and tooling up had been as interesting as theorizing and thinking up, she would have fired up a new factory every week, and chaired several hundred corporations.

"It grieves me," she would say, "it grieves my heart," that the company that made one superior product packaged it poorly, or took the wrong tack in its advertising. She knew, as she held the thing mournfully in her two hands, that she'd never find another. She was right. We children wholly sympathized, and so did Father; what could she do, what could anyone do, about it? She was Samson in chains. She paced.

She didn't like the taste of stamps so she didn't lick stamps; she licked the corner of the envelope instead. She glued sandpaper to the sides of kitchen drawers, and under kitchen cabinets, so she always had a handy place to strike a match. She designed, and hounded workmen to build against all norms, doubly wide kitchen counters and elevated bathroom sinks. To splint a finger, she stuck it in a lightweight cigar tube. Conversely, to protect a pack of cigarettes, she carried it in a BandAid box. She drew plans for an over-the-finger toothbrush for babies, an oven rack that slid up and down, and—the family favorite—Lendalarm. Lendalarm was a beeper you attached to books (or tools) you loaned friends. After ten days, the beeper sounded. Only the rightful owner could silence it.

She repeatedly reminded us of P. T. Barnum's dictum: You could sell anything to anybody if you marketed it right. The adman who thought of making Americans believe they needed underarm deodorant was a visionary. So, too, was the hero who made a success of a new product, Ivory soap. The executives were horrified, Mother told me, that a cake of this stuff floated. Soap wasn't supposed to float. Anyone would be able to tell it was mostly whipped-up air. Then some inspired adman made a leap: Advertise that it floats. Flaunt it. The rest is history.

She respected the rare few who broke through to new ways. "Look," she'd say, "here's an intelligent apron." She called upon us to admire intelligent control knobs and intelligent pan handles, intelligent andirons and picture frames and knife sharpeners. She questioned everything, every pair of scissors, every knitting needle, gardening glove, tape dispenser. Hers was a restless mental vigor that just about ignited the dumb household objects with its force.

Torpid conformity was a kind of sin; it was stupidity itself, the mighty stream against which Mother would never cease to struggle. If you held no minority opinions, or if you failed to risk total ostracism for them daily, the world would be a better place without you.

Always I heard Mother's emotional voice asking Amy and me the same few questions: "Is that your own idea? Or somebody else's?" "*Giant* is a good movie," I pronounced to the family at dinner. "Oh, really?" Mother warmed to these occasions. She all but rolled up her sleeves. She knew I hadn't seen it. "Is that your considered opinion?"

She herself held many unpopular, even fantastic, positions. She was scathingly sarcastic about the McCarthy hearings while they took place, right on our living-room television; she frantically opposed Father's wait-and-see calm. "We don't know enough about it," he said. "I do," she said. "I know all I need to know."

She asserted, against all opposition, that people who lived in trailer parks were not bad but simply poor, and had as much right to settle on beautiful land, such as rural Ligonier, Pennsylvania, as did the oldest of families in the finest of hidden houses. Therefore, the people who owned trailer parks, and sought zoning changes to permit trailer parks, needed our help. Her profound belief that the country-club pool sweeper was a person, and that the department-store saleslady, the bus driver, telephone operator, and house-painter were people, and even in groups the steelworkers who carried pickets and the Christmas shoppers who clogged intersections were people—this was a conviction common enough in democratic Pittsburgh, but not altogether common among our friends' parents, or even, perhaps, among our parents' friends.

Opposition emboldened Mother, and she would take on anybody on any issue—the chairman of the board, at a cocktail party, on the current strike; she would fly at him in a flurry of passion, as a songbird selflessly attacks a big hawk.

"Eisenhower's going to win," I announced after school. She lowered her magazine and looked me in the eyes: "How do you know?" I was doomed. It was fatal to say, "Everyone says so." We all knew well what happened. "Do you consult this Everyone before you make your decisions? What if Everyone decided to round up all the Jews?" Mother knew there was no danger of cowing me. She simply tried to keep us all awake. And in fact it was always clear to Amy and me, and to Molly when she grew old enough to listen, that if our classmates came to cruelty, just as much as if the neighborhood or the nation came to madness, we were expected to take, and would be each separately capable of taking, a stand.

My Father's Life

Raymond Carver

Raymond Carver (1938–1988) was born in Chatskanie, Oregon. He received a B.A. from Humboldt State College (1963) and studied creative writing at the University of Iowa and (with the late novelist John Gardner) at Chico State College. A dedicated writer with a worldwide following, Carver is one of the better known short-story writers of the late 20th century. His books include the short story collections Will You Please Be Quiet, Please *(1976) (a National Book Award nominee),* What We Talk About When We Talk About Love *(1981),* Cathedral *(1983), and* Where I'm Calling From *(1988); the miscellaneous collection* Fires: Essays, Poems, Stories *(1983); and the poetry collections* In a Marine Light *(1987) and—posthumously—*A New Path to the Waterfall *(1989). In addition, he published stories in* The Atlantic Monthly, Esquire, *and* The New Yorker. *Carver's stories are often sparse and seldom without the poignancy of the dark side of life—such as depression, unemployment, alcoholism, and divorce. This essay—originally published in* Esquire *in 1984—exhibits Carver's sensitivity for human relationships. Notice how he reveals his own pain as he describes his father's charm and weaknesses.*

1 My dad's name was Clevie Raymond Carver. His family called him Raymond and friends called him C.R. I was named Raymond Clevie Carver Jr. I hated the "Junior" part. When I was little my dad called me Frog, which was okay. But later, like everybody else in the family, he began calling me Junior. He went on calling me this until I was thirteen or fourteen and announced that I

From *Fires: Essays, Poems, Stories.* Originally appeared in *Esquire* (September, 1994).

wouldn't answer to that name any longer. So he began calling me Doc. From then until his death, on June 17, 1967, he called me Doc, or else Son.

When he died, my mother telephoned my wife with the news. I was away from my family at the time, between lives, trying to enroll in the School of Library Science at the University of Iowa. When my wife answered the phone, my mother blurted out, "Raymond's dead!" For a moment, my wife thought my mother was telling her that I was dead. Then my mother made it clear *which* Raymond she was talking about and my wife said, "Thank God. I thought you meant *my* Raymond."

My dad walked, hitched rides, and rode in empty boxcars when he went from Arkansas to Washington State in 1934, looking for work. I don't know whether he was pursuing a dream when he went out to Washington. I doubt it. I don't think he dreamed much. I believe he was simply looking for steady work at decent pay. Steady work was meaningful work. He picked apples for a time and then landed a construction laborer's job on the Grand Coulee Dam. After he'd put aside a little money, he bought a car and drove back to Arkansas to help his folks, my grandparents, pack up for the move west. He said later that they were about to starve down there, and this wasn't meant as a figure of speech. It was during that short while in Arkansas, in a town called Leola, that my mother met my dad on the sidewalk as he came out of a tavern.

"He was drunk," she said. "I don't know why I let him talk to me. His eyes were glittery. I wish I'd had a crystal ball." They'd met once, a year or so before, at a dance. He'd had girlfriends before her, my mother told me. "Your dad always had a girlfriend, even after we married. He was my first and last. I never had another man. But I didn't miss anything."

They were married by a justice of the peace on the day they left for Washington, this big, tall country girl and a farmhand-turned-construction worker. My mother spent her wedding night with my dad and his folks, all of them camped beside the road in Arkansas.

In Omak, Washington, my dad and mother lived in a little place not much bigger than a cabin. My grandparents lived next door. My dad was still working on the dam, and later, with the huge turbines producing electricity and the water backed up for a hundred miles into Canada) he stood in the crowd and heard Franklin D. Roosevelt when he spoke at the construction site. "He never mentioned those guys who died building that dam," my dad said. Some of his friends had died there, men from Arkansas, Oklahoma, and Missouri.

He then took a job in a sawmill in Clatskanie, Oregon, a little town alongside the Columbia River. I was born there, and my mother has a picture of my dad standing in front of the gate to the mill, proudly holding me up to face the camera. My bonnet is on crooked and about to come untied. His hat is pushed back on his forehead, and he's wearing a big grin. Was he going in to work or just finishing his shift? It doesn't matter. In either case, he had a job and a family. These were his salad days.

In 1941 we moved to Yakima, Washington, where my dad went to work as a saw filer, a skilled trade he'd learned in Clatskanie. When war broke out, he was given a deferment because his work was considered necessary to the war effort. Finished lumber was in demand by the armed services, and he kept his saws so sharp they could shave the hair off your arm.

After my dad had moved us to Yakima, he moved his folks into the same neighborhood. By the mid-1940s the rest of my dad's family—his brother, his sister, and her husband, as well as uncles, cousins, nephews, and most of their extended family and friends—had come out from Arkansas. All because my dad came out first. The men went to work at Boise Cascade, where my dad worked, and the women packed apples in the canneries. And in just a little while, it seemed—according to my mother—everybody was better off than my dad. "Your dad couldn't keep money," my mother said. "Money burned a hole in his pocket. He was always doing for others."

The first house I clearly remember living in, at 1515 South Fifteenth Street, in Yakima, had an outdoor toilet. On Halloween night, or just any night, for the hell of it, neighbor kids, kids in their early teens, would carry our toilet away and leave it next to the road. My dad would have to get somebody to help him bring it home. Or these kids would take the toilet and stand it in somebody else's backyard. Once they actually set it on fire, but ours wasn't the only house that had an outdoor toilet. When I was old enough to know what I was doing, I threw rocks at the other toilets when I'd see someone go inside. This was called bombing the toilets. After a while, though, everyone went to indoor plumbing until, suddenly, our toilet was the last outdoor one in the neighborhood. I remember the shame I felt when my third-grade teacher, Mr. Wise, drove me home from school one day. I asked him to stop at the house just before ours, claiming I lived there.

I can recall what happened one night when my dad came home late to find that my mother had locked all the doors on him from the inside. He was drunk, and we could feel the house shudder as he rattled the door. When he'd managed to force open a window, she hit him between the eyes with a colander and knocked him out. We could see him down there on the grass. For years afterward, I used to pick up this colander—it was as heavy as a rolling pin—and imagine what it would feel like to be hit in the head with something like that.

It was during this period that I remember my dad taking me into the bedroom, sitting me down on the bed, and telling me that I might have to go live with my Aunt LaVon for a while. I couldn't understand what I'd done that meant I'd have to go away from home to live. But this, too—whatever prompted it—must have blown over, more or less, anyway, because we stayed together, and I didn't have to go live with her or anyone else.

I remember my mother pouring his whiskey down the sink. Sometimes she'd pour it all out and sometimes, if she was afraid of getting caught, she'd only pour half of it out and then add water to the rest. I tasted some of his whiskey once myself. It was terrible stuff, and I don't see how anybody could drink it.

After a long time without one, we finally got a car, in 1949 or 1950, a 1938 Ford. But it threw a rod the first week we had it, and my dad had to have the motor rebuilt.

"We drove the oldest car in town," my mother said. "We could have had a Cadillac for all he spent on car repairs." One time she found someone else's tube of lipstick on the floorboard, along with a lacy handkerchief. "See this?" she said to me. "Some floozy left this in the car."

Once I saw her take a pan of warm water into the bedroom where my dad was sleeping. She took his hand from under the covers and held it in the water. I stood in the doorway and watched. I wanted to know what was going on. This would make him talk in his sleep, she told me. There were things she needed to know, things she was sure he was keeping from her.

Every year or so, when I was little, we would take the North Coast Limited across the Cascade Range from Yakima to Seattle and stay in the Vance Hotel and eat, I remember, at a place called the Dinner Bell Cafe. Once we went to Ivar's Acres of Clams and drank glasses of warm clam broth.

In 1956, the year I was to graduate from high school, my dad quit his job at the mill in Yakima and took a job in Chester, a little sawmill town in northern California. The reasons given at the time for his taking the job had to do with a higher hourly wage and the vague promise that he might, in a few years' time, succeed to the job of head filer in this new mill. But I think, in the main, that my dad had grown restless and simply wanted to try his luck elsewhere. Things had gotten a little too predictable for him in Yakima. Also, the year before, there had been the deaths, within six months of each other, of both his parents.

But just a few days after graduation, when my mother and I were packed to move to Chester, my dad penciled a letter to say he'd been sick for a while. He didn't want us to worry, he said, but he'd cut himself on a saw. Maybe he'd got a tiny sliver of steel in his blood. Anyway, something had happened and he'd had to miss work, he said. In the same mail was an unsigned postcard from somebody down there telling my mother that my dad was about to die and that he was drinking "raw whiskey."

When we arrived in Chester, my dad was living in a trailer that belonged to the company. I didn't recognize him immediately. I guess for a moment I didn't want to recognize him. He was skinny and pale and looked bewildered. His pants wouldn't stay up. He didn't look like my dad. My mother began to cry. My dad put his arm around her and patted her shoulder vaguely, like he didn't know what this was all about, either. The three of us took up life together in the trailer, and we looked after him as best we could. But my dad was sick, and he couldn't get any better. I worked with him in the mill that summer and part of the fall. We'd get up in the mornings and eat eggs and toast while we listened to the radio, and then go out the door with our lunch pails. We'd pass through the gate together at eight in the morning, and I wouldn't see him again until quitting time. In November I went back to Yakima to be closer to my girlfriend, the girl I'd made up my mind I was going to marry.

He worked at the mill in Chester until the following February, when he collapsed on the job and was taken to the hospital. My mother asked if I would come down there and help. I caught a bus from Yakima to Chester, intending to drive them back to Yakima. But now, in addition to being physically sick, my dad was in the midst of a nervous breakdown, though none of us knew to call it that at the time. During the entire trip back to Yakima, he didn't speak, not even when asked a direct question. ("How do you feel, Raymond?" "You okay, Dad?") He'd communicate if he communicated at all, by moving his head or by turning his palms up as if to say he didn't know or care. The only time he said anything on the trip, and for nearly a month afterward, was when I was speeding down a gravel road in Oregon and the car muffler came loose. "You were going too fast," he said.

Back in Yakima a doctor saw to it that my dad went to a psychiatrist. My mother and dad had to go on relief, as it was called, and the county paid for the psychiatrist. The psychiatrist asked my dad, "Who is the President?" He'd had a question put to him that he could answer. "Ike," my dad said. Nevertheless, they put him on the fifth floor of Valley Memorial Hospital and began giving him electroshock treatments. I was married by then and about to start my own family. My dad was still locked up when my wife went into this same hospital, just one floor down, to have our first baby. After she had delivered, I went upstairs to give my dad the news. They let me in through a steel door and showed me where I could find him. He was sitting on a couch with a blanket over his lap. *Hey,* I thought. *What in hell is happening to my dad?* I sat down next to him and told him he was a grandfather. He waited a minute and then said, "I feel like a grandfather." That's all he said. He didn't smile or move. He was in a big room with a lot of other people. Then I hugged him, and he began to cry.

Somehow he got out of there. But now came the years when he couldn't work and just sat around the house trying to figure what next and what he'd done wrong in his life that he'd wound up like this. My mother went from job to crummy job. Much later she referred to that time he was in the hospital, and those years just afterward, as "when Raymond was sick." The word *sick* was never the same for me again.

In 1964, through the help of a friend, he was lucky enough to be hired on at a mill in Klamath, California. He moved down there by himself to see if he could hack it. He lived not far from the mill, in a one-room cabin not much different from the place he and my mother had started out living in when they went west. He scrawled letters to my mother, and if I called she'd read them aloud to me over the phone. In the letters, he said it was touch and go. Every day that he went to work, he felt like it was the most important day of his life. But every day, he told her, made the next day that much easier. He said for her to tell me he said hello. If he couldn't sleep at night, he said, he thought about me and the good times we used to have. Finally, after a couple of months, he regained some of his confidence. He could do the work and didn't think he had to worry that he'd let anybody down ever again. When he was sure, he sent for my mother.

He'd been off from work for six years and had lost everything in that time—home, car, furniture, and appliances, including the big freezer that had been my mother's pride and joy. He'd lost his good name too—Raymond Carver was someone who couldn't pay his bills—and his self-respect was gone. He'd even lost his virility. My mother told my wife, "All during that time Raymond was sick we slept together in the same bed, but we didn't have relations. He wanted to a few times, but nothing happened. I didn't miss it, but I think he wanted to, you know."

During those years I was trying to raise my own family and earn a living. But, one thing and another, we found ourselves having to move a lot. I couldn't keep track of what was going down in my dad's life. But I did have a chance one Christmas to tell him I wanted to be a writer. I might as well have told him I wanted to become a plastic surgeon. "What are you going to write about?" he wanted to know. Then, as if to help me out, he said, "Write about stuff you know about. Write about some of those fishing trips we took." I said I would, but I knew I wouldn't. "Send me what you write," he said. I said I'd do that, but then I didn't. I wasn't writing anything about fishing, and I didn't think he'd particularly care about, or even necessarily understand, what I was writing in those days. Besides, he wasn't a reader. Not the sort, anyway, I imagined I was writing for.

Then he died. I was a long way off, in Iowa City, with things still to say to him. I didn't have the chance to tell him goodbye, or that I thought he was doing great at his new job. That I was proud of him for making a comeback.

My mother said he came in from work that night and ate a big supper. Then he sat at the table by himself and finished what was left of a bottle of whiskey, a bottle she found hidden in the bottom of the garbage under some coffee grounds a day or so later. Then he got up and went to bed, where my mother joined him a little later. But in the night she had to get up and make a bed for herself on the couch. "He was snoring so loud I couldn't sleep," she said. The next morning when she looked in on him, he was on his back with his mouth open, his cheeks caved in. *Graylooking,* she said. She knew he was dead—she didn't need a doctor to tell her that. But she called one anyway, and then she called my wife.

Among the pictures my mother kept of my dad and herself during those early days in Washington was a photograph of him standing in front of a car, holding a beer and a stringer of fish. In the photograph he is wearing his hat back on his forehead and has this awkward grin on his face. I asked her for it and she gave it to me, along with some others. I put it up on my wall, and each time we moved, I took the picture along and put it up on another wall. I looked at it carefully from time to time, trying to figure out some things about my dad, and maybe myself in the process. But I couldn't. My dad just kept moving further and further away from me and back into time. Finally, in the course of another move, I lost the photograph. It was then that I tried to recall it, and at the same time make an attempt to say something about my dad, and how I thought that in some important ways we might be alike. I wrote the poem when I was living in an apartment house in an urban area south of San Francisco, at a time when I found myself, like my dad, having trouble with alcohol. The poem was a way of trying to connect up with him.

Photograph of My Father in His Twenty-Second Year

October. Here in this dank, unfamiliar kitchen
I study my father's embarrassed young man's face.
Sheepish grin, he holds in one hand a string
of spiny yellow perch, in the other
a bottle of Carlsberg beer.

In jeans and flannel shirt, he leans
against the front fender of a 1934 Ford.
He would like to pose brave and hearty for his posterity,
wear his old hat cocked over his ear.
All his life my father wanted to be bold.

But the eyes give him away, and the hands
that limply offer the string of dead perch
and the bottle of beer. Father, I love you,
yet how can I say thank you, I who can't hold my liquor either
and don't even know the places to fish.

30 The poem is true in its particulars, except that my dad died in June and not October, as the first word of the poem says. I wanted a word with more than one syllable to it to make it linger a little. But more than that, I wanted a month appropriate to what I felt at the time I wrote the poem—a month of short days and failing light, smoke in the air, things perishing. June was summer nights and days, graduations, my wedding anniversary, the birthday of one of my children. June wasn't a month your father died in. 30

After the service at the funeral home, after we had moved outside, a woman I didn't know came over to me and said, "He's happier where he is now." I stared at this woman until she moved away. I still remember the little knob of a hat she was wearing. Then one of my dad's cousins—I didn't know the man's name—reached out and took my hand, "We all miss him," he said, and I knew he wasn't saying it just to be polite.

I began to weep for the first time since receiving the news. I hadn't been able to before. I hadn't had the time, for one thing. Now, suddenly, I couldn't stop. I held my wife and wept while she said and did what she could do to comfort me there in the middle of that summer afternoon.

I listened to people say consoling things to my mother, and I was glad that my dad's family had turned up, had come to where he was. I thought I'd remember everything that was said and done that day and maybe find a way to tell it sometime. But I didn't. I forgot it all, or nearly. What I do remember is that I heard our name used a lot that afternoon, my dad's name and mine. But I knew they were talking about my dad. *Raymond,* these people kept saying in their beautiful voices out of my childhood. *Raymond.*

Big Two-Hearted River

Ernest Hemingway

Ernest Hemingway was born in Oak Park, Illinois in 1899. The son of a doctor who would eventually commit suicide, Hemingway did not bother with college but went straight to work as a journalist for the Kansas City Star, *a job that is sometimes cited as a cause of his famous and oft-parodied prose style. During World War I, he drove an ambulance for the Red Cross and was wounded in the line of duty. After the war, he resumed work as a journalist for the* Toronto Star, *and was assigned duties as a foreign correspondent, which resulted in his association with the famous "Lost Generation" of writers in Paris in the twenties. When Hemingway's second novel,* The Sun Also Rises, *was published, he was suddenly successful and his style—short, simple sentences and a focus on details—became famous. He won the Nobel Prize for literature in 1954. In 1961, he committed suicide at his home in the wilderness of Idaho. "Big Two-Hearted River" tells the story of a strong male character's fishing trip into the backcountry, where he hopes to find peace.*

Part I

1 The train went on up the track out of sight, around one of the 1
hills of burnt timber. Nick sat down on the bundle of canvas and bedding the baggage man had pitched out of the door of the baggage car. There was no town, nothing but the rails and the burned-over country. The thirteen saloons that had lined the one street of Seney had not left a trace. The foundations of the Mansion

House hotel stuck up above the ground. The stone was chipped and split by the fire. It was all that was left of the town of Seney. Even the surface had been burned off the ground.

Nick looked at the burned-over stretch of hillside, where he had expected to find the scattered houses of the town and then walked down the railroad track to the bridge over the river. The river was there. It swirled against the log spiles of the bridge. Nick looked down into the clear, brown water, colored from the pebbly bottom, and watched the trout keeping themselves steady in the current with wavering fins. As he watched them they changed their positions by quick angles, only to hold steady in the fast water again. Nick watched them a long time.

He watched them holding themselves with their noses into the current, many trout in deep, fast moving water, slightly distorted as he watched far down through the glassy convex surface of the pool, its surface pushing and swelling smooth against the resistance of the log-driven piles of the bridge. At the bottom of the pool were the big trout. Nick did not see them at first. Then he saw them at the bottom of the pool, big trout looking to hold themselves on the gravel bottom in a varying mist of gravel and sand, raised in spurts by the current.

Nick looked down into the pool from the bridge. It was a hot day. A kingfisher flew up the stream. It was a long time since Nick had looked into a stream and seen trout. They were very satisfactory. As the shadow of the kingfisher moved up the stream, a big trout shot upstream in a long angle, only his shadow marking the angle, then lost his shadow as he came through the surface of the water, caught the sun, and then, as he went back into the stream under the surface, his shadow seemed to float down the stream with the current, unresisting, to his post under the bridge where he tightened facing up into the current.

Nick's heart tightened as the trout moved. He felt all the old feeling.

He turned and looked down the stream. It stretched away, pebbly-bottomed with shallows and big boulders and a deep pool as it curved away around the foot of a bluff.

Nick walked back up the ties to where his pack lay in the cinders beside the railway track. He was happy. He adjusted the pack harness around the bundle, pulling straps tight, slung the pack on his back, got his arms through the shoulder straps and took some of the pull off his shoulders by leaning his forehead against the wide band of the tump-line. Still, it was too heavy. It was much too heavy. He had his leather rodcase in his hand and leaning forward to keep the weight of the pack high on his shoulders he walked along the road that paralleled the railway track, leaving the burned town behind in the heat, and then turned off around a hill with a high, fire-scarred hill on either side onto a road that went back into the country. He walked along the road feeling the ache from the pull of the heavy pack. The road climbed steadily. It was hard work walking up-hill. His muscles ached and the day was hot, but Nick felt happy. He felt he had left everything behind, the need for thinking, the need to write, other needs. It was all back of him.

From the time he had gotten down off the train and the baggage man had thrown his pack out of the open car door things had been different. Seney was burned, the country was burned over and changed, but it did not matter. It could not all be burned. He knew that. He hiked along the road, sweating in the sun, climbing to cross the range of hills that separated the railway from the pine plains.

The road ran up, dipping occasionally, but always climbing. Nick went on up. Finally the road after going parallel to the burnt hillside reached the top. Nick leaned back against a stump and slipped out of the pack harness. Ahead of him, as far as he could see, was the pine plain. The burned country stopped off at the left with the range of hills. On ahead islands of dark pine trees rose out of the plain. Far off to the left was the line of the river. Nick followed it with his eye and caught glints of the water in the sun.

There was nothing but the pine plain ahead of him, until the far blue hills that marked the Lake Superior height of land. He could hardly see them, faint and far away in the heat-light over the plain. If he looked too steadily they were gone. But if he only half-looked they were there, the far-off hills of the height of land.

Nick sat down against the charred stump and smoked a cigarette. His pack balanced on the top of the stump, harness holding ready, a hollow molded in it from his back. Nick sat smoking, looking out over the country. He did not need to get his map out. He knew where he was from the position of the river.

As he smoked, his legs stretched out in front of him, he noticed a grasshopper walk along the ground and up onto his woolen sock.

The grasshopper was black. As he had walked along the road, climbing, he had started many grasshoppers from the dust. They were all black. They were not the big grasshoppers with yellow and black or red and black wings whirring out from their black wing sheathing as they fly up. These were just ordinary hoppers, but all a sooty black in color. Nick had wondered about them as he walked, without really thinking about them. Now, as he watched the black hopper that was nibbling at the wool of his sock with its fourway lip, he realized that they had all turned black from living in the burned-over land. He realized that the fire must have come the year before, but the grasshoppers were all black now. He wondered how long they would stay that way.

Carefully he reached his hand down and took hold of the hopper by the wings. He turned him up, all his legs walking in the air, and looked at his jointed belly. Yes, it was black too, iridescent where the back and head were dusty.

"Go on, hopper," Nick said, speaking out loud for the first time. "Fly away somewhere."

He tossed the grasshopper up into the air and watched him sail away to a charcoal stump across the road.

Nick stood up. He leaned his back against the weight of his pack where it rested upright on the stump and got his arms through the shoulder straps. He stood with the pack on his back on the brow of the hill looking out across the country, toward the distant river and then struck down the hillside away from the road. Underfoot the ground was good walking. Two hundred yards down the hillside the fire line stopped. Then it was sweet fern, growing ankle high, to walk through, and clumps of jack pines; a long undulating country with frequent rises and descents, sandy underfoot and the country alive again.

Nick kept his direction by the sun. He knew where he wanted to strike the river and he kept on through the pine plain, mounting small rises to see other rises ahead of him and sometimes from the top of a rise a great solid island of pines off to his right or his left. He broke off some sprigs of the heathery sweet fern, and put them under his pack straps. The chafing crushed it and he smelled it as he walked.

He was tired and very hot, walking across the uneven, shadeless pine plain. At any time he knew he could strike the river by turning off to his left. It could not be more than a mile away. But he kept on toward the north to hit the river as far upstream as he could go in one day's walking.

For some time as he walked Nick had been in sight of one of the big islands of pine standing out above the rolling high ground he was crossing. He dipped down and then as he came slowly up to the crest of the bridge he turned and made toward the pine trees.

There was no underbrush in the island of pine trees. The trunks of the trees went straight up or slanted toward each other. The trunks were straight and brown without branches. The branches were high above. Some interlocked to make a solid shadow on the brown forest floor. Around the grove of trees was a bare space. It was brown and soft underfoot as Nick walked on it. This was the over-lapping of the pine needle floor, extending out beyond the width of the high branches. The trees had grown tall and the branches moved high, leaving in the sun this bare space they had once covered with shadow. Sharp at the edge of this extension of the forest floor commenced the sweet fern.

Nick slipped off his pack and lay down in the shade. He lay on his back and looked up into the pine trees. His neck and back and the small of his back rested as he stretched. The earth felt good against his back. He looked up at the sky, through the branches, and then shut his eyes. He opened them and looked up again. There was a wind high up in the branches. He shut his eyes again and went to sleep.

Nick woke stiff and cramped. The sun was nearly down. His pack was heavy and the straps painful as he lifted it on. He leaned over with the pack on and picked up the leather rod-case and started out from the pine trees across the sweet fern swale, toward the river. He knew it could not be more than a mile.

He came down a hillside covered with stumps into a meadow. At the edge of the meadow flowed the river. Nick was glad to get to the river. He walked upstream through the meadow. His trousers were soaked with the dew as he walked. After the hot day, the dew had come quickly and heavily. The river made no sound. It was too fast and smooth. At the edge of the meadow, before he mounted to a piece of high ground to make camp, Nick looked down the river at the trout rising. They were rising to insects come from the swamp on the other side of the stream when the sun went down. The trout jumped out of water to take them. While Nick walked through the little stretch of meadow alongside the stream, trout had jumped high out of water.

Now as he looked down the river, the insects must be settling on the surface, for the trout were feeding steadily all down the stream. As far down the long stretch as he could see, the trout were rising, making circles all down the surface of the water, as though it were starting to rain.

The ground rose, wooded and sandy, to overlook the meadow, the stretch of river, and the swamp. Nick dropped his pack and rod-case and looked for a level piece of ground. He was very hungry and he wanted to make his camp before he cooked. Between two jack pines, the ground was quite level. He took the ax out of the pack and chopped out two projecting roots. That leveled a piece of ground large enough to sleep on. He smoothed out the sandy soil with his hand and pulled all the sweet fern bushes by their roots. His hands smelled good from the sweet fern. He smoothed the uprooted earth. He did not want anything making lumps under the blankets. When he had the ground smooth, he spread his three blankets. One he folded double, next to the ground. The other two he spread on top.

With the ax he slit off a bright slab of pine from one of the stumps and split it into pegs for the tent. He wanted them long and solid to hold in the ground. With the tent unpacked and spread on the ground, the pack, leaning against a jackpine, looked much smaller. Nick tied the rope that served the tent for a ridge-pole to the trunk of one of the pine trees and pulled the tent up off the ground with the other end of the rope and tied it to the other pine. The tent hung on the rope like a canvas blanket on a clothesline. Nick poked a pole he had cut up under the back peak of the canvas and then made it a tent by pegging out the sides. He pegged the sides out taut and drove the pegs deep, hitting them down into the ground with the flat of the ax until the rope loops were buried and the canvas was drum tight.

Across the open mouth of the tent Nick fixed cheesecloth to keep out mosquitoes. He crawled inside under the mosquito bar with various things from the pack to put at the head of the bed under the slant of the canvas. Inside the tent the light came through the brown canvas. It smelled pleasantly of canvas. Already there was something mysterious and homelike. Nick was happy as he crawled inside the tent. He had not been unhappy all day. This was different though. Now things were done. There had been this to do. Now it was done. It had been a hard trip. He was very tired. That was done. He had made his camp. He was settled. Nothing could touch him. It was a good place to camp. He was there, in the good place. He was in his home where he had made it. Now he was hungry.

He came out, crawling under the cheesecloth. It was quite dark outside. It was lighter in the tent.

Nick went over to the pack and found, with his fingers, a long nail in a paper sack of nails, in the bottom of the pack. He drove it into the pine tree, holding it close and hitting it gently with the flat of the ax. He hung the pack up on the nail. All his supplies were in the pack. They were off the ground and sheltered now.

Nick was hungry. He did not believe he had ever been hungrier. He opened and emptied a can of pork and beans and a can of spaghetti into the frying pan.

I've got a right to eat this kind of stuff, if I'm willing to carry it, Nick said. His voice sounded strange in the darkening woods. He did not speak again.

He started a fire with some chunks of pine he got with the ax from a stump. Over the fire he stuck a wire grill, pushing the four legs down into the ground with his boot. Nick put the frying pan on the grill over the flames. He was hungrier. The beans and spaghetti warmed. Nick stirred them and mixed them together. They began to bubble, making little bubbles that rose with difficulty to the surface. There was a good smell. Nick got out a bottle of tomato catchup and cut four slices of bread. The little bubbles were coming faster now. Nick sat down beside the fire and lifted the frying pan off. He poured about half the contents out into the tin plate. It spread slowly on the plate. Nick knew it was too hot. He poured on some tomato catchup. He knew the beans and spaghetti were still too hot. He looked at the fire, then at the tent, he was not going to spoil it all by burning his tongue. For years he had never enjoyed fried bananas because he had never been able to wait for them to cool. His tongue was very sensitive. He was very hungry. Across the river in the swamp, in the almost dark, he saw a mist rising. He looked at the tent once more. All right. He took a full spoonful from the plate.

"Chrise," Nick said, "Geezus Chrise," he said happily.

He ate the whole plateful before he remembered the bread. Nick finished the second plateful with the bread, mopping the plate shiny. He had not eaten since a cup of coffee and a ham sandwich in the station restaurant at St. Ignace. It had been a very fine experience. He had been that hungry before, but had not been able to satisfy it. He could have made camp hours before if he had wanted to. There were plenty of good places to camp on the river. But this was good.

Nick tucked two big chips of pine under the grill. The fire flared up. He had forgotten to get water for the coffee. Out of the pack he got a folding canvas bucket and walked down the hill, across the edge of the meadow, to the stream. The other bank was in the white mist. The grass was wet and cold as he knelt on the bank and dipped the canvas bucket into the stream. It bellied and pulled hard in the current. The water was ice cold. Nick rinsed the bucket and carried it full up to the camp. Up away from the stream it was not so cold.

Nick drove another big nail and hung up the bucket full of water. He dipped the coffee pot half full, put some more chips under the grill onto the fire, and put the pot on. He could not remember which way he made coffee. He could remember an argument about it with Hopkins, but not which side he had taken. He decided to bring it to a boil. He remembered now that was Hopkins's way. He had once argued about everything with Hopkins. While he waited for the coffee to boil, he opened a small can of apricots. He liked to open cans. He emptied the can of apricots out into a tin cup. While he watched the coffee on the fire, he drank the juice syrup of the apricots, carefully at first to keep from spilling, then meditatively, sucking the apricots down. They were better than fresh apricots.

The coffee boiled as he watched. The lid came up and coffee and grounds ran down the side of the pot. Nick took it off the gill. It was a triumph for Hopkins. He put sugar in the empty apricot cup and poured some of the coffee out to cool. It was too hot to pour and he used his hat to hold the handle of the coffee pot. He would not let it steep in the pot at all. Not the first cup. It should be straight Hopkins all the way. Hop deserved that. He was a very serious coffee drinker. He was the most serious man Nick had ever known. Not heavy, serious. That was a long time ago. Hopkins spoke without moving his lips. He had played polo. He made millions of dollars in Texas. He had borrowed carfare to go to Chicago, when the wire came that his first big well had come in. He could have wired for money. That would have been too slow. They called Hop's girl the Blonde Venus. Hop did not mind because she was not his real girl. Hopkins said very confidently that none of them would make fun of his real girl. He was right. Hopkins went away when the telegram came. That was on the Black River. It took eight days for the telegram to reach him. Hopkins gave away his .22 caliber Colt automatic pistol to Nick. He gave his camera to Bill. It was to remember him always by. They were all going fishing again next summer. The Hop Head was rich. He would get a yacht and they would all cruise along the north shore of Lake Superior. He was excited but serious. They said good-bye and all felt bad. It broke up the trip. They never saw Hopkins again. That was a long time ago on the Black River.

Nick drank the coffee, the coffee according to Hopkins. The coffee was bitter. Nick laughed. It made a good ending to the story. His mind was starting to work. He knew he could choke it because he was tired enough. He spilled the coffee out of the pot and shook the grounds loose into the fire. He lit a cigarette and went inside the tent. He took off his shoes and trousers, sitting on the blankets, rolled the shoes up inside the trousers for a pillow, and got in between the blankets.

Out through the front of the tent he watched the glow of the fire, when th night wind blew on it. It was a quiet night. The swamp was perfectly quiet. Nick stretched under the blanket comfortably. A mosquito hummed close to his ear. Nick sat up and lit a match. The mosquito was on the canvas, over his head. Nick moved the match quickly up to it. The mosquito made a satisfactory hiss in the flame. The match went out. Nick lay down again under the blanket. He turned on his side and shut his eyes. He was sleepy. He felt sleep coming. He curled up under the blanket and went to sleep.

[1925]

Part II

In the morning the sun was up and the tent was starting to get hot. Nick crawled out under the mosquito netting stretched across the mouth of the tent, to look at the morning. The grass was wet on his hands as he came out. He held his trousers and his shoes in his hands The river sun was just up over the hill. There was the meadow, the river, and the swamp. There were birch trees in the green of the swamp on the other side of the river.

The river was clear and smoothly fast in the early morning. Down about two hundred yards were three logs all the way across the stream They made the water smooth and deep above them. As Nick watched, a mink crossed the river on the logs and went into the swamp. Nick was excited. He was excited by the early morning and the river. He was really too hurried to eat breakfast, but he knew he must. He built a little fire and put on the coffee pot.

While the water was heating in the pot he took an empty bottle and went down over the edge of the high ground to the meadow. The meadow was wet with dew and Nick wanted to catch grasshoppers for bait before the sun dried the grass. He found plenty of good grasshoppers. They were at the base of the grass stems. Sometimes they clung to a grass stem. They were cold and wet with the dew, and could not jump until the sun warmed them. Nick picked them up, taking only the medium-sized brown ones, and put them into the bottle. He turned over a log and just under the shelter of the edge were several hundred hoppers. It was a grasshopper lodging house. Nick put about fifty of the medium browns into the bottle. While he was picking up the hoppers the others warmed in the sun and commenced to hop away. They flew when they hopped. At first they made one flight and stayed stiff when they landed, as though they were dead.

Nick knew that by the time he was through with breakfast they would be as lively as ever. Without dew in the grass it would take him all day to catch a bottle full of good grasshoppers and he would have to crush many of them, slamming at them with his hat. He washed his hands at the stream. He was excited to be near it. Then he walked up to the tent. The hoppers were already jumping stiffly in the grass. In the bottle, warmed by the sun, they were jumping in a mass. Nick put in a pine stick as a cork. It plugged the mouth of the bottle enough, so the hoppers could not get out and left plenty of air passage.

He had rolled the log back and knew he could get grasshoppers there every morning.

Nick laid the bottle full of jumping grasshoppers against a pine trunk. Rapidly he mixed some buckwheat flour with water and stirred it smooth, one cup of flour, one cup of water. He put a handful of coffee in the pot and dipped a lump of grease out of a can and slid it sputtering across the hot skillet. On the smoking skillet he poured smoothly the buckwheat batter. It spread like lava, the grease spitting sharply. Around the edges the buckwheat cake began to firm, then brown, then crisp. The surface was bubbling slowly to porousness. Nick pushed under the browned under surface with a fresh pine chip. He shook the skillet sideways and the cake was loose on the surface.

I won't try and flop it, he thought. He slid the chip of clean wood all the way under the cake, and flopped it over onto its face. It sputtered in the pan.

45 When it was cooked Nick regreased the skillet. He used all the batter. It made another big flapjack and one smaller one. 45

Nick ate a big flapjack and a smaller one, covered with apple butter. He put apple butter on the third cake, folded it over twice, wrapped it in oiled paper, and put it in his shirt pocket. He put the apple butter jar back in the pack and cut bread for two sandwiches.

In the pack he found a big onion. He sliced it in two and peeled the silky outer skin. Then he cut one half into slices and made onion sandwiches. He wrapped them in oiled paper and buttoned them in the other pocket of his khaki shirt. He turned the skillet upside down on the grill, drank the coffee, sweetened and yellow brown with the condensed milk in it, and tidied up the camp. It was a good camp.

Nick took his fly rod out of the leather rod-case, jointed it, and shoved the rod-case back into the tent. He put on the reel and threaded the line through the guides. He had to hold it from hand to hand, as he threaded it, or it would slip back through its own weight. It was a heavy, double tapered fly line. Nick had paid eight dollars for it a long time ago. It was made heavy to lift back in the air and come forward flat and heavy and straight to make it possible to cast a fly which has no weight. Nick opened the aluminum leader box. The leaders were coiled between the damp flannel pads. Nick had wet the pads at the water cooler on the train up to St. Ignace. In the damp pads the gut leaders had softened and Nick unrolled one and tied it by a loop at the end to the heavy fly line. He fastened a hook on the end of the leader. It was a small hook; very thin and springy.

Nick took it from his hook book, sitting with the rod across his lap. He tested the knot and the spring of the rod by pulling the line taut. It was a good feeling. He was careful not to let the hook bite into his finger.

50 He started down to the stream, holding his rod, the bottle of grasshoppers hung from his neck by a thong tied in half hitches around the neck of the bottle. His landing net hung by a hook from his belt. Over his shoulder was a long flour sack tied at each comer into an ear. The cord went over his shoulder. The sack flapped against his legs. 50

Nick felt awkward and professionally happy with all his equipment hanging from him. The grasshopper bottle swung against his chest. In his shirt the breast pockets bulged against him with the lunch and his fly book.

He stepped into the stream. It was a shock. His trousers clung tight to his legs. His shoes felt the gravel. The water was a rising cold shock.

Rushing, the current sucked against his legs. Where he stepped in, the water was over his knees. He waded with the current. The gravel slid under his shoes. He looked down at the swirl of water below each leg and tipped up the bottle to get a grasshopper.

The first grasshopper gave a jump in the neck of the bottle and went out into the water. He was sucked under in the whirl by Nick's right leg and came to the surface a little way down stream. He floated rapidly, kicking. In a quick circle, breaking the smooth surface of the water, he disappeared. A trout had taken him.

Another hopper poked his face out of the bottle. His antennae wavered. He was getting his front legs out of the bottle to jump. Nick took him by the head and held him while he threaded the slim hook under his chin, down through his thorax, and into the last segments of his abdomen. The grasshopper took hold of the hook with his front feet, spitting tobacco juice on it. Nick dropped him into the water.

Holding the rod in his right hand he let out line against the pull of the grasshopper in the current. He stripped off line from the reel with his left hand and let it run free. He could see the hopper in the little waves of the current. It went out of sight.

There was a tug on the line. Nick pulled against the taut line. It was his first strike. Holding the now living rod across the current, he brought in the line with his left hand. The rod bent in jerks, the trout pumping against the current. Nick knew it was a small one. He lifted the rod straight up in the air. It bowed with the pull.

He saw the trout in the water jerking with his head and body against the shifting tangent of the line in the stream.

Nick took the line in his left hand and pulled the trout, thumping tiredly against the current, to the surface. His back was mottled the clear, water- over-gravel color, his side flashing in the sun. The rod under his right arm, Nick stooped, dipping his right hand into the current. He held the trout, never still, with his moist right hand, while he unhooked the barb from his mouth, then dropped him back into the stream.

60 He hung unsteadily in the current, then settled to the bottom beside a stone. Nick reached down his hand to touch him, his arm to the elbow under water. The trout was steady in the moving stream, resting on the gravel, beside a stone. As Nick's fingers touched him, touched his smooth, cool, underwater feeling he was gone, gone in a shadow across the bottom of the stream.

He's all right, Nick thought. He was only tired.

He had wet his hand before he touched the trout, so he would not disturb the delicate mucus that covered him. If a trout was touched with a dry hand, a white fungus attacked the unprotected spot. Years before when he had fished crowded streams, with fly fishermen ahead of him and behind him, Nick had again and again come on dead trout, furry with white fungus, drifted against a rock, or floating belly up in some pool. Nick did not like to fish with other men on the river. Unless they were of your party, they spoiled it.

He wallowed down the stream, above his knees in the current, through the fifty yards of shallow water above the pile of logs that crossed the stream. He did not rebait his hook and held it in his hand as he waded. He was certain he could catch small trout in the shallows, but did not want them. There would be no big trout in the shallows this time of day.

Now the water deepened up his thighs sharply and coldly. Ahead was the smooth dammed-back flood of water above the logs. The water was smooth and dark; on the left, the lower edge of the meadow; on the right of the swamp.

65 Nick leaned back against the current and took a hopper from the bottle. He threaded the hopper on the hook and spat on him for good luck. Then he pulled several yards of line from the reel and tossed the hopper out ahead onto the fast, dark water. It floated down towards the logs, then the weight of the line pulled the bait under the surface. Nick held the rod in his right hand, letting the line run out through his fingers.

There was a long tug. Nick struck and the rod came alive and dangerous, bent double, the line tightening, coming out of water, tightening, all in a heavy, dangerous, steady pull. Nick felt the moment when the leader would break if the strain increased and let the line go.

The reel ratcheted into a mechanical shriek as the line went out in a rush. Too fast. Nick could not check it, the line rushing out, the reel note rising as the line ran out.

With the core of the reel showing, his heart feeling stopped with the excitement, leaning back against the current that mounted icily his thighs, Nick thumbed the reel hard with his left hand. It was awkward getting his thumb inside the fly reel frame.

As he put on pressure the line tightened into sudden hardness and beyond the logs a huge trout went high out of water. As he jumped, Nick lowered the tip of the rod. But he felt, as he dropped the tip to ease the strain, the moment when the strain was too great; the hardness too tight. Of course, the leader had broken. There was no mistaking the feeling when all spring left the line and it became dry and hard. Then it went slack.

His mouth dry, his heart down, Nick reeled in. He had never seen so big a trout. There was a heaviness, a power not to be held, and then the bulk of him, as he jumped. He looked as broad as a salmon.

Nick's hand was shaky. He reeled in slowly. The thrill had been too much. He felt, vaguely, a little sick, as though it would be better to sit down.

The leader had broken where the hook was tied to it. Nick took it in his hand. He thought of the trout somewhere on the bottom, holding himself steady over the gravel, far down below the light, under the logs, with the hook in his jaw. Nick knew the trout's teeth would cut through the snell of the hook. The hook would imbed itself in his jaw. He'd bet the trout was angry. Anything that size would be angry. That was a trout. He had been solidly hooked. Solid as a rock. He felt like a rock, too, before he started off. By God, he was a big one. By God, he was the biggest one I ever heard of.

Nick climbed out onto the meadow and stood, water running down his trousers and out of his shoes, his shoes squlchy. He went over and sat on the logs. He did not want to rush his sensations any.

He wriggled his toes in the water, in his shoes, and got out a cigarette from his breast pocket. He lit it and tossed the match into the fast water below the logs. A tiny trout rose at the match, as it swung around in the fast current. Nick laughed. He would finish the cigarette.

He sat on the logs, smoking, drying in the sun, the sun warm on his back, the river shallow ahead entering the woods, curving into the woods, shallows, light glittering, big water-smooth rocks, cedars along the bank and white birches, the logs warm in the sun, smooth to sit on, without bark, gray to the touch; slowly the feeling of disappointment left him. It went away slowly, the feeling of disappointment that came sharply after the thrill that made his shoulders ache. It was all right now. His rod lying out on the logs, Nick tied a new hook on the leader, pulling the gut tight until it grimped into itself in a hard knot.

He baited up, then picked up the rod and walked to the far end of the logs to get into the water, where it was not too deep. Under and beyond the logs was a deep pool. Nick walked around the shallow shelf near the swamp shore until he came out on the shallow bed of the stream.

On the left, where the meadow ended and the woods began, a great elm tree was uprooted. Gone over in a storm, it lay back into the woods, its roots clotted with dirt, grass growing in them, rising a solid bank beside the stream. The river cut to the edge of the uprooted tree. From where Nick stood he could see deep channels, like ruts, cut in the shallow bed of the stream by the flow of the current. Pebbly where he stood and pebbly and full of boulders beyond; where it curved near the tree roots the bed of the stream was marly and between the ruts of deep water green weed fronds swung in the current.

Nick swung the rod back over his shoulder and forward, and the line, curving forward, laid the grasshopper down on one of the deep channels in the weeds. A trout struck and Nick hooked him.

Holding the rod far out toward the uprooted tree and sloshing backward in the current, Nick worked the trout, plunging, the rod bending alive, out of the danger of the weeds into the open river. Holding the rod, pumping alive against the current, Nick brought the trout in. He rushed, but always came, the spring of the rod yielding to the rushes, sometimes jerking under water, but always bringing him in. Nick eased downstream with the rushes. The rod above his head he led the trout over the net, then lifted.

80 The trout hung heavy in the net, mottled trout back and silver sides in the meshes. Nick unhooked him; heavy sides, good to hold, big undershot jaw, and slipped him, heaving and big sliding, into the long sack that hung from his shoulders in the water.

Nick spread the mouth of the sack against the current and it filled, heavy with water. He held it up, the bottom in the stream, and the water poured out through the sides. Inside at the bottom was the big trout, alive in the water.

Nick moved downstream. The sack out ahead of him sunk heavy in the water, pulling from his shoulders.

It was getting hot, the sun hot on the back of his neck.

Nick had one good trout. He did not care about getting many trout. Now the stream was shallow and wide. There were trees along both banks. Thc trees of the left bank made short shadows on the current in the forenoon sun. Nick knew there were trout in each shadow In the afternoon, after the sun had crossed toward the hills, the trout would be in the cool shadows on the other side of the stream.

85 The very biggest ones would he up close to the bank. You could always pick them up there on the Black. When the sun was down they all moved out into the current. Just when the sun made the water blinding in the glare before it went down, you were liable to strike a big trout anywhere in the current. It was almost impossible to fish then, the surface of the water was blinding as a mirror in the sun. Of course, you could fish upstream, but in a stream like the Black, or this, you had to wallow against the current and in a deep place, the water piled up on you. It was no fun to fish upstream with this much current.

Nick moved along through the shallow stretch watching the banks for deep holes. A beech tree grew close beside the river, so that the branches hung down into the water. The stream went back in under the leaves. There were always trout in a place like that.

Nick did not care about fishing that hole. He was sure he would get hooked in the branches.

It looked deep though. He dropped the grasshopper so the current took it under water, back in under the overhanging branch. The line pulled hard and Nick struck. The trout threshed heavily, half out of water in the leaves and branches. The line was caught. Nick pulled hard and the trout was off. He reeled in and holding the hook in his hand, walked down the stream.

Ahead, close to the left bank, was a big log. Nick saw it was hollow; pointing up river the current entered it smoothly, only a little ripple spread each side of the log. The water was deepening. The top of the hollow log was gray and dry. It was partly in the shadow.

90 Nick took the cork out of the grasshopper bottle and a hopper clung to it. He picked him off, hooked him, and tossed him out. He

held the rod far out so that the hopper on the water moved into the current flowing into the hollow log. Nick lowered the rod and the hopper floated in. There was a heavy strike. Nick swung the rod against the pull. It felt as though he were hooked into the log itself, except for the live feeling.

He tried to force the fish out into the current. It came, heavily.

The line went slack and Nick thought the trout was gone. Then he saw him, very near, in the current, shaking his head, trying to get the hook out. His mouth was clamped shut. He was fighting the hook in the clear flowing current.

Looping in the line with his left hand, Nick swung the rod to make the line taut and tried to lead the trout toward the net, but he was gone, out of sight, the line pumping. Nick fought him against the current, letting him thump in the water against the spring of the rod. He lifted the rod to his left hand, worked the trout upstream, holding his weight, fighting on the rod, and then let him down into the net. He lifted him clear of the water, a heavy half circle in the net, the net dripping, unhooked him and slid him into the sack.

He spread the mouth of the sack and looked down in at the two big trout alive in the water.

95 Through the deepening water, Nick waded over to the hollow log. He took the sack off, over his head, the trout flopping as it came out of water, and hung it so the trout were deep in the water. Then he pulled himself up on the log and sat, the water from his trouser and boots running down into the stream. He laid his rod down, moved along to the shady end of the log and took the sandwiches out of his pocket. He dipped the sandwiches in the cold water. The current carried away the crumbs. He ate the sandwiches and dipped his hat full of water to drink, the water running out through his hat just ahead of his drinking.

It was cool in the shade, sitting on the log. He took a cigarette out and struck a match to light it. The match sunk into the gray wood, making a tiny furrow. Nick leaned over the side of the log, found a hard place, and lit the match. He sat smoking and watching the river.

Ahead the river narrowed and went into a swamp. The river became smooth and deep and the swamp looked solid with cedar trees, their trunks close together, their branches solid. It would not be possible to walk through a swamp like that. The branches grew so low.

You would have to keep almost level with the ground to move at all. You could not crash through the branches. That must be why the animals that lived in swamps were built the way they were, Nick thought.

He wished he had brought something to read. He felt like reading. He did not feel like going on into the swamp. He looked down the river. A big cedar slanted all the way across the stream. Beyond that the river went into the swamp.

Nick did not want to go in there now. He felt a reaction against deep wading with the water deepening up under his armpits, to hook big trout in places impossible to land them. In the swamp the banks were bare, the big cedars came together overhead, the sun did not come through, except in patches; in the fast deep water, in the half light, the fishing would be tragic. In the swamp fishing was a tragic adventure. Nick did not want it. He did not want to go down the stream any further today.

He took out his knife, opened it, and stuck it in the log. Then he pulled up the sack, reached into it, and brought out one of the trout. Holding him near the tail, hard to hold, alive, in his hand, he whacked him against the log. The trout quivered, rigid. Nick laid him on the log in the shade and broke the neck of the other fish the same way. He laid them side by side on the log. They were fine trout.

Nick cleaned them, slitting them from the vent to the tip of the jaw. All the insides and the gills and tongue came out in one piece. They were both males; long gray-white strips of milt, smooth and clean. All the insides clean and compact, coming out all together. Nick tossed the offal ashore for the minks to find.

He washed the trout in the stream. When he held them back up in the water they looked like live fish. Their color was not gone yet. He washed his hands and dried them on the log. Then he laid the trout on the sack spread out on the log, rolled them up in it, tied the bundle, and put it in the landing net. His knife was still standing, blade stuck in the log. He cleaned it on the wood and put it in his pocket.

Nick stood up on the log, holding his rod, the landing net hanging heavy, then stepped into the water and splashed ashore. He climbed the bank and cut up into the woods, toward the high ground. He was going back to camp. He looked back. The river just showed through the trees. There were plenty of days coming when he could fish the swamp.

[1925]

Harrison Bergeron

Kurt Vonnegut Jr.

Kurt Vonnegut (1922–2007) was born in Indianapolis, Indiana. He was educated at Cornell, Carnegie-Mellon, and the University of Chicago, where his master's thesis was unanimously rejected by the department of anthropology. He served in the Army in World War II and was a prisoner of war in Dresden, Germany, during the Allied fire bombing of that city. He worked as a police reporter, a public relations writer, a Saab dealer, and a teacher. Vonnegut was that rarity, a popular writer who also has considerable standing among critics and intellectuals. The novels he wrote during the sixties, especially Cat's Cradle *(1963), found a cult following among students. Slaughterhouse Five (1969), perhaps his best, depicted the destruction by fire-bombing of Dresden. The satire and absurdity that are the trademarks of his novels occur also in "Harrison Bergeron," where Vonnegut sides with the non-conformist, the rule-breaker, the person who stands outside the narrow moral universe of conventional society.*

1 The year was 2081, and everybody was finally equal. They 1
weren't only equal before God and the law. They were equal every which way. Nobody was smarter than anybody else. Nobody was better looking than anybody else. Nobody was stronger or quicker than anybody else. All this equality was due to the 211th, 212th, and 213th Amendments to the Constitution, and to the unceasing vigilance of agents of the United States Handicapper General.

Some things about living still weren't quite right, though. April, for instance, still drove people crazy by not being springtime. And it

---

Reprinted from *Welcome to the Monkey House* (1961), by permission of Bantam Dell Publishing, a division of Random House, Inc.

was in that clammy month that the H-G men took George and Hazel Bergeron's fourteen-year-old son, Harrison, away.

It was tragic, all right, but George and Hazel couldn't think about it very hard. Hazel had a perfectly average intelligence, which meant she couldn't think about anything except in short bursts. And George, while his intelligence was way above normal, had a little mental handicap radio in his ear. He was required by law to wear it at all times. It was tuned to a government transmitter. Every twenty seconds or so, the transmitter would send out some sharp noise to keep people like George from taking unfair advantage of their brains.

George and Hazel were watching television. There were tears on Hazel's cheeks, but she'd forgotten for the moment what they were about.

On the television screen were ballerinas.

A buzzer sounded in George's head. His thoughts fled in panic, like bandits from a burglar alarm.

"That was a real pretty dance, that dance they just did," said Hazel.

"Huh?" said George.

"That dance—it was nice," said Hazel.

"Yup," said George. He tried to think a little about the ballerinas. They weren't really very good—no better than anybody else would have been, anyway. They were burdened with sashweights and bags of birdshot, and their faces were masked, so that no one, seeing a free and graceful gesture or a pretty face, would feel like something the cat drug in. George was toying with the vague notion that maybe dancers shouldn't be handicapped. But he didn't get very far with it before another noise in his ear radio scattered his thoughts.

George winced. So did two out of the eight ballerinas.

Hazel saw him wince. Having no mental handicap herself, she had to ask George what the latest sound had been.

"Sounded like somebody hitting a milk bottle with a ball peen hammer," said George

"I'd think it would be real interesting, hearing all the different sounds," said Hazel, a little envious. "All the things they think up."

"Um," said George.

"Only, if I was Handicapper General, you know what I would do?" said Hazel. Hazel, as a matter of fact, bore a strong resemblance to the Handicapper General, a woman named Diana Moon Glampers. "If I was Diana Moon Glampers," said Hazel, "I'd have chimes on Sunday—just chimes. Kind of in honor of religion."

"I could think, if it was just chimes," said George.

"Well—maybe make 'em real loud," said Hazel. "I think I'd make a good Handicapper General."

"Good as anybody else," said George.

"Who knows better'n I do what normal is?" said Hazel.

"Right," said George. He began to think glimmeringly about his abnormal son who was now in jail, about Harrison, but a twenty-one-gun salute in his head stopped that.

"Boy!" said Hazel, "that was a doozy, wasn't it?"

It was such a doozy that George was white and trembling, and tears stood on the rims of his red eyes. Two of the eight ballerinas had collapsed to the studio floor, [and] were holding their temples.

"All of a sudden you look so tired," said Hazel. "Why don't you stretch out on the sofa, so's you can rest your handicap bag on the pillows, honeybunch." She was referring to the forty-seven pounds of birdshot in a canvas bag, which was padlocked around George's neck. "Go on and rest the bag for a little while," she said. "I don't care if you're not equal to me for a while."

George weighed the bag with his hands. "I don't mind it," he said. "I don't notice it any more. It's just a part of me."

"You been so tired lately—kind of wore out," said Hazel. "if there was just some way we could make a little hole in the bottom of the bag, and just take out a few of them lead balls. Just a few."

"Two years in prison and two thousand dollars fine for every ball I took out," said George. "I don't call that a bargain."

"If you could just take a few out when you came home from work," said Hazel. "I mean—you don't compete with anybody around here. You just set around."

"If I tried to get away with it," said George, "then other people'd get away with it—and pretty soon we'd be right back to the dark ages again, with everybody competing against everybody else. You wouldn't like that, would you?"

"I'd hate it," said Hazel.

"There you are," said George. "The minute people start cheating on laws, what do you think happens to society?"

If Hazel hadn't been able to come up with an answer to this question George couldn't have supplied one. A siren was going off in his head.

"Reckon it'd fall all apart," said Hazel.

"What would?" said George blankly.

35 "Society," said Hazel uncertainly. "Wasn't that what you just said?"

"Who knows?" said George.

The television program was suddenly interrupted for a news bulletin. It wasn't clear at first as to what the bulletin was about, since the announcer, like all announcers, had a serious speech impediment. For about half a minute, and in a state of high excitement, the announcer tried to say, "Ladies and gentlemen—"

He finally gave up, handed the bulletin to a ballerina to read.

"That's all right—" Hazel said of the announcer, "he tried. That's the big thing. He tried to do the best he could with what God gave him. He should get a nice raise for trying so hard."

40 "Ladies and gentlemen—" said the ballerina, reading the bulletin. She must have been extraordinarily beautiful, because the mask she wore was hideous. And it was easy to see that she was the strongest and most graceful of all the dancers, for her handicap bags were as big as those worn by two-hundred-pound men.

And she had to apologize at once for her voice, which was a very unfair voice for a woman to use. Her voice was a warm, luminous, timeless melody. "Excuse me—" she said, and she began again, making her voice absolutely uncompetitive.

"Harrison Bergeron, age fourteen," she said in a grackle squawk, "has just escaped from jail, where he was held on suspicion of plotting to overthrow the government. He is a genius and an athlete, is under-handicapped, and should be regarded as extremely dangerous."

A police photograph of Harrison Bergeron was flashed on the screen upside down, then sideways, upside down again, then right side up. The picture showed the full length of Harrison against a background calibrated in feet and inches. He was exactly seven feet tall.

The rest of Harrison's appearance was Halloween and hardware. Nobody had ever borne heavier handicaps. He had outgrown hindrances faster than the H-G men could think them up. Instead of a little ear radio for a mental handicap, he wore a tremendous pair of earphones, and spectacles with thick wavy lenses. The spectacles were intended to make him not only half blind, but to give him whanging headaches besides.

45 Scrap metal was hung all over him. Ordinarily, there was a certain symmetry, a military neatness to the handicaps issued to strong people, but Harrison looked like a walking junkyard. In the race of life, Harrison carried three hundred pounds.

And to offset his good looks, the H-G men required that he wear at all times a red rubber ball for a nose, keep his eyebrows shaved off, and cover his even white teeth with black caps at snaggle-tooth random.

"If you see this boy," said the ballerina, "do not—I repeat, do not—try to reason with him."

There was the shriek of a door being torn from its hinges.

Screams and barking cries of consternation came from the television set. The photograph of Harrison Bergeron on the screen jumped again and again, as though dancing to the tune of an earthquake.

50 George Bergeron correctly identified the earthquake, and well he might have—for many was the time his own home had danced to the same crashing tune. "My God—" said George, "that must be Harrison!"

The realization was blasted from his mind instantly by the sound of an automobile collision in his head.

When George could open his eyes again, the photograph of Harrison was gone. A living, breathing Harrison filled the screen.

Clanking, clownish, and huge, Harrison stood in the center of the studio. The knob of the uprooted studio door was still in his hand. Ballerinas, technicians, musicians, and announcers cowered on their knees before him, expecting to die.

"I am the Emperor!" cried Harrison. "Do you hear? I am the Emperor! Everybody must do what I say at once!" He stamped his foot and the studio shook.

55 "Even as I stand here—-" he bellowed, "crippled, hobbled, sickened—I am a greater ruler than any man who ever lived. Now watch me become what I *can* become!"

Harrison tore the straps of his handicap harness like wet tissue paper, tore straps guaranteed to support five thousand pounds.

Harrison's scrap-iron handicaps crashed to the floor.

Harrison thrust his thumbs under the bar of the padlock that secured his head harness. The bar snapped like celery. Harrison smashed his headphones and spectacles against the wall.

He flung away his rubber-ball nose, revealed a man that would have awed Thor, the god of thunder.

60 "I shall now select my Empress!" he said, looking down on the cowering people. "Let the first woman who dares rise to her feet claim her mate and her throne!"

A moment passed, and then a ballerina arose swaying like a willow.

Harrison plucked the mental handicap from her ear, snapped off her physical handicaps with marvelous delicacy. Last of all, he removed her mask.

She was blindingly beautiful.

"Now—" said Harrison, taking her hand, "shall we show the people the meaning of the word dance? Music!" he commanded.

The musicians scrambled back into their chairs, and Harrison stripped them of their handicaps, too. "Play your best," he told them, "and I'll make you barons and dukes and earls."

The music began. It was normal at first—cheap, silly, false. But Harrison snatched two musicians from their chairs, waved them like batons as he sang the music as he wanted it played. He slammed them back into their chairs.

The music began again and was much improved.

Harrison and his Empress merely listened to the music for a while—listened gravely, as though synchronizing their heartbeats with it.

They shifted their weights to their toes.

Harrison placed his big hands on the girl's tiny waist, letting her sense the weightlessness that would soon be hers.

And then, in an explosion of joy and grace, into the air they sprang!

Not only were the laws of the land abandoned, but the law of gravity and the laws of motion as well.

They reeled, whirled, swiveled, flounced, capered, gamboled, and spun.

They leaped like deer on the moon.

The studio ceiling was thirty feet high, but each leap brought the dancers nearer to it.

It became their obvious intention to kiss the ceiling.

They kissed it.

And then, neutralizing gravity with love and pure will, they remained suspended in air inches below the ceiling, and they kissed each other for a long, long time.

It was then that Diana Moon Glampers, the Handicapper General, came into the studio with a double-barreled ten-gauge shotgun. She fired twice and the Emperor and the Empress were dead before they hit the floor.

Diana Moon Glampers loaded the gun again. She aimed it at the musicians and told them they had ten seconds to get their handicaps back on.

It was then that the Bergerons' television tube burned out. Hazel turned to comment about the blackout to George. But George had gone out into the kitchen for a can of beer.

George came back in with the beer, paused while a handicap signal shook him up. And then he sat down again.

"You been crying?" he said to Hazel.

"Yup," she said.

"What about?" he said.

"I forget," she said. "Something real sad on television."

"What was it?" he said.

"It's all kind of mixed up in my mind," said Hazel.

"Forget sad things," said George.

"I always do," said Hazel.

"That's my girl," said George. He winced. There was the sound of a riveting gun in his head.

"Gee— I could tell that one was a doozy," said Hazel.

"You can say that again," said George.

"Gee—" said Hazel, "I could tell that one was a doozy."

Me Talk Pretty One Day

David Sedaris

David Sedaris is considered a master of satire and his readings sell out concert halls across the country. He has a CD entitled David Sedaris at Carnegie Hall. *He read his stories on stage and on the radio, and has had plays produced in New York at La Mama and at Lincoln Center. He has written essays for* Esquire *and* The New Yorker. *His works include* Book of Liz *(2002),* Me Talk Pretty One Day *(2001),* Holidays on Ice *(1998) and* Naked *(1998). He won an Obie Award for a theater production created with his sister, Amy Sedaris, called* One Women Shoe. *Sedaris is a regular contributor to National Public Radio's "This American Life."*

1 At the age of forty-one, I am returning to school and have to 1 think of myself as what my French textbook calls "a true debutant." After paying my tuition, I was issued a student ID, which allows me a discounted entry fee at movie theaters, puppet shows, and Festyland, a far-flung amusement park that advertises with billboards picturing a cartoon stegosaurus sitting in a canoe and eating what appears to be a ham sandwich.

I've moved to Paris with hope of learning the language. My school is an easy ten-minute walk from my apartment, and on the first day of class I arrived early, watching as the returning students greeted one another in the school lobby. Vacations were recounted, and questions were raised concerning mutual friends with names like Kang and Vlatnya. Regardless of their nationalities, everyone spoke in what sounded to me like excellent French. Some accents were better than others, but the students exhibited an ease and confidence I found intimidating. As an added discomfort, they were all young, attractive, and well dressed, causing me to feel not unlike Pa Kettle trapped backstage after a fashion show.

The first day of class was nerve-racking because I knew I'd be expected to perform. That's the way they do it here—it's everybody into the language pool, sink or swim. The teacher marched in, deeply tanned from a recent vacation, and proceeded to rattle off a series of administrative announcements. I've spent quite a few summers in Normandy, and I took a monthlong French class before leaving New York. I'm not completely in the dark, yet I understood only half of what this woman was saying.

"If you have not *meimslsxp* or *lgpdmurct* by this time, then you should not be in this room. Has everyone *apzkiubjxow?* Everyone? Good, we shall begin." She spread out her lesson plan and sighed, saying, "All right, then, who knows the alphabet?"

It was startling because (a) I hadn't been asked that question in a while and (b) I realized, while laughing, that I myself did *not* know the alphabet. They're the same letters, but in France they're pronounced differently. I know the shape of the alphabet but had no idea what it actually sounded like.

"Ahh." The teacher went to the board and sketched the letter *a*. "Do we have anyone in the room whose first name commences with an *ahh?*"

Two Polish Annas raised their hands, and the teacher instructed them to present themselves by stating their names, nationalities, occupations, and a brief list of things they liked and disliked in this world. The first Anna hailed from an industrial town outside of Warsaw and had front teeth the size of tombstones. She worked as a seamstress, enjoyed quiet times with friends, and hated the mosquito.

"Oh, really," the teacher said. "How very interesting. I thought that everyone loved the mosquito, but here, in front of all the world, you claim to detest him. How is it that we've been blessed with someone as unique and original as you? Tell us, please."

The seamstress did not understand what was being said but knew that this was an occasion for shame. Her rabbity mouth huffed for breath, and she stared down at her lap as though the appropriate comeback were stitched somewhere alongside the zipper of her slacks.

The second Anna learned from the first and claimed to love sunshine and detest lies. It sounded like a translation of one of those Playmate of the Month data sheets, the answers always written in the same loopy handwriting: "Turn-ons: Mom's famous five-alarm chili! Turnoffs: insecurity and guys who come on too strong!!!!"

The two Polish Annas surely had clear notions of what they loved and hated, but like the rest of us, they were limited in terms of vocabulary, and this made them appear less than sophisticated. The teacher forged on, and we learned that Carlos, the Argentine bandonion player, loved wine, music, and in his words, "making sex with the womens of the world." Next came a beautiful young Yugoslav who identified herself as an optimist, saying that she loved everything that life had to offer.

The teacher licked her lips, revealing a hint of the saucebox we would later come to know. She crouched low for her attack, placed her hands on the young woman's desk, and leaned close, saying, "Oh yeah? And do you love your little war?"

While the optimist struggled to defend herself, I scrambled to think of an answer to what had obviously become a trick question. How often is one asked what he loves in this world? More to the point, how often is one asked and then publicly ridiculed for his answer? I recalled my mother, flushed with wine, pounding the tabletop late one night, saying, "Love? I love a good steak cooked rare. I love my cat, and I love . . ." My sisters and I leaned forward, waiting to hear our names. "Tums," our mother said. "I love Tums."

The teacher killed some time accusing the Yugoslavian girl of masterminding a program of genocide, and I jotted frantic notes in the margins of my pad. While I can honestly say that I love leafing through medical textbooks devoted to severe dermatological conditions, the hobby is beyond the reach of my French vocabulary, and acting it out would only have invited controversy.

When called upon, I delivered an effortless list of things that I detest: blood sausage, intestinal pâtés, brain pudding. I'd learned these words the hard way. Having given it some thought, I then declared my love for IBM typewriters, the French word for *bruise,* and my electric floor waxer. It was a short list, but still I managed to mispronounce *IBM* and assign the wrong gender to both the floor waxer and the typewriter. The teacher's reaction led me to believe that these mistakes were capital crimes in the country of France.

"Were you always this *palicmkrexis?*" she asked. "Even a *fiuscrzsa ticiwelmun* knows that a typewriter is feminine."

I absorbed as much of her abuse as I could understand, thinking—but not saying—that I find it ridiculous to assign a gender to an inanimate object incapable of disrobing and making an occasional fool of itself. Why refer to Lady Crack Pipe or Good Sir Dishrag when these things could never live up to all that their sex implied?

The teacher proceeded to belittle everyone from German Eva, who hated laziness, to Japanese Yukari, who loved paintbrushes and soap. Italian, Thai, Dutch, Korean, and Chinese—we all left class foolishly believing that the worst was over. She'd shaken us up a little, but surely that was just an act designed to weed out the deadweight. We didn't know it then, but the coming months would teach us what it was like to spend time in the presence of a wild animal, something completely unpredictable. Her temperament was not based on a series of good and bad days but, rather, good and bad moments. We soon learned to dodge chalk and protect our heads and stomachs whenever she approached us with a question. She hadn't yet punched anyone, but it seemed wise to protect ourselves against the inevitable.

Though we were forbidden to speak anything but French, the teacher would occasionally use us to practice any of her five fluent languages.

"I hate you," she said to me one afternoon. Her English was flawless. "I really, really hate you." Call me sensitive, but I couldn't help but take it personally.

After being singled out as a lazy *kfdtinvfm,* I took to spending four hours a night on my homework, putting in even more time whenever we were assigned an essay. I suppose I could have gotten by with less, but I was determined to create some sort of identity for myself: David the hard worker, David the cut-up. We'd have one of those "complete this sentence" exercises, and I'd fool with the thing for hours, invariably settling on something like "A quick run around the lake? I'd love to! Just give me a moment while I strap on my wooden leg." The teacher, through word and action, conveyed the message that if this was my idea of an identity, she wanted nothing to do with it.

My fear and discomfort crept beyond the borders of the classroom and accompanied me out onto the wide boulevards. Stopping for a coffee, asking directions, depositing money in my bank account:

these things were out of the question, as they involved having to speak. Before beginning school, there'd been no shutting me up, but now I was convinced that everything I said was wrong. When the phone rang, I ignored it. If someone asked me a question, I pretended to be deaf. I knew my fear was getting the best of me when I started wondering why they don't sell cuts of meat in vending machines.

My only comfort was the knowledge that I was not alone. Huddled in the hallways and making the most of our pathetic French, my fellow students and I engaged in the sort of conversation commonly overheard in refugee camps.

"Sometime me cry alone at night."

"That be common for I, also, but be more strong, you. Much work and someday you talk pretty. People start love you soon. Maybe tomorrow, okay."

Unlike the French class I had taken in New York, here there was no sense of competition. When the teacher poked a shy Korean in the eyelid with a freshly sharpened pencil, we took no comfort in the fact that, unlike Hyeyoon Cho, we all knew the irregular past tense of the verb *to defeat.* In all fairness, the teacher hadn't meant to stab the girl, but neither did she spend much time apologizing, saying only, "Well, you should have been *vkkdyo* more *kdeynfulh.*"

Over time it became impossible to believe that any of us would ever improve. Fall arrived and it rained every day, meaning we would now be scolded for the water dripping from our coats and umbrellas. It was mid-October when the teaching singled me out, saying, "Every day spent with you is like having a cesarean section." And it struck me that, for the first time since arriving in France, I could understand every word that someone was saying.

Understanding doesn't mean that you can suddenly speak the language. Far from it. It's a small step, nothing more, yet its rewards are intoxicating and deceptive. The teacher continued her diatribe and I settled back, bathing in the subtle beauty of each new curse and insult.

"You exhaust me with your foolishness and reward my efforts with nothing but pain, do you understand me?"

The world opened up, and it was with great joy that I responded, "I know the thing that you speak exact now. Talk me more, you, plus, please, plus."

Shooting an Elephant

George Orwell

George Orwell is the pen name used by the British author Eric Blair (1903–1950). Orwell was born in the Indian village of Motihari, near Nepal, where his father was stationed in the Civil Service. India was then part of the British Empire; Orwell's grandfather too had served the Empire in the Indian Army. From 1907 to 1922 Orwell lived in England, returning to India and Burma and a position in the Imperial Police, which he held until 1927. This is the period about which he writes in "Shooting an Elephant." Thereafter he lived in England, Paris, Spain, and elsewhere, writing on a wide range of topics. He fought in the Spanish Civil War and was actively engaged in several political movements, always against totalitarianism of any kind. He is best known today for two novels of political satire: Animal Farm *(1945) and* 1984 *(1949). He was also a prolific journalist and essayist, with his essays collected in five volumes. "Shooting an Elephant" was first published in 1936 and later collected in a book of the same name in 1950. Note that Orwell is writing as an older, wiser man about events that took place when he was in his early twenties some two decades previously. This combined perspective of the young man experiencing the incident and the older man looking back on it is part of the rich reading experience.*

1 In Moulmein, in Lower Burma, I was hated by large numbers of 1
people—the only time in my life that I have been important enough for this to happen to me. I was sub-divisional police officer of the town, and in an aimless, petty, kind of way anti-European feel-

From *Shooting an Elephant and Other Essays* by George Orwell. Published by Harcourt Brace and Company. Harcourt Brace and Company and Heath & Co., Ltd.

ing was very bitter. No one had the guts to raise a riot, but if a European woman went through the bazaars alone somebody would probably spit betel juice over her dress. As a police officer I was an obvious target and was baited whenever it seemed safe to do so. When a nimble Burman tripped me up on the football field and the referee (another Burman) looked the other way, the crowd yelled with hideous laughter. This happened more than once. In the end the sneering yellow faces of young men that met me everywhere, the insults hooted after me when I was at a safe distance, got badly on my nerves. The young Buddhist priests were the worst of all. There were several thousand of them in the town and none of them seemed to have anything to do except stand on street corners and jeer at Europeans.

All this was perplexing and upsetting. For at that time I had already made up my mind that imperialism was an evil thing and the sooner I chucked up my job and got out of it the better. Theoretically—and secretly, of course—I was all for the Burmese and all against their oppressors, the British. As for the job I was doing, I hated it more bitterly than I can perhaps make clear. In a job like that you see the dirty work of Empire at close quarters. The wretched prisoners huddling in the stinking cages of the lock-ups, the grey, cowed faces of the long-term convicts, the scarred buttocks of the men who had been flogged with bamboos—all these oppressed me with an intolerable sense of guilt. But I could get nothing into perspective. I was young and ill-educated and I had had to think out my problems in the utter silence that is imposed on every Englishman in the East. I did not even know that the British Empire is dying, still less did I know that it is a great deal better than the younger empires that are going to supplant it. All I knew was that I was stuck between my hatred of the empire I served and my rage against the evil-spirited little beasts who tried to make my job impossible. With one part of my mind I thought of the British Raj as an unbreakable tyranny, as something clamped down, in *saecula saeculorum,* upon the will of prostrate peoples; with another part I thought that the greatest joy in the world would be to drive a bayonet into a Buddhist priest's guts. Feelings like these are the normal by-products of imperialism; ask any Anglo-Indian official, if you can catch him off duty.

One day something happened which in a roundabout way was enlightening. It was a tiny incident in itself, but it gave me a better glimpse than I had had before of the real nature of imperialism—the real motives for which despotic governments act. Early one morning the sub-inspector at a police station the other end of the town rang me up on the 'phone and said that an elephant was ravaging the bazaar. Would I please come and do something about it? I did not know what I could do, but I wanted to see what was happening and I got on to a pony and started out. I took my rifle, an old .44 Winchester and much too small to kill an elephant, but I thought the noise might be useful *in terrorem.* Various Burmans stopped me on the way and told me about the elephant's doings. It was not, of course, a wild elephant, but a tame one which had gone "must." It had been chained up, as tame elephants always are when their attack of "must" is due, but on the previous night it had broken its chain and escaped. Its mahout, the only person who could manage it when it was in that state, had set out in pursuit, but had taken the wrong direction and was now twelve hours' journey away, and in the morning the elephant had suddenly reappeared in the town. The Burmese population had no weapons and were quite helpless against it. It had already destroyed somebody's bamboo hut, killed a cow and raided some fruit-stalls and devoured the stock; also it had met the municipal rubbish van and, when the driver jumped out and took to his heels, had turned the van over and inflicted violence upon it.

The Burmese sub-inspector and some Indian constables were waiting for me in the quarter where the elephant had been seen. It was a very poor quarter, a labyrinth of squalid bamboo huts, thatched with palm-leaf, winding all over a steep hillside. I remember that it was a cloudy, stuffy, morning at the beginning of the rains. We began questioning the people as to where the elephant had gone and, as usual, failed to get any definite information. That is invariably the case in the East; a story always sounds clear enough at a distance, but the nearer you get to the scene of events the vaguer it becomes. Some of the people said that the elephant had gone in one direction, some said that he had gone in another, some professed not even to have heard of any elephant. I had almost made up my mind that the whole story was a pack of lies, when we heard yells a little distance away. There was a loud, scandalized cry of "Go away, child! Go away this instant!" and an old woman with a switch in her hand came round the corner of a hut, violently shooing away a crowd of naked children. Some more women followed, clicking their tongues and exclaiming; evidently there was something that the children ought not to have seen. I rounded the hut and saw a man's dead body sprawling in the mud. He was an Indian, a black Dravidian coolie, almost naked, and he could not have been dead many minutes. The people said that the elephant had come suddenly upon him round the corner of the hut, caught him with its trunk, put its foot on his back and ground him into the earth. This was the rainy season and the ground was soft, and his face had scored a trench a foot deep and a couple of yards long. He was lying on his belly with arms crucified and head sharply twisted to one side. His face was coated with mud, the eyes wide open, the teeth bared and grinning with an expression of unendurable agony. (Never tell me, by the way, that the dead look peaceful. Most of the corpses I have seen looked devilish.) The friction of the great beast's foot had stripped the skin from his back as neatly as one skins a rabbit. As soon as I saw the dead man I sent an orderly to a friend's house nearby to borrow an elephant rifle. I had already sent back the pony, not wanting it to go mad with fright and throw me if it smelt the elephant.

5 The orderly came back in a few minutes with a rifle and five cartridges, and meanwhile some Burmans had arrived and told us that the elephant was in the paddy fields below, only a few hundred yards away. As I started forward practically the whole population of the quarter flocked out of the houses and followed me. They had seen the rifle and were all shouting excitedly that I was going to shoot the elephant. They had not shown much interest in the elephant when he was merely ravaging their homes, but it was different now that he was going to be shot. It was a bit of fun to them, as it would be to an English crowd; besides they wanted the meat. It made me vaguely uneasy. I had no intention of shooting the elephant—I had merely sent for the rifle to defend myself if necessary—and it is always unnerving to have a crowd following you. I marched down the hill, looking and feeling a fool, with the rifle over my shoulder and an evergrowing army of people jostling at my heels. At the bottom, when you got away from the huts, there was a metalled road and beyond that a miry waste of paddy fields a thousand yards across, not yet ploughed but soggy from the first rains and dotted with coarse grass. The elephant was standing eight yards from the road, his left side towards us. He took not the slightest notice of the crowd's approach. He was tearing up bunches of grass, beating them against his knees to clean them and stuffing them into his mouth.

I had halted on the road. As soon as I saw the elephant I knew with perfect certainty that I ought not to shoot him. It is a serious matter to shoot a working elephant—it is comparable to destroying a huge and costly piece of machinery—and obviously one ought not to do it if it can possibly be avoided. And at that distance, peacefully eating, the elephant looked no more dangerous than a cow. I thought then and I think now that his attack of "must" was already passing off; in which case he would merely wander harmlessly about until the mahout came back and caught him. Moreover, I did not in the least want to shoot him. I decided that I would watch him for a little while to make sure that he did not turn savage again, and then go home.

But at that moment I glanced round at the crowd that had followed me. It was an immense crowd, two thousand at the least and growing every minute. It blocked the road for a long distance on either side. I looked at the sea of yellow faces above the garish clothes—faces all happy and excited over this bit of fun, all certain that the elephant was going to be shot. They were watching me as they would watch a conjurer about to perform a trick. They did not like me, but with the magical rifle in my hands I was momentarily worth watching. And suddenly I realized that I should have to shoot the elephant after all. The people expected it of me and I had got to do it; I could feel their two thousand wills pressing me forward, irresistibly. And it was at this moment, as I stood there with the rifle in my hands, that I first grasped the hollowness, the futility of the white man's dominion in the East. Here was I, the white man with his gun, standing in front of the unarmed native crowd—seemingly the leading actor of the piece; but in reality I was only an absurd puppet pushed to and fro by the will of those yellow faces behind. I perceived in this moment that when the white man turns tyrant it is his own freedom that he destroys. He becomes a sort of hollow, posing dummy, the conventionalized figure of a sahib. For it is the condition of his rule that he shall spend his life in trying to impress the "natives," and so in every crisis he has got to do what the "natives" expect of him. He wears a mask, and his face grows to fit it. I had got to shoot the elephant. I had committed myself to doing it when I sent for the rifle. A sahib has got to act like a sahib; he has got to appear resolute, to know his own mind and do definite things. To come all that way, rifle in hand, with a thousand people marching at my heels, and then to trail feebly away, having done nothing—no, that was impossible. The crowd would laugh at me. And my whole life, every white man's life in the East, was one long struggle not to be laughed at.

But I did not want to shoot the elephant. I watched him beating his bunch of grass against his knees, with that preoccupied grandmotherly air that elephants have. It seemed to me that it would be murder to shoot him. At that age I was not squeamish about killing animals, but I had never shot an elephant and never wanted to. (Somehow it always seems worse to kill a *large* animal.) Besides, there was the beast's owner to be considered. Alive, the elephant was worth at least a hundred pounds; dead, he would only be worth the value of his tusks, five pounds, possibly. But I had got to act quickly. I turned to some experienced-looking Burmans who had been there when we arrived, and asked them how the elephant had been behaving. They all said the same thing: he took no notice of you if you left him alone, but he might charge if you went too close to him.

It was perfectly clear to me what I ought to do. I ought to walk up to within, say, twenty-five yards of the elephant and test his behavior. If he charged, I could shoot; if he took no notice of me, it would be safe to leave him until the mahout came back. But also I knew that I was going to do no such thing. I was a poor shot with a rifle and the ground was soft mud into which one would sink at every step. If the elephant charged and I missed him, I should have about as much chance as a toad under a steam-roller. But even then I was not thinking particularly of my own skin, only of the watchful yellow faces behind. For at that moment, with the crowd watching me, I was not afraid in the ordinary sense, as I would have been if I had been alone. A white man mustn't be frightened in front of "natives"; and so, in general, he isn't frightened. The sole thought in my mind was that if anything went wrong those two thousand Burmans would see me pursued, caught, trampled on and reduced to a grinning corpse like that Indian up the hill. And if that happened it was quite probable that some of them would laugh. That would never do. There was only one alternative. I shoved the cartridges into the magazine and lay down on the road to get a better aim.

10 The crowd grew very still, and a deep, low, happy sigh, as of people who see the theatre curtain go up at last, breathed from innumerable throats. They were going to have their bit of fun after all. The rifle was a beautiful German thing with cross-hair sights. I did not then know that in shooting an elephant one would shoot to cut an imaginary bar running from ear-hole to ear-hole. I ought, therefore, as the elephant was sideways on, to have aimed straight at his ear-hole; actually

I aimed several inches in front of this, thinking the brain would be further forward.

When I pulled the trigger I did not hear the bang or feel the kick—one never does when a shot goes home—but I heard the devilish roar of glee that went up from the crowd. In that instant, in too short a time, one would have thought, even for the bullet to get there, a mysterious, terrible change had come over the elephant. He neither stirred nor fell, but every line of his body had altered. He looked suddenly stricken, shrunken, immensely old, as though the frightful impact of the bullet had paralysed him without knocking him down. At last, after what seemed a long time—it might have been five seconds, I dare say—he sagged flabbily to his knees. His mouth slobbered. An enormous senility seemed to have settled upon him. One could have imagined him thousands of years old. I fired again into the same spot. At the second shot he did not collapse but climbed with desperate slowness to his feet and stood weakly upright, with legs sagging and head drooping. I fired a third time. That was the shot that did for him. You could see the agony of it jolt his whole body and knock the last remnant of strength from his legs. But in falling he seemed for a moment to rise, for as his hind legs collapsed beneath him he seemed to tower upward like a huge rock toppling, his trunk reaching skywards like a tree. He trumpeted, for the first and only time. And then down he came, his belly towards me, with a crash that seemed to shake the ground even where I lay.

I got up. The Burmans were already racing past me across the mud. It was obvious that the elephant would never rise again, but he was not dead. He was breathing very rhythmically with long rattling gasps, his great mound of a side painfully rising and falling. His mouth was wide open—I could see far down into caverns of pale pink throat. I waited a long time for him to die, but his breathing did not weaken. Finally I fired my two remaining shots into the spot where I thought his heart must be. The thick blood welled out of him like red velvet, but still he did not die. His body did not even jerk when the shots hit him, the tortured breathing continued without a pause. He was dying, very slowly and in great agony, but in some world remote from me where not even a bullet could damage him further. I felt that I had got to put an end to that dreadful noise. It seemed dreadful to see the great beast lying there, powerless to move and yet powerless to die, and not even to be able to finish him. I sent back for my small rifle and poured shot after shot into his heart and down his throat. They seemed to make no impression. The tortured gasps continued as steadily as the ticking of a clock.

In the end I could not stand it any longer and went away. I heard later that it took him half an hour to die. Burmans were bringing dahs and baskets even before I left, and I was told they had stripped his body almost to the bones by the afternoon.

Afterwards, of course, there were endless discussions about the shooting of the elephant. The owner was furious, but he was only an Indian and could do nothing. Besides, legally I had done the right thing, for a mad elephant has to be killed, like a mad dog, if its owner fails to control it. Among the Europeans opinion was divided. The older men said I was right, the younger men said it was a damn shame to shoot an elephant for killing a coolie, because an elephant was worth more than any damn Coringhee coolie. And afterwards I was very glad that the coolie had been killed; it put me legally in the right and it gave me a sufficient pretext for shooting the elephant. I often wondered whether any of the others grasped that I had done it solely to avoid looking a fool.

Little Snow White

Jacob and Wilhelm Grimm

The brothers Grimm, Jacob Ludwig Carl (1785–1863) and Wilhelm Carl (1786–1859), were born in Hanau, Germany, the sons of a lawyer. Upon the death of their father, they decided to follow his profession, studying law at the University of Marburg (1802–1806), but they both found themselves more drawn to other studies. There they became interested in folk poetry and began to collect folk stories and poetry. They worked together for decades, publishing their three volume Ger Kinder und Hausmarchen *(Fairy Tales) between 1812 and 1822, in which "Little Snow White" appears. Jacob also wrote the reknowned* Germanic Grammar *(1818 and revised 1822–1840) and devised the influential Grimm's law of sound changes. The two became respected professors at the University of Berlin.*

1 Once upon a time in the middle of winter, when the flakes of snow were falling like feathers from the sky, a queen sat at a window sewing, and the frame of the window was made of black ebony. And whilst she was sewing and looking out of the window at the snow, she pricked her finger with the needle, and three drops of blood fell upon the snow. And the red looked pretty upon the white snow, and she thought to herself, would that I had a child as white as snow, as red as blood, and as black as the wood of the window-frame. 1

Soon after that she had a little daughter, who was as white as snow, and as red as blood, and her hair was as black as ebony, and she was therefore called little Snow White. And when the child was born, the queen died.

After a year had passed the king took to himself another wife. She was a beautiful woman, but proud and haughty, and she could not bear that anyone else should surpass her in beauty. She had a wonderful looking-glass, and when she stood in front of it and looked at herself in it, and said,

> looking-glass, looking-glass, on the wall,
> who in this land is the fairest of all.

The looking-glass answered,

> thou, oh queen, art the fairest of all.

Then she was satisfied, for she knew that the looking-glass spoke the truth. But Snow White was growing up, and grew more and more beautiful, and when she was seven years old she was as beautiful as the day, and more beautiful than the queen herself. And once when the queen asked her looking-glass,

> looking-glass, looking-glass, on the wall,
> who in this land is the fairest of all.

It answered,

> thou art fairer than all who are here, lady queen.
> But more beautiful still is Snow White, as I ween.

Then the queen was shocked, and turned yellow and green with envy. From that hour, whenever she looked at Snow White, her heart heaved in her breast, she hated the girl so much. And envy and pride grew higher and higher in her heart like a weed, so that she had no peace day or night. She called a huntsman, and said, take the child away into the forest. I will no longer have her in my sight. Kill her, and bring me back her lung and liver as a token. The huntsman obeyed, and took her away but when he had drawn his knife, and was about to pierce Snow White's innocent heart, she began to weep, and said, ah dear huntsman, leave me my life. I will run away into the wild forest, and never come home again.

And as she was so beautiful the huntsman had pity on her and said, run away, then, you poor child. The wild beasts will soon have devoured you, thought he, and yet it seemed as if a stone had been rolled from his heart since it was no longer needful for him to kill her.

And as a young bear just then came running by he stabbed it, and cut out its lung and liver and took them to the queen as proof that the child was dead. The cook had to salt them, and the wicked queen ate them, and thought she had eaten the lung and liver of Snow White.

But now the poor child was all alone in the great forest, and so terrified that she looked at all the leaves on the trees, and did not know what to do. Then she began to run, and ran over sharp stones and through thorns, and the wild beasts ran past her, but did her no harm.

She ran as long as her feet would go until it was almost evening, then she saw a little cottage and went into it to rest herself. Everything in the cottage was small, but neater and cleaner than can be told. There was a table on which was a white cover, and seven little plates, and on each plate a little spoon, moreover, there were seven little knives and forks, and seven little mugs. Against the wall stood seven little beds side by side, and covered with snow-white counterpanes.

Little Snow White was so hungry and thirsty that she ate some vegetables and bread from each plate and drank a drop of wine out of each mug, for she did not wish to take all from one only. Then, as she was so tired, she laid herself down on one of the little beds, but none of them suited her, one was too long, another too short, but at last she found that the seventh one was right, and so she remained in it, said a prayer and went to sleep.

When it was quite dark the owners of the cottage came back. They were seven dwarfs who dug and delved in the mountains for ore. They lit their seven candles, and as it was now light within the cottage they saw that someone had been there, for everything was not in the same order in which they had left it.

The first said, who has been sitting on my chair.

The second, who has been eating off my plate.

The third, who has been taking some of my bread.

The fourth, who has been eating my vegetables.

The fifth, who has been using my fork.

The sixth, who has been cutting with my knife.

The seventh, who has been drinking out of my mug.

Then the first looked round and saw that there was a little hollow on his bed, and he said, who has been getting into my bed. The others came up and each called out, somebody has been lying in my bed too. But the seventh when he looked at his bed saw little Snow

White, who was lying asleep therein. And he called the others, who came running up, and they cried out with astonishment, and brought their seven little candles and let the light fall on little Snow White. Oh, heavens, oh, heavens, cried they, what a lovely child. And they were so glad that they did not wake her up, but let her sleep on in the bed. And the seventh dwarf slept with his companions, one hour with each, and so passed the night.

When it was morning little Snow White awoke, and was frightened when she saw the seven dwarfs. But they were friendly and asked her what her name was. My name is Snow White, she answered. How have you come to our house, said the dwarfs. Then she told them that her step-mother had wished to have her killed, but that the huntsman had spared her life, and that she had run for the whole day, until at last she had found their dwelling.

The dwarfs said, if you will take care of our house, cook, make the beds, wash, sew and knit, and if you will keep everything neat and clean you can stay with us and you shall want for nothing.

Yes, said Snow White, with all my heart. And she stayed with them. She kept the house in order for them. In the mornings they went to the mountains and looked for copper and gold, in the evenings they came back, and then their supper had to be ready. The girl was alone the whole day, so the good dwarfs warned her and said, beware of your step-mother, she will soon know that you are here, be sure to let no one come in.

But the queen, believing that she had eaten Snow White's lung and liver, could not but think that she was again the first and most beautiful of all, and she went to her looking-glass and said,

> looking-glass, looking-glass, on the wall,
> who in this land is the fairest of all.

And the glass answered,

> oh, queen, thou art fairest of all I see,
> but over the hills, where the seven dwarfs dwell,
> Snow White is still alive and well,
> and none is so fair as she.

Then she was astounded, for she knew that the looking-glass never spoke falsely, and she knew that the huntsman had betrayed her, and that little Snow White was still alive.

And so she thought and thought again how she might kill her, for so long as she was not the fairest in the whole land, envy let her have no rest. And when she had at last thought of something to do, she painted her face, and dressed herself like an old pedlar-woman, and no one could have known her. In this disguise she went over the seven mountains to the seven dwarfs, and knocked at the door and cried, pretty things to sell, very cheap, very cheap. Little Snow White looked out of the window and called out, good-day my good woman, what have you to sell. Good things, pretty things, she answered, stay-laces of all colors, and she pulled out one which was woven of bright-colored silk. I may let the worthy old woman in, thought Snow White, and she unbolted the door and bought the pretty laces. Child, said the old woman, what a fright you look, come, I will lace you properly for once. Snow-white had no suspicion, but stood before her, and let herself be laced with the new laces. But the old woman laced so quickly and so tightly that Snow White lost her breath and fell down as if dead. Now I am the most beautiful, said the queen to herself, and ran away.

Not long afterwards, in the evening, the seven dwarfs came home, but how shocked they were when they saw their dear little Snow White lying on the ground, and that she neither stirred nor moved, and seemed to be dead. They lifted her up, and, as they saw that she was laced too tightly, they cut the laces, then she began to breathe a little, and after a while came to life again. When the dwarfs heard what had happened they said, the old pedlar-woman was no one else than the wicked queen, take care and let no one come in when we are not with you.

But the wicked woman when she had reached home went in front of the glass and asked,

> looking-glass, looking-glass, on the wall,
> who in this land is the fairest of all.

And it answered as before,

> oh, queen, thou art fairest of all I see,
> but over the hills, where the seven dwarfs dwell,
> Snow White is still alive and well,
> and none is so fair as she.

When she heard that, all her blood rushed to her heart with fear, for she saw plainly that little Snow White was again alive. But now, she said, I will think of something that shall really put an end to you.

And by the help of witchcraft, which she understood, she made a poisonous comb. Then she disguised herself and took the shape of another old woman. So she went over the seven mountains to the seven dwarfs, knocked at the door, and cried, good things to sell, cheap, cheap. Little Snow White looked out and said, go away, I cannot let anyone come in. I suppose you can look, said the old woman, and pulled the poisonous comb out and held it up. It pleased the girl so well that she let herself be beguiled, and opened the door. When they had made a bargain the old woman said, now I will comb you properly for once. Poor little Snow White had no suspicion, and let the old woman do as she pleased, but hardly had she put the comb in her hair than the poison in it took effect, and the girl fell down senseless. You paragon of beauty, said the wicked woman, you are done for now, and she went away.

But fortunately it was almost evening, when the seven dwarfs came home. When they saw Snow White lying as if dead upon the ground they at once suspected the step-mother, and they looked and found the poisoned comb. Scarcely had they taken it out when Snow White came to herself, and told them what had happened. Then they warned her once more to be upon her guard and to open the door to no one.

The queen, at home, went in front of the glass and said,

> looking-glass, looking-glass, on the wall,
> who in this land is the fairest of all.

Then it answered as before,

> oh, queen, thou art fairest of all I see,
> but over the hills, where the seven dwarfs dwell,
> Snow White is still alive and well,
> and none is so fair as she.

When she heard the glass speak thus she trembled and shook with rage. Snow White shall die, she cried, even if it costs me my life.

There upon she went into a quite secret, lonely room, where no one ever came, and there she made a very poisonous apple. Outside it looked pretty, white with a red cheek, so that everyone who saw it longed for it, but whoever ate a piece of it must surely die.

When the apple was ready she painted her face, and dressed herself up as a farmer's wife, and so she went over the seven mountains to the seven dwarfs. She knocked at the door. Snow White put her head out of the window and said, I cannot let anyone in, the seven dwarfs have forbidden me. It is all the same to me, answered the woman, I shall soon get rid of my apples. There, I will give you one.

No, said Snow White, I dare not take anything. Are you afraid of poison, said the old woman, look, I will cut the apple in two pieces, you eat the red cheek, and I will eat the white. The apple was so cunningly made that only the red cheek was poisoned. Snow White longed for the fine apple, and when she saw that the woman ate part of it she could resist no longer, and stretched out her hand and took the poisonous half. But hardly had she a bit of it in her mouth than she fell down dead. Then the queen looked at her with a dreadful look, and laughed aloud and said, white as snow, red as blood, black as ebony-wood, this time the dwarfs cannot wake you up again.

And when she asked of the looking-glass at home,

> looking-glass, looking-glass, on the wall,
> who in this land is the fairest of all.

And it answered at last,

> oh, queen, in this land thou art fairest of all.

Then her envious heart had rest, so far as an envious heart can have rest.

The dwarfs, when they came home in the evening, found Snow White lying upon the ground, she breathed no longer and was dead. They lifted her up, looked to see whether they could find anything poisonous, unlaced her, combed her hair, washed her with water and wine, but it was all of no use, the poor child was dead, and remained dead. They laid her upon a bier, and all seven of them sat around it and wept for her, and wept three days long.

Then they were going to bury her, but she still looked as if she were living, and still had her pretty red cheeks. They said, we could not bury her in the dark ground, and they had a transparent coffin of glass made, so that she could be seen from all sides, and they laid her in it, and wrote her name upon it in golden letters, and that she was a king's daughter. Then they put the coffin out upon the mountain, and one of them always stayed by it and watched it. And birds came too, and wept for Snow White, first an owl, then a raven, and last a dove.

And now Snow White lay a long, long time in the coffin, and she did not change, but looked as if she were asleep, for she was as white as snow, as red as blood, and her hair was as black as ebony.

It happened, however, that a king's son came into the forest, and went to the dwarfs house to spend the night. He saw the coffin on the mountain, and the beautiful Snow White within it, and read what was written upon it in golden letters. Then he said to the dwarfs, let me have the coffin, I will give you whatever you want for it. But the dwarfs answered, we will not part with it for all the gold in the world. Then he said, let me have it as a gift, for I cannot live without seeing Snow White. I will honor and prize her as my dearest possession. As he spoke in this way the good dwarfs took pity upon him, and gave him the coffin.

And now the king's son had it carried away by his servants on their shoulders. And it happened that they stumbled over a tree-stump, and with the shock the poisonous piece of apple which Snow White had bitten off came out of her throat. And before long she opened her eyes, lifted up the lid of the coffin, sat up, and was once more alive. Oh, heavens, where am I, she cried. The king's son, full of joy, said, you are with me. And told her what had happened, and said, I love you more than everything in the world, come with me to my father's palace, you shall be my wife.

And Snow White was willing, and went with him, and their wedding was held with great show and splendor. But Snow White's wicked step-mother was also bidden to the feast. When she had arrayed herself in beautiful clothes she went before the looking-glass, and said,

> looking-glass, looking-glass, on the wall,
> who in this land is the fairest of all.

The glass answered,

> oh, queen, of all here the fairest art thou,
> but the young queen is fairer by far as I trow.

Then the wicked woman uttered a curse, and was so wretched, so utterly wretched that she knew not what to do. At first she would not go to the wedding at all, but she had no peace, and had to go to see the young queen. And when she went in she recognized Snow White, and she stood still with rage and fear, and could not stir. But iron slippers had already been put upon the fire, and they were brought in with tongs, and set before her. Then she was forced to put on the red-hot shoes, and dance until she dropped down dead.

Comparison

Ravens and Crows: What's the Difference?

Raven J. Brown

Ravens and Crows *is a Web site devoted to crows and related birds of all sorts, hosted online at www.shades-of-night.com/aviary/difs.html by ornithology enthusiast Raven J. Brown. The site features textual information, photographs from famous bird photographers, and audio clips of bird calls. The site invites users to travel among a variety of choice pages devoted to every type of crow relative—from blue jays to Edgar Allen Poe's raven. This particular page focuses on the scientific differences between old-world and new-world crows.*

A web page from *The Aviary* (a site devoted to ravens, crows, and the rest of the corvidae).

1 Many people use the terms 'raven' and 'crow' interchangeably, 1
but they are actually quite different. Technically, since ravens belong to the crow (*corvus*) family of birds, they can be called crows—but not all crows are ravens. The two differ in a variety of ways.

Size

First, and most noticeably, ravens are larger than crows. They are (on average) about the size of a hawk, where crows are approximately the size of a pigeon.

"Ravens and Crows: What's the Difference?" a web page from "The Aviary (A site devoted to Ravens, Crows, and the rest of the Corvidae)," online at <http://www.shades-of-night.com/aviary/difs.html>, 2000. Reprinted with permission of author.

Call

If you're familiar with the call which crows make, you'd probably recognize the raven's call as being different. Crows have a more nasal, higher pitched call, where a raven's call is lower, and hoarser . . . almost a croaking sound. I've frequently been approached by people saying "I heard this really funny-sounding crow the other day . . ." and when I ask "Was it a really big crow?" the answer has almost invariably been yes. In which case, chances are pretty good that it wasn't a crow at all, but a raven. If you want to hear the difference for yourself, click here for a raven's call and crow's call. [Go to *The Aviary* site to do this.]

Tail Feathers

Crows have a very fan-shaped tail, where raven's tails have more of a wedge-shape to them. This isn't very easy to tell if the bird is sitting on the ground, but when flying overhead, you can often get a good look at the shape of the tail.

Feather Shape

5 Ravens' feathers are also a slightly different shape than crows' feathers. 5
Crow feathers tend to be more rounded at the tip, while ravens have feathers which are slightly pointed. This is most noticeable on the breast feathers, especially when the bird fluffs itself up. The feathers on the crow's breast lie comfortably against each other and provide a nice, even, rounded covering. The feathers on a raven lie a little more jaggedly, and when a raven fluffs up, its breast tends to took ragged. In fact, when a raven really fluffs up and all its feathers look like they're standing on end, the raven appears to have a short fluffy mane (called a 'ruff').

Habitat

Ravens and crows can often be found living side by side in the same areas, but where there's a choice, Ravens prefer wilder areas while crows will live quite close to cities. The bigger the city, the less likely ravens will make it their home—and when they do, they tend to live in or near parks and natural spaces. Crows, on the other hand, are more likely to live near buildings, and will venture farther into human developments to compete for food.

There are more differences between crows and ravens, including their social habits and life span (ravens live longer), but these are the key points. They should help you determine whether the bird you're looking at is a raven or just a very large crow.

Grant and Lee: A Study in Contrasts

Bruce Catton

Bruce Catton (1899–1978) is best known for his popular histories of the American Civil War. He wrote a dozen books and many articles about the War, including A Stillness at Appomattox, *which won the Pulitzer Prize and the National Book Award in 1954. Having first worked as a newspaper journalist, Catton was interested in writing for the popular press rather than scholarly historians, and his writing always sought to make history real and living. "Grant and Lee: A Study in Contrasts" was published in 1956 in a book of essays by various historians called* The American Story. *As you read it, notice how Catton takes us far beyond just the story of these two Civil War generals meeting at the end of the War—he is indeed writing a chapter in an American story. As you read this focused exploration of the character of these two men and the times they embody, you will also be learning something about the Civil War itself and the nature of great men.*

1 When Ulysses S. Grant and Robert E. Lee met in the parlor 1
of a modest house at Appomattox Court House, Virginia, on April 9, 1865, to work out the terms for the surrender of Lee's Army of Northern Virginia, a great chapter in American life came to a close, and a great new chapter began.

These men were bringing the Civil War to its virtual finish. To be sure, other armies had yet to surrender, and for a few days the fugitive Confederate government would struggle desperately and vainly, trying to find some way to go on living now that its chief support was gone.

From *The American Story*, edited by Earl Schenck Miers. Published by the U.S. Capitol Historical Society.

But in effect it was all over when Grant and Lee signed the papers. And the little room where they wrote out the terms was the scene of one of the poignant, dramatic contrasts in American history.

They were two strong men, these oddly different generals, and they represented the strengths of two conflicting currents that, through them, had come into final collision.

Back of Robert E. Lee was the notion that the old aristocratic concept might somehow survive and be dominant in American life.

5 Lee was tidewater Virginia, and in his background were family, culture, and tradition . . . the age of chivalry transplanted to a New World which was making its own legends and its own myths. He embodied a way of life that had come down through the age of knighthood and the English country squire. America was a land that was beginning all over again, dedicated to nothing much more complicated than the rather hazy belief that all men had equal rights and should have an equal chance in the world. In such a land Lee stood for the feeling that it was somehow of advantage to human society to have a pronounced inequality in the social structure. There should be a leisure class, backed by ownership of land; in turn, society itself should be keyed to the land as the chief source of wealth and influence. It would bring forth (according to this ideal) a class of men with a strong sense of obligation to the community; men who lived not to gain advantage for themselves, but to meet the solemn obligations which had been laid on them by the very fact that they were privileged. From them the country would get its leadership; to them it could look for the higher values—of thought, of conduct, of personal deportment—to give it strength and virtue.

Lee embodied the noblest elements of this aristocratic ideal. Through him, the landed nobility justified itself. For four years, the Southern states had fought a desperate war to uphold the ideals for which Lee stood. In the end, it almost seemed as if the Confederacy fought for Lee; as if he himself was the Confederacy . . . the best thing that the way of life for which the Confederacy stood could ever have to offer. He had passed into legend before Appomattox. Thousands of tired, underfed, poorly clothed Confederate soldiers, long since past the simple enthusiasm of the early days of the struggle, somehow considered Lee the symbol of everything for which they had been willing to die. But they could not quite put this feeling into words. If the Lost Cause, sanctified by so much heroism and so many deaths, had a living justification, its justification was General Lee.

Grant, the son of a tanner on the Western frontier, was everything Lee was not. He had come up the hard way and embodied nothing in particular except the eternal toughness and sinewy fiber of the men who grew up beyond the mountains. He was one of a body of men who owed reverence and obeisance to no one, who were self-reliant to a fault, who cared hardly anything for the past but who had a sharp eye for the future.

These frontier men were the precise opposites of the tidewater aristocrats. Back of them, in the great surge that had taken people over the Alleghenies and into the opening Western country, there was a deep, implicit dissatisfaction with a past that had settled into grooves. They stood for democracy, not from any reasoned conclusion about the proper ordering of human society, but simply because they had grown up in the middle of democracy and knew how it worked. Their society might have privileges, but they would be privileges each man had won for himself. Forms and patterns meant nothing. No man was born to anything, except perhaps to a chance to show how far he could rise. Life was competition.

Yet along with this feeling had come a deep sense of belonging to a national community. The Westerner who developed a farm, opened a shop, or set up in business as a trader, could hope to prosper only as his own community prospered—and his community ran from the Atlantic to the Pacific and from Canada down to Mexico. If the land was settled, with towns and highways and accessible markets, he could better himself. He saw his fate in terms of the nation's own destiny. As its horizons expanded, so did his. He had, in other words, an acute dollars-and-cents stake in the continued growth and development of his country.

10 And that, perhaps, is where the contrast between Grant and Lee 10 becomes most striking. The Virginia aristocrat, inevitably, saw himself in relation to his own region. He lived in a static society which could endure almost anything except change. Instinctively, his first loyalty would go to the locality in which that society existed. He would fight to the limit of endurance to defend it, because in defending it he was defending everything that gave his own life its deepest meaning.

The Westerner, on the other hand, would fight with an equal tenacity for the broader concept of society. He fought so because everything he lived by was tied to growth, expansion, and a constantly widening horizon. What he lived by would survive or fall with the nation itself. He could not possibly stand by unmoved in the face of an attempt to destroy the Union. He would combat it with everything he had, because he could only see it as an effort to cut the ground out from under his feet.

So Grant and Lee were in complete contrast, representing two diametrically opposed elements in American life. Grant was the modern man emerging; beyond him, ready to come on the stage, was the great age of steel and machinery, of crowded cities and a restless burgeoning vitality. Lee might have ridden down from the old age of chivalry, lance in hand, silken banner fluttering over his head. Each man was the perfect champion of his cause, drawing both his strengths and his weaknesses from the people he led.

Yet it was not all contrast, after all. Different as they were—in background, in personality, in underlying aspiration—these two great soldiers had much in common. Under everything else, they were marvelous fighters. Furthermore, their fighting qualities were really very much alike.

Each man had, to begin with, the great virtue of utter tenacity and fidelity. Grant fought his way down the Mississippi Valley in spite of acute personal discouragement and profound military handicaps. Lee hung on in the trenches at Petersburg after hope itself had died. In each man there was an indomitable quality . . . the born fighter's refusal to give up as long as he can still remain on his feet and lift his two fists.

15 Daring and resourcefulness they had, too; the ability to think 15
faster and move faster than the enemy. These were the qualities which gave Lee the dazzling campaigns of Second Manassas and Chancellorsville and won Vicksburg for Grant.

Lastly, and perhaps greatest of all, there was the ability, at the end, to turn quickly from war to peace once the fighting was over. Out of the way these two men behaved at Appomattox came the possibility of a peace of reconciliation. It was a possibility not wholly realized, in the years to come, but which did, in the end, help the two sections to become one nation again . . . after a war whose bitterness might have seemed to make such a reunion wholly impossible. No part of either man's life became him more than the part he played in this brief meeting in the McLean house at Appomattox. Their behavior there put all succeeding generations of Americans in their debt. Two great Americans, Grant and Lee—very different, yet under everything very much alike. Their encounter at Appomattox was one of the great moments of American history.

Neat People vs. Sloppy People

Suzanne Britt Jordan

Suzanne Britt Jordan was born in Winston-Salem, North Carolina. Educated at Salem College and Washington University, where she received an M.A. in English, she has taught English at Meredith College. Widely published, Jordan has written columns for North Carolina Gardens & Homes *and* The Dickens Dispatch *(a national newsletter for Charles Dickens devotees) and articles for* The Baltimore Sun, Books and Religion, The Boston Globe, Long Island Newsday, The New York Times, *and* Newsweek. *Her essays have been collected in* Skinny People Are Dull and Crunchy Like Carrots *(1982) and* Show and Tell *(1983). She has also published a history of Meredith College and two English textbooks. This essay, published in* Show and Tell, *pokes fun at ethics, values, and how well we clean our rooms.*

1 I've finally figured out the difference between neat people and 1
sloppy people. The distinction is, as always, moral. Neat people are lazier and meaner than sloppy people.

Sloppy people, you see, are not really sloppy. Their sloppiness is merely the unfortunate consequence of their extreme moral rectitude. Sloppy people carry in their mind's eye a heavenly vision, a precise plan, that is so stupendous, so perfect, it can't be achieved in this world or the next.

Sloppy people live in Never-Never-Land. Someday is their metier. Someday they are planning to alphabetize all their books and set up home catalogues. Someday they will go through their wardrobes and mark certain items for tentative mending and certain items for passing on to relatives of similar shape and size. Someday sloppy people will make family scrapbooks into which they will put newspaper clippings, postcards, locks of hair, and the dried corsage from their senior prom. Someday they will file everything on the surface of their desks, including the cash receipts from coffee purchases at the snack shop. Someday they will sit down and read all the back issues of *The New Yorker.*

For all these noble reasons and more, sloppy people never get neat. They aim too high and wide. They save everything, planning someday to file, order, and straighten out the world. But while these ambitious plans take clearer and clearer shape in their heads, the books spill from the shelves onto the floor, the clothes pile up in the hamper and closet, the family mementos accumulate in every drawer, the surface of the desk is buried under mounds of paper, and the unread magazines threaten to reach the ceiling.

5 Sloppy people can't bear to part with anything. They give loving 5
attention to every detail. When sloppy people say they're going to tackle the surface of the desk, they really mean it. Not a paper will go unturned; not a rubber band will go unboxed. Four hours or two weeks into the excavation, the desk looks exactly the same, primarily because the sloppy person is meticulously creating new piles of papers with new headings and scrupulously stopping to read all the old book catalogues before he throws them away. A neat person would just bulldoze the desk.

Neat people are bums and clods at heart. They have cavalier attitudes toward possessions, including family heirlooms. Everything is just another dust-catcher to them. If anything collects dust, it's got to go and that's that. Neat people will toy with the idea of throwing the children out of the house just to cut down the clutter.

Neat people don't care about process. They like results. What they want to do is get the whole thing over with so they can sit down and watch the rasslin' on TV. Neat people operate on two unvarying principles: Never handle any item twice, and throw everything away.

The only thing messy in a neat person's house is the trash can. The minute something comes to a neat person's hand, he will look at it, try to decide if it has immediate use and, finding none, throw it in the trash.

Neat people are especially vicious with mail. They never go through their mail unless they are standing directly over a trash can. If the trash can is beside the mailbox, even better. All ads, catalogues, pleas for charitable contributions, church bulletins, and money-saving coupons go straight into the trash can without being opened. All letters from home, postcards from Europe, bills and paychecks are opened, immediately responded to, then dropped in the trash can. Neat people keep their receipts only for tax purposes. That's it. No sentimental salvaging of birthday cards or the last letter a dying relative ever wrote. Into the trash it goes.

10 Neat people place neatness above everything, even economics. 10 They are incredibly wasteful. Neat people throw away several toys every time they walk through the den. I knew a neat person once who threw away a perfectly good dish drainer because it had mold on it. The drainer was too much trouble to wash. And neat people sell their furniture when they move. They will sell a La-Z-Boy recliner while you are reclining in it.

Neat people are no good to borrow from. Neat people buy everything in expensive little single portions. They get their flour and sugar in two-pound bags. They wouldn't consider clipping a coupon, saving a leftover, reusing plastic nondairy whipped cream containers, or rinsing off tin foil and draping it over the unmoldy dish drainer. You can never borrow a neat person's newspaper to see what's playing at the movies. Neat people have the paper all wadded up and in the trash by 7:05 A.M.

Neat people cut a clean swath through the organic as well as the inorganic world. People, animals, and things are all one to them. They are so insensitive. After they've finished with the pantry, the medicine cabinet, and the attic, they will throw out the red geranium (too many leaves), sell the dog (too many fleas), and send the children off to boarding school (too many scuff marks on the hardwood floors).

The Spider and the Wasp

Alexander Petrunkevitch

Alexander Petrunkevitch (1875–1967) was born in Russia and educated in Germany and Russia. After coming to the United States in the early 1900s he taught biology at Yale University and other colleges. He wrote a number of publications about spiders, including two books: Index Catalogue of Spiders of North, Central, and South America *(1911) and* An Inquiry into the Natural Classification of Spiders *(1933). Petrunkevitch also wrote poetry and nonfiction on a number of different topics, including philosophy and history. His natural curiosity and interest in broad perspectives combine with his scientific knowledge as he tries to understand a particular natural phenomenon in the following selection, which was first published in* Scientific American *in 1952.*

1 To hold its own in the struggle for existence, every species of animal must have a regular source of food, and if it happens to live on other animals, its survival may be very delicately balanced. The hunter cannot exist without the hunted; if the latter should perish from the earth, the former would, too. When the hunted also prey on some of the hunters, the matter may become complicated. 1

This is nowhere better illustrated than in the insect world. Think of the complexity of a situation such as the following: There is a certain wasp, *Pimpla inquisitor,* whose larvae feed on the larvae of the tussock moth. *Pimpla* larvae in turn serve as food for the larvae of a second wasp, and the latter in their turn nourish still a third wasp.

What subtle balance between fertility and mortality must exist in the case of each of these four species to prevent the extinction of all of them! An excess of mortality over fertility in a single member of the group would ultimately wipe out all four.

This is not a unique case. The two great orders of insects, Hymenoptera and Diptera, are full of such examples of interrelationship. And the spiders (which are not insects but members of a separate order of arthropods) also are killers and victims of insects.

In the feeding and safeguarding of their progeny the insects and spiders exhibit some interesting analogies to reasoning and some crass examples of blind instinct. The case I propose to describe here is that of the tarantula spiders and their arch-enemy, the digger wasps of the genus Pepsis. It is a classic example of what looks like intelligence pitted against instinct—a strange situation in which the victim, though fully able to defend itself, submits unwittingly to its destruction.

5 A fertilized female tarantula lays from 200 to 400 eggs at a time; 5
thus it is possible for a single tarantula to produce several thousand young. She takes no care of them beyond weaving a cocoon of silk to enclose the eggs. After they hatch, the young walk away, find convenient places in which to dig their burrows and spend the rest of their lives in solitude. Tarantulas feed mostly on insects and millipedes. Once their appetite is appeased, they digest the food for several days before eating again. Their sight is poor, being limited to sensing a change in the intensity of light and to the perception of moving objects. They apparently have little or no sense of hearing, for a hungry tarantula will pay no attention to a loudly chirping cricket placed in its cage unless the insect happens to touch one of its legs.

But all spiders, and especially hairy ones, have an extremely delicate sense of touch. Laboratory experiments prove that tarantulas can distinguish three types of touch: pressure against the body wall, stroking of the body hair and riffling of certain very fine hairs on the legs called trichobothria. Pressure against the body, by a finger or the end of a pencil, causes the tarantula to move off slowly for a short distance. The touch excites no defensive response unless the approach is from above where the spider can see the motion, in which case it rises on its hind legs, lifts its front legs, opens its fangs and holds this threatening posture as long as the object continues to move. When the motion stops, the spider drops back to the ground, remains quiet for a few seconds and then moves slowly away.

The entire body of a tarantula, especially its legs, is thickly clothed with hair. Some of it is short and woolly, some long and stiff. Touching this body hair produces one of two distinct reactions. When the spider is hungry, it responds with an immediate and swift attack. At the touch of a cricket's antennae the tarantula seizes the insect so swiftly that a motion picture taken at the rate of 64 frames per second shows only the result and not the process of capture. But when the spider is not hungry, the stimulation of its hairs merely causes it to shake the touched limb. An insect can walk under its hairy belly unharmed.

The trichobothria, very fine hairs growing from disklike membranes on the legs, were once thought to be the spider's hearing organs, but we now know that they have nothing to do with sound. They are sensitive only to air movement. A light breeze makes them vibrate slowly without disturbing the common hair. When one blows gently on the trichobothria, the tarantula reacts with a quick jerk of its four front legs. If the front and hind legs are stimulated at the same time, the spider makes a sudden jump. This reaction is quite independent of the state of its appetite.

These three tactile responses—to pressure on the body wall, to moving of the common hair and to flexing of the trichobothria—are so different from one another that there is no possibility of confusing them. They serve the tarantula adequately for most of its needs and enable it to avoid most annoyances and dangers. But they fail the spider completely when it meets its deadly enemy, the digger wasp Pepsis.

10 These solitary wasps are beautiful and formidable creatures. Most species are either a deep shiny blue all over, or deep blue with rusty wings. The largest have a wing span of about four inches. They live on nectar. When excited, they give off a pungent odor—a warning that they are ready to attack. The sting is much worse than that of a bee or common wasp, and the pain and swelling last longer. In the adult stage the wasp lives only a few months. The female produces but a few eggs, one at a time at intervals of two or three days. For each egg the mother must provide one adult tarantula, alive but paralyzed. The tarantula must be of the correct species to nourish the larva. The mother wasp attaches the egg to the paralyzed spider's abdomen. Upon hatching from the egg, the larva is many hundreds of times smaller than its living but helpless victim. It eats no other food and drinks no water. By the time it has finished its single gargantuan meal and become ready

for wasphood, nothing remains of the tarantula but its indigestible chitinous skeleton.

The mother wasp goes tarantula-hunting when the egg in her ovary is almost ready to be laid. Flying low over the ground late on a sunny afternoon, the wasp looks for its victim or for the mouth of a tarantula burrow, a round hole edged by a bit of silk. The sex of the spider makes no difference, but the mother is highly discriminating as to species. Each species of Pepsis requires a certain species of tarantula, and the wasp will not attack the wrong species. In a cage with a tarantula which is not its normal prey the wasp avoids the spider, and is usually killed by it in the night.

Yet when a wasp finds the correct species, it is the other way about. To identify the species the wasp apparently must explore the spider with her antennae. The tarantula shows an amazing tolerance to this exploration. The wasp crawls under it and walks over it without evoking any hostile response. The molestation is so great and so persistent that the tarantula often rises on all eight legs, as if it were on stilts. It may stand this way for several minutes. Meanwhile the wasp, having satisfied itself that the victim is of the right species, moves off a few inches to dig the spider's grave. Working vigorously with legs and jaws, it excavates a hole 8 to 10 inches deep with a diameter slightly larger than the spider's girth. Now and again the wasp pops out of the hole to make sure that the spider is still there.

When the grave is finished, the wasp returns to the tarantula to complete her ghastly enterprise. First she feels it all over once more with her antennae. Then her behavior becomes more aggressive. She bends her abdomen, protruding her sting, and searches for the soft membrane at the point where the spider's leg joins its body—the only spot where she can penetrate the horny skeleton. From time to time, as the exasperated spider slowly shifts ground, the wasp turns on her back and slides along with the aid of her wings, trying to get under the tarantula for a shot at the vital spot. During all this maneuvering, which can last for several minutes, the tarantula makes no move to save itself. Finally the wasp corners it against some obstruction and grasps one of its legs in her powerful jaws. Now at last the harassed spider tries a desperate but vain defense. The two contestants roll over and over on the ground. It is a terrifying sight and the outcome is always the same. The wasp finally manages to thrust her sting into the soft spot and holds it there for a few seconds while she pumps in the poison. Almost immediately the tarantula falls paralyzed on its back. Its legs stop twitching; its heart stops beating, yet it is not dead, as is shown by the fact that if taken from the wasp it can be restored to some sensitivity by being kept in a moist chamber for several months.

After paralyzing the tarantula, the wasp cleans herself by dragging her body along the ground and rubbing her feet, sucks the drop of blood oozing from the wound in the spider's abdomen, then grabs a leg of the flabby, helpless animal in her jaws and drags it down to the bottom of the grave. She stays there for many minutes, sometimes for several hours, and what she does all that time in the dark we do not know. Eventually she lays her egg and attaches it to the side of the spider's abdomen with a sticky secretion. Then she emerges, fills the grave with soil carried bit by bit in her jaws, and finally tramples the ground all around to hide any trace of the grave from prowlers. Then she flies away, leaving her descendant safely started in life.

In all this the behavior of the wasp evidently is qualitatively different from that of the spider. The wasp acts like an intelligent animal. This is not to say that instinct plays no part or that she reasons as man does. But her actions are to the point; they are not automatic and can be modified to fit the situation. We do not know for certain how she identifies the tarantula—probably it is by some olfactory or chemo-tactile sense—but she does it purposefully and does not blindly tackle a wrong species.

On the other hand, the tarantula's behavior shows only confusion. Evidently the wasp's pawing gives it no pleasure, for it tries to move away. That the wasp is not simulating sexual stimulation is certain, because male and female tarantulas react in the same way to its advances. That the spider is not anesthetized by some odorless secretion is easily shown by blowing lightly at the tarantula and making it jump suddenly. What, then, makes the tarantula behave as stupidly as it does?

No clear, simple answer is available. Possibly the stimulation by the wasp's antennae is masked by a heavier pressure on the spider's body, so that it reacts as when prodded by a pencil. But the explanation may be much more complex. Initiative in attack is not in the nature of tarantulas; most species fight only when cornered so that escape is impossible. Their inherited patterns of behavior apparently prompt them to avoid problems rather than attack them. For example, spiders always weave their webs in three dimensions, and when a spider finds that there is insufficient space to attach certain threads in the third dimension, it leaves the place and seeks another, instead of finishing the web in a single plane. This urge to escape seems to arise under all circumstances, in all phases of life and to take the place of reasoning. For a spider to change the pattern of its web is as impossible as for an inexperienced man to build a bridge across a chasm obstructing his way.

In a way the instinctive urge to escape is not only easier but often more efficient than reasoning. The tarantula does exactly what is most efficient in all cases except in an encounter with a ruthless and determined attacker dependent for the existence of her own species on killing as many tarantulas as she can lay eggs. Perhaps in this case the spider follows its usual pattern of trying to escape, instead of seizing and killing the wasp, because it is not aware of its danger. In any case, the survival of the tarantula species as a whole is protected by the fact that the spider is much more fertile than the wasp.

A Tale of Two Sitcoms

Steven D. Stark

Steven D. Stark is a writer and cultural commentator living in Cambridge, Massachusetts. He is a graduate of Harvard College and Yale Law School. Stark has been a sports columnist for the Montreal Gazette, *an analyst for Weekend Edition Sunday and The Voice of America, produced for National Public Radio, and a writer for the* Atlantic Monthly, The Boston Globe, Boston Phoenix, The Los Angeles Times, *and* The New York Times. *He is a commentator on CNN's Showbiz Today. In 2006 he published a highly regarded study of The Beatles' significance to popular culture, titled* Meet the Beatles: A Cultural History of the Band That Shook Youth, Gender, and the World. *The following selection is taken from his 1997 book* Glued to the Set: The 60s Television Shows and Events That Made Us Who We Are Today.

1 The popular shows of a decade are usually a lot alike. In many ways *Dallas* and *Dynasty* were indistinguishable, and it would take Wyatt Earp himself to discern great differences between *Wagon Train* and *Gunsmoke.* In the late seventies *Happy Days, Laverne and Shirley,* and *Three's Company* often seemed to form one long seamless web. 1

Yet sometimes, in eras of cultural conflict or confusion, no one type of show can accurately capture the public mood. In the early 1970s, for example, *All in the Family* made a hero of a conservative traditionalist while *The Mary Tyler Moore Show* romanticized the life of a single career woman blazing new ground. In their own ways, both shows reflected their times, and both were popular—often with the same viewers.

In much the same fashion, popular programming in the nineties offered a contrast, as it struggled with an emerging question which had no clear answer: What does it mean to be a man in a postfeminist age? Two very different situation comedies which hit Number 1 in that decade tried to provide an answer. On the one hand, there was ABC's *Home Improvement*—the top-rated show for the 1993–94 season. And then, there was NBC's *Seinfeld*—which hit Number 1 the following season.

Even the reaction to both shows provided a sharp contrast. Critics regularly lavished *Seinfeld* with praise for its postmodern plots; its technical innovations were hailed as breakthroughs; and the show was always an Emmy contender in several categories. Novelist Jay McInerney went so far in a 1996 issue of *TV Guide* to ask, "Is Seinfeld the Best Comedy Ever?" By comparison, *Home Improvement* was perhaps the quietest Number 1 in TV history, eliciting a few critical comments and winning little more than a slew of (what else?) People's Choice awards, in which the public does the voting.

5 There were indeed surface similarities between the two shows. 5
Both starred male comedians, who took their standup nightclub acts and transformed them for television. Both comedians wrote best-selling books once they hit it big, and both shows featured subplots about television itself. Both presented memorable supporting players, like Kramer of *Seinfeld,* or next-door neighbor Wilson of *Home Improvement,* whose full face is never shown over his fence. Both ran in prime time and in syndication over roughly the same period with similar ratings—though the one time *Seinfeld* was matched directly against *Home Improvement* in 1992–93, *Seinfeld* got plastered in the ratings.

Yet the differences between the shows were more revealing. *Home Improvement* was set in suburban Detroit, in the white-bread heartland. Though actually filmed in L.A., *Seinfeld* was a New York show which roughly approximated the lifestyles of influential New York critics and Madison Avenue types. *Home Improvement* was solidly suburban middle class; *Seinfeld* was a portrait of life in yuppie Upper Manhattan.

Home Improvement was a rather traditional family sitcom about a wife, three kids, and a bumbling Dad; the *Seinfeld* family of friends featured no children and no workplace either, at least in the traditional sense. With its "morality tale" quality, *Home Improvement* was a cousin of *Leave It to Beaver* and *My Three Sons*—an anachronism in an era when wisecracking shows like *Friends* or *Murphy Brown* dispensed with nuclear families altogether.

By contrast, *Seinfeld* was closer to Jack Benny, or even Milton Berle. That was a remarkable turnaround for a medium which for much of its bland and homogeneous entertainment life took single Jews like Seinfeld, changed their names, converted them to Christianity, married them off to attractive WASP housewives, and moved them to the suburbs. New York *Newsday* once called *Seinfeld* "the most fully realized schlemiel in the history of television."

What encouraged programmers to take these chances was the way that cable television had atomized the viewing audience. Because of cable competition, network television was not the mass medium in 1995 that it was in 1975; it took far fewer viewers to make a hit. *Seinfeld* won the 1994–95 ratings race with a rating that two decades earlier wouldn't have even placed in the Top Twenty-five. Such a disintegration of the network audience meant that the networks no longer had to program for as large a mass to make money, and shows like *Seinfeld*—which appealed to upscale viewers—often were the result. By 1995, half the sitcoms on TV seemed to feature singles living in cities like New York, if only because these series appealed to viewers similarly situated who, in turn, appealed to advertisers because they have lots of discretionary income.

10 Yet even though television was finally acknowledging the nation's diversity, that didn't mean that shows like *Seinfeld* were realistic national self-portraits either. After all, the more that television sitcoms have moved in the direction of "realism," the less authentic they have often become. For all the praise that *All in the Family* received, Archie Bunker was a parody; even the witty comedy of *Mary Tyler Moore* hardly reflected a workplace anyone could recognize with honest assurance. Similarly, no one—not even an Upper East Sider—has hours every day to spend chatting with friends in a diner. Yet critics were fond of praising the realism of *Seinfeld.* "Men probably laughed louder than women at the episode in which Elaine discovered that her nipple was exposed on her Christmas card photo," wrote McInerney. "This stuff happens to all of us." Oh, really?

Seinfeld did have considerable strengths, however. The show was genuinely funny, a rare treat on prime-time television. Some of the series episodes, like the one on the "soup Nazi" or on losing a car in a parking lot, were inspired, and the supporting cast of Elaine, Kramer, and George was exceptional. "It's about nothing, everything else is about something; this, it's about nothing," said George in pitching his and Jerry's sitcom proposal to a network, as *Seinfeld* became a show within a show. Already some of its lines have become pop culture classics: "I'm Cosmo Kramer, the Assman!"; "Not that there's anything wrong with that"; and "Master of your Domain."

Seinfeld was also a hit because it appealed to men more than did many other sitcoms, as it reflected a new adolescent sensibility sweeping America in the 1990s. Along with the comedy of David Letterman, the cartoon series *Beavis and Butthead,* megamovies like *Jurassic Park,* and syndicated radio talkmeisters Howard Stern and Don Imus, *Seinfeld* often echoed the world of 11- to 15-year-old boys. The radio style of Stern and Imus, for example, was that of the narcissistic class cutup in seventh grade: Both sat in a playhouse-like radio studio with a bunch of guys and horsed around for hours talking about sex, sports, and politics, all the while laughing at their own loutish, subversive jokes.

Seinfeld shared a similar sensibility, albeit softened somewhat for television. Like a group of 14-year-olds, the men on *Seinfeld* seemed not to hold real regular jobs, the better to devote time to "the gang." (One woman, Elaine, was allowed to tag along with the boys, much like those younger sisters who are permitted to hang out with their brothers.) Not only was every man in Seinfeld's gang unmarried and pushing fortysomething, but it also was difficult to imagine any having a real relationship with any woman but his mother. Note how much more often parents of adult children appeared here than on other shows.

Or compare *Seinfeld* to its predecessor in its NBC Thursday night time slot, *Cheers.* If the men on that show didn't spend much time at work either, they did hang out in a traditional domain of adults—the tavern—and the hero, Sam Malone, spent many of his waking hours chasing women. Seinfeld, by contrast, was better known for sitting in a restaurant eating french fries with his pals. One of the most celebrated risqué *Seinfeld* episodes was about (what else?) masturbation, while others dealt with urinating in the shower or on couches. That's usually big stuff in the seventh grade, but not much beyond.

The *Seinfeld* evocation of early male adolescence did reflect deeper cultural strains. This country has always venerated "bad boys," from Huck Finn to Holden Caulfield. Moreover, many psychologists consider that preteen stage of life, when one is acutely aware of being powerless, as the time when individuals are most subversive of the society at-large. That sentiment fit a nineties cultural mood, as America became full of the defiant, oppositional anger that often characterizes the early adolescent—witness the tearing down of public figures with the ready help of the tabloid press, and the flocking to antiestablishment talk radio whereon the humor grew more derisive by the day. In a similar vein, one could imagine the whole *Seinfeld* cast of perpetual adolescents on the Clinton White House staff working with George Stephanopolous or Craig Livingstone. Yet boys will be boys: Maybe that's why much of the country viewed the Clinton administration's missteps as benignly as they viewed George Costanza's.

Because this country has always had tendencies that remind observers of a 14-year-old boy, no one would blame *Seinfeld* alone for society's failure to grow up and take care of its real children; its current ambivalence about paternal authority; or its vulgarity and exhibitionist inclinations. Yet the show definitely played a role, along with its cultural cousins. In much the same way that *Roseanne* had domesticated tabloid television for the masses, *Seinfeld* did the same for sophomoric talk radio, as embodied by fellow Manhattanites Stern and Imus.

By contrast, *Home Improvement* had the gentle ring of mainstream truth. It's no accident that 14- to 30-year-olds in a *TV Guide* poll voted Jill and Tim the TV parents most like their own. Naturally, that state of affairs sometimes drew the critics' ire. "'Home Improvement' is a reactionary return, after 'Roseanne' and 'Married with Children' and all those Census Bureau reports, to the semi-extinct idea of a nuclear family whose members actually like each other," wrote Chuck Eddy in a review of the show for *millennium pop.*

Unlike *Seinfeld, Home Improvement* was about grown-ups. Take the premiere episode: Tim (the Toolman) Taylor, host of a cable show called *Tool Time,* wants to rewire his dishwasher to make it more powerful but ends up breaking it. When he tries to comfort his wife after she doesn't get a job, he inadvertently ends up making her feel worse. In just such a fashion *Home Improvement* was built around that preoccupation central to the zeitgeist of the nineties: If television once told us *Father Knows Best,* this show probed what it meant to be the best father and husband in an age of feminism and embattled male identity.

When Matt Williams and David McFadzean were developing ideas for this show, they were both reading the work of noted linguist Deborah Tannen on male-female communication. "Her book deals with the fact that men and women speak different languages," Williams once remembered. "That right there is the piston that drives this television series. Jill and Tim will never do the same thing the same way, and both sides are valid." On another occasion, Williams noted:

> The biggest challenge for us is to take absurd situations, or extreme points of view or actions, and root them in some kind of truth. . . . If we do our job correctly, those are the things the audience will never think twice about, because we've rooted them in some kind of behavioral truth.

And so the show went in the 1990s, quietly drawing better in rural than urban areas yet still doing well among professionals. Like Jerry Seinfeld, Tim Allen's persona became a new cultural icon—the post-feminist handyman. His was a sitcom prototype with the qualities that many Americans in the 1990s held dear—low-key, predictable, intelligent but not particularly well-educated, with a little dirt under his fingernails. If he'd been a politician in the nineties, he would have had little in common with Bill Clinton or Newt Gingrich—Washington insiders and policy preachers to the core. (Colin Powell would be another story.) For different reasons, Taylor also would have had little to talk about with Seinfeld, who never would have tuned in to *Tool Time,* much less own a hammer. (Like many Manhattanites, Seinfeld always seemed to prefer the movies to television anyway.)

Here, then, were two conflicting strains in the American character: *Seinfeld,* a popular urban show about eccentric individualism and the flight from adulthood, versus *Home Improvement,* a popular suburban show about commitment and ultimately about family. The forces which create "the buzz" in this country—the press, the public relations establishment, and Madison Avenue—simply loved *Seinfeld,* which tells us as much about their makeup and tastes as about the show itself. We also had our Seinfeld-esque White House.

The guess here, however, is that *Home Improvement* was still a better reflection of who we are, despite major social changes over decades. In the not-so-grand tradition of television, viewers still feel more comfortable with the Cleavers, the Andersons, and the Bradys than they do with the *Seinfeld* alternative. Viewers want happy, traditional families, even when they realize that a TV family and setting is idealized—or perhaps *especially* when they realize it. The perfect man for the nineties? It's OK to have that fling with the "bad boy"—who, after all, has always been part of the greater American family. But when it's time to settle down, he isn't the guy you're going to want to bring into your living rooms and bedrooms, night after night.

Public and Private Language

Richard Rodriguez

Richard Rodriguez (1944–) was born in San Francisco. A child of Mexican immigrants, Rodriguez spoke Spanish until he went to a Catholic school at age 6. As a youth, he delivered newspapers and worked as a gardener. Rodriguez received a B.A. from Stanford University, an M.A. from Columbia University, and a Ph.D. in English Renaissance literature from the University of California at Berkeley; he later attended the Warburg Institute in London on a Fulbright fellowship. A noted prose stylist, Rodriguez has worked as a teacher, journalist, and educational consultant, in addition to writing, lecturing, and appearing frequently on the Public Broadcast System (PBS) program, "The MacNeil-Lehrer News Hour." Rodriguez's books include Hunger of Memory: The Education of Richard Rodriguez *(1982), a collection of autobiographical essays;* Mexico's Children *(1990); and* Days of Obligation: An Argument With My Mexican Father *(1992), which was nominated for a National Book Award. In addition, he has been published in* The American Scholar, Change, College English, Harper's, Mother Jones, Reader's Digest, *and* Time. *A controversial writer, Rodriguez often speaks out against affirmative action and bilingual education. Rodriguez uses the concept of a "private language" of the family and a "public language" of the community in this essay to push his argument against bilingual education.*

---

1 I remember to start with that day in Sacramento—a California now nearly thirty years past—when I first entered a classroom, able to understand some fifty stray English words.

The third of four children, I had been preceded to a neighborhood Roman Catholic school by an older brother and sister. But neither of them had revealed very much about their classroom experiences. Each afternoon they returned, as they left in the morning, always together, speaking in Spanish as they climbed the five steps of the porch. And their mysterious books, wrapped in shopping-bag paper, remained on the table next to the door, closed firmly behind them.

An accident of geography sent me to a school where all my classmates were white, many the children of doctors and lawyers and business executives. All my classmates certainly must have been uneasy on that first day of school—as most children are uneasy—to find themselves apart from their families in the first institution of their lives. But I was astonished.

The nun said, in a friendly but oddly impersonal voice, "Boys and girls, this is Richard Rodriguez." (I heard her sound out: *Rich-heard Road-ree-guess.*) It was the first time I had heard anyone name me in English. "Richard," the nun repeated more slowly, writing my name down in her black leather book. Quickly I turned to see my mother's face dissolve in a watery blur behind the pebbled glass door.

5 Many years later there is something called bilingual education—a scheme proposed in the late 1960s by Hispanic-American social activists, later endorsed by a congressional vote. It is a program that seeks to permit non-English-speaking children, many from lower-class homes, to use their family language as the language of school. (Such is the goal its supporters announce.) I hear them and am forced to say no: It is not possible for a child—any child—ever to use his family's language in school. Not to understand this is to misunderstand the public uses of schooling and to trivialize the nature of intimate life—a family's "language."

Memory teaches me what I know of these matters; the boy reminds the adult. I was a bilingual child, a certain kind—socially disadvantaged—the son of working-class parents, both Mexican immigrants.

In the early years of my boyhood, my parents coped very well in America. My father had steady work. My mother managed at home.

They were nobody's victims. Optimism and ambition led them to a house (our home) many blocks from the Mexican south side of town. We lived among *gringos* and only a block from the biggest, whitest houses. It never occurred to my parents that they couldn't live wherever they chose. Nor was the Sacramento of the fifties bent on teaching them a contrary lesson. My mother and father were more annoyed than intimidated by those two or three neighbors who tried initially to make us unwelcome. ("Keep your brats away from my sidewalk!") But despite all they achieved, perhaps because they had so much to achieve, any deep feeling of ease, the confidence of "belonging" in public was withheld from them both. They regarded the people at work, the faces in crowds, as very distant from us. They were the others, *los gringos.* That term was interchangeable in their speech with another, even more telling, *los americanos.*

I grew up in a house where the only regular guests were my relations. For one day, enormous families of relatives would visit and there would be so many people that the noise and the bodies would spill out to the backyard and front porch. Then, for weeks, no one came by. (It was usually a salesman who rang the doorbell.) Our house stood apart. A gaudy yellow in a row of white bungalows. We were the people with the noisy dog. The people who raised pigeons and chickens. We were the foreigners on the block. A few neighbors smiled and waved. We waved back. But no one in the family knew the names of the old couple who lived next door; until I was seven years old, I did not know the names of the kids who lived across the street.

In public, my father and mother spoke a hesitant, accented, not always grammatical English. And they would have to strain—their bodies tense—to catch the sense of what was rapidly said by *los gringos.* At home they spoke Spanish. The language of their Mexican past sounded in counterpoint to the English of public society. The words would come quickly, with ease. Conveyed through those sounds was the pleasing, soothing, consoling reminder of being at home.

10 During those years when I was first conscious of hearing, my mother and father addressed me only in Spanish; in Spanish I learned to reply. By contrast, English *(inglés),* rarely heard in the house, was the language I came to associate with *gringos.* I learned my first words of English overhearing my parents speak to strangers. At five years age, I knew just enough English for my mother to trust me on errands to stores one block away. No more.

I was a listening child, careful to hear the very different sounds of Spanish and English. Wide-eyed with hearing, I'd listen to sounds more than words. First, there were English *(gringo)* sounds. So many words were still unknown that when the butcher or the lady at the drugstore said something to me, exotic polysyllabic sounds would bloom in the midst of their sentences. Often, the speech of people in public seemed to me very loud, booming with confidence. The man behind the counter would literally ask, "What can I do for you?" But by being so firm and so clear, the sound of his voice said that he was a *gringo;* he belonged in public society.

I would also hear then the high nasal notes of middle-class American speech. The air stirred with sound. Sometimes, even now, when I have been traveling abroad for several weeks, I will hear what I heard as a boy. In hotel lobbies or airports, in Turkey or Brazil, some Americans will pass, and suddenly I will hear it again—the high sound of American voices. For a few seconds I will hear it with pleasure, for it is now the sound of *my* society—a reminder of home. But inevitably—already on the flight headed for home—the sound fades with repetition. I will be unable to hear it anymore.

When I was a boy, things were different. The accent of *los gringos* was never pleasing nor was it hard to hear. Crowds at Safeway or at bus stops would be noisy with sound. And I would be forced to edge away from the chirping chatter above me.

I was unable to hear my own sounds, but I knew very well that I spoke English poorly. My words could not stretch far enough to form complete thoughts. And the words I did speak I didn't know well enough to make into distinct sounds. (Listeners would usually lower their heads, better to hear what I was trying to say.) But it was one thing for *me* to speak English with difficulty. It was more troubling for me to hear my parents speak in public: their high-whining vowels and guttural consonants; their sentences that got stuck with "ch" and "ah" sounds; the confused syntax; the hesitant rhythm of sounds so different from the way *gringos* spoke. I'd notice, moreover, that my parents' voices were softer than those of *gringos* we'd meet.

15 I am tempted now to say that none of this mattered. In adulthood 15
I am embarrassed by childhood fears. And, in a way, it didn't matter very much that my parents could not speak English with ease. Their linguistic difficulties had no serious consequences. My mother and father made themselves understood at the county hospital clinic and at

government offices. And yet, in another way, it mattered very much—it was unsettling to hear my parents struggle with English. Hearing them, I'd grow nervous, my clutching trust in their protection and power weakened.

There were many times like the night at a brightly lit gasoline station (a blaring white memory) when I stood uneasily, hearing my father. He was talking to a teenaged attendant. I do not recall what they were saying, but I cannot forget the sounds my father made as he spoke. At one point his words slid together to form one word—sounds as confused as the threads of blue and green oil in the puddle next to my shoes. His voice rushed through what he had left to say. And, toward the end, reached falsetto notes, appealing to his listener's understanding. I looked away to the lights of passing automobiles. I tried not to hear anymore. But I heard only too well the calm, easy tones in the attendant's reply. Shortly afterward, walking toward home with my father, I shivered when he put his hand on my shoulder. The very first chance that I got, I evaded his grasp and ran on ahead into the dark, skipping with feigned boyish exuberance.

But then there was Spanish. *Español:* my family's language. *Español:* the language that seemed to me a private language. I'd hear strangers on the radio and in the Mexican Catholic church across town speaking in Spanish, but I couldn't really believe that Spanish was a public language, like English. Spanish speakers, rather, seemed related to me, for I sensed that we shared—through our language—the experience of feeling apart from *los gringos.* It was thus a ghetto Spanish that I heard and I spoke. Like those whose lives are bound by a barrio, I was reminded by Spanish of my separateness from *los otros, los gringos* in power. But more intensely than for most barrio children—because I did not live in a barrio—Spanish seemed to me the language of home. (Most days it was only at home that I'd hear it.) It became the language of joyful return.

A family member would say something to me and I would feel myself specially recognized. My parents would say something to me and I would feel embraced by the sounds of their words. Those sounds said: *I am speaking with ease in Spanish. I am addressing you in words I never use with* los gringos. *I recognize you as someone special, close, like no one outside. You belong with us. In the family.*

(Ricardo.)

20 At the age of five, six, well past the time when most other children no longer easily notice the difference between sounds uttered at

home and words spoken in public, I had a different experience. I lived in a world magically compounded of sounds. I remained a child longer than most; I lingered too long, poised at the edge of language—often frightened by the sounds of *los gringos,* delighted by the sounds of Spanish at home. I shared with my family a language that was startlingly different from that used in the great city around us.

For me there were none of the gradations between public and private society so normal to a maturing child. Outside the house was public society; inside the house was private. Just opening or closing the screen door behind me was an important experience. I'd rarely leave home all alone or without reluctance. Walking down the sidewalk, under the canopy of tall trees, I'd warily notice the—suddenly—silent neighborhood kids who stood warily watching me. Nervously, I'd arrive at the grocery store to hear there the sounds of the *gringo*—foreign to me—reminding me that in this world so big, I was a foreigner. But then I'd return. Walking back toward our house, climbing the steps from the sidewalk, when the front door was open in summer, I'd hear voices beyond the screen door talking in Spanish. For a second or two, I'd stay, linger there, listening. Smiling, I'd hear my mother call out, saying in Spanish (words): "Is that you, Richard?" All the while her sounds would assure me: *You are home now; come closer; inside. With us.*

"Sí,' I'd reply.

Once more inside the house I would resume (assume) my place in the family. The sounds would dim, grow harder to hear. Once more at home, I would grow less aware of that fact. It required, however, no more than the blurt of the doorbell to alert me to listen to sounds all over again. The house would turn instantly still while my mother went to the door. I'd hear her hard English sounds. I'd wait to hear her voice return to soft-sounding Spanish, which assured me, as surely as did the clicking tongue of the lock on the door, that the stranger was gone.

Plainly, it is not healthy to hear such sounds so often. It is not healthy to distinguish public words from private sounds so easily. I remained cloistered by sounds, timid and shy in public, too dependent on voices at home. And yet it needs to be emphasized: I was an extremely happy child at home. I remember many nights when my father would come back from work, and I'd hear him call out to my mother in Spanish, sounding relieved. In Spanish, he'd sound light and free notes he never could manage in English. Some nights I'd jump up just at hearing his voice. With *mis hermanos* I would come running into the room where he was with my mother. Our laughing (so deep was the pleasure!) became screaming. Like others who know the pain of public alienation, we transformed the knowledge of our public separateness and made it consoling—the reminder of intimacy. *We are speaking now the way we never speak out in public. We are alone—together,* voices sounded, surrounded to tell me. Some nights, no one seemed willing to loosen the hold sounds had on us. At dinner, we invented new words. (Ours sounded Spanish, but made sense only to us.) We pieced together new words by taking, say, an English verb and giving it Spanish endings. My mother's instructions at bedtime would be lacquered with mock-urgent tones. Or a word like *sí* would become, in several notes, able to convey added measures of feeling. Tongues explored the edges of words, especially the fat vowels. And we happily sounded that military drum roll, the twirling roar of the Spanish *rr.* Family language: my family's sounds. The voices of my parents and sisters and brother. Their voices insisting: *You belong here. We are family members. Related. Special to one another. Listen!* Voices singing and sighing, rising, straining, then surging, teeming with pleasure that burst syllables into fragments of laughter. At times it seemed there was steady quiet only when, from another room, the rustling whispers of my parents faded and I moved closer to sleep.

25 Supporters of bilingual education today imply that students like me miss a great deal by not being taught in their family's language. What they seem not to recognize is that, as a socially disadvantaged child, I considered Spanish to be a private language. What I needed to learn in school was that I had the right—and the obligation—to speak the public language of *los gringos.* The odd truth is that my first-grade classmates could have become bilingual, in the conventional sense of that word, more easily than I. Had they been taught (as upper-middle-class children are often taught early) a second language like Spanish or French, they could have regarded it simply as that: another public language. In my case such bilingualism could not have been so quickly achieved. What I did not believe was that I could speak a single public language.

Without question, it would have pleased me to hear my teachers address me in Spanish when I entered the classroom. I would have felt much less afraid. I would have trusted them and responded with ease. But I would have delayed—for how long postponed?—having to learn the language of public society. I would have evaded—and for how long could I have afforded to delay?—learning the great lesson of school, that I had a public identity.

Fortunately, my teachers were unsentimental about their responsibility. What they understood was that I needed to speak a public language. So their voices would search me out, asking me questions. Each time I'd hear them, I'd look up in surprise to see a nun's face frowning at me. I'd mumble, not really meaning to answer. The nun would persist, "Richard, stand up. Don't look at the floor. Speak up. Speak to the entire class, not just to me!" But I couldn't believe that the English language was mine to use. (In part, I did not want to believe it.) I continued to mumble. I resisted the teacher's demands. (Did I somehow suspect that once I learned public language my pleasing family life would be changed?) Silent, waiting for the bell to sound, I remained dazed, diffident, afraid.

Because I wrongly imagined that English was intrinsically a public language and Spanish an intrinsically private one, I easily noted the difference between classroom language and the language of home. At school, words were directed to a general audience of listeners. ("Boys and girls.") Words were meaningfully ordered. And the point was not self-expression alone but to make oneself understood by many others. The teacher quizzed: "Boys and girls, why do we use that word in this sentence? Could we think of a better word to use there? Would the sentence change its meaning if the words were differently arranged? And wasn't there a better way of saying much the same thing?" (I couldn't say. I wouldn't try to say.)

Three months. Five. Half a year passed. Unsmiling, ever watchful, my teachers noted my silence. They began to connect my behavior with the difficult progress my older sister and brother were making. Until one Saturday morning three nuns arrived at the house to talk to our parents. Stiffly, they sat on the blue living room sofa. From the doorway of another room, spying the visitors, I noted the incongruity—the clash of two worlds, the faces and voices of school intruding upon the familiar setting of home. I overheard one voice gently wondering, "Do your children speak only Spanish at home, Mrs. Rodriguez?" While another voice added, "That Richard especially seems so timid and shy."

30 *That Rich-heard!* 30

With great tact the visitors continued, "Is it possible for you and your husband to encourage your children to practice their English when they are home?" Of course, my parents complied. What would they not do for their children's well-being? And how could they have questioned the Church's authority which those women represented? In an instant, they agreed to give up the language (the sounds) that had revealed and accentuated our family's closeness. The moment after the visitors left, the change was observed. "*Ahora,* speak to us *en inglés,*" my father and mother united to tell us.

At first, it seemed a kind of game. After dinner each night, the family gathered to practice "our" English. (It was still then *inglés,* a language foreign to us, so we felt drawn as strangers to it.) Laughing, we would try to define words we could not pronounce. We played with strange English sounds, often overanglicizing our pronunciations. And we filled the smiling gaps of our sentences with familiar Spanish sounds. But that was cheating, somebody shouted. Everyone laughed. In school, meanwhile, like my brother and sister, I was required to attend a daily tutoring session. I needed a full year of special attention. I also needed my teachers to keep my attention from straying in class by calling out, *Rich-heard*—their English voices slowly prying loose my ties to my other name, its three notes, *Ri-car-do.* Most of all I needed to hear my mother and father speak to me in a moment of seriousness in broken—suddenly heartbreaking—English. The scene was inevitable: One Saturday morning I entered the kitchen where my parents were talking in Spanish. I did not realize that they were talking in Spanish however until, at the moment they saw me, I heard their voices change to speak English. Those *gringo* sounds they uttered startled me. Pushed me away. In that moment of trivial misunderstanding and profound insight, I felt my throat twisted by unsounded grief. I turned quickly and left the room. But I had no place to escape to with Spanish. (The spell was broken.) My brother and sisters were speaking English in another part of the house.

Again and again in the days following, increasingly angry, I was obliged to hear my mother and father: "Speak to us *en inglés. (Speak.)*" Only then did I determine to learn classroom English. Weeks after, it happened: One day in school I raised my hand to volunteer an answer. I spoke out in a loud voice. And I did not think it remarkable when the entire class understood. That day, I moved very far from the disadvantaged child I had been only days earlier. The belief, the calming assurance that I belonged in public, had at last taken hold.

Shortly after, I stopped hearing the high and loud sounds Of *los gringos.* A more and more confident speaker of English, I didn't trouble to listen to *how* strangers sounded, speaking to me. And there simply were too many English-speaking people in my day for me to hear American accents anymore. Conversations quickened. Listening to persons who sounded eccentrically pitched voices, I usually noted their sounds for an initial few seconds before I concentrated on *what* they were saying. Conversations became content-full. Transparent. Hearing someone's *tone* of voice—angry or questioning or sarcastic or happy or sad—I didn't distinguish it from the words it expressed. Sound and word were thus tightly wedded. At the end of a day, I was often bemused, always relieved to realize how "silent," though crowded with words, my day in public had been. (This public silence measured and quickened the change in my life.)

35 At last, seven years old, I came to believe what had been technically true since my birth: I was an American citizen.

But the special feeling of closeness at home was diminished by then. Gone was the desperate, urgent, intense feeling of being at home; rare was the experience of feeling myself individualized by family intimates. We remained a loving family, but one greatly changed. No longer so close; no longer bound tight by the pleasing and troubling knowledge of our public separateness. Neither my older brother nor sister rushed home after school anymore. Nor did I. When I arrived home there would often be neighborhood kids in the house. Or the house would be empty of sounds.

The silence at home, however, was finally more than a literal silence. Fewer words passed between parent and child, but more profound was the silence that resulted from my inattention to sounds. At about the time I no longer bothered to listen with care to the sounds of English in public, I grew careless about listening to the sounds family members made when they spoke. Most of the time I heard someone speaking at home and didn't distinguish his sounds from the words people uttered in public. I didn't even pay much attention to my parents' accented and ungrammatical speech. At least not at home. Only when I was with them in public would I grow alert to their accents. Though, even then, their sounds caused me less and less concern. For I was increasingly confident of my own public identity.

I would have been happier about my public success had I not sometimes recalled what it had been like earlier, when my family had conveyed its intimacy through a set of conveniently private sounds. Sometimes in public, hearing a stranger, I'd hark back to my past. A Mexican farmworker approached me downtown to ask directions to somewhere. "*¿Hijito . . . ?*" he said. And his voice summoned deep longing. Another time, standing beside my mother in the visiting room of a Carmelite convent, before the dense screen which rendered the nuns shadowy figures, I heard several Spanish-speaking nuns—their busy, singsong overlapping voices—assure us that yes, yes, we were remembered, all our family was remembered in their prayers. (Their voices echoed faraway family sounds.) Another day, a dark-faced old woman—her hand light on my shoulder—steadied herself against me as she boarded a bus. She murmured something I couldn't quite comprehend. Her Spanish voice came near, like the face of a never-before-seen relative in the instant before I was kissed. Her voice, like so many of the Spanish voices I'd hear in public, recalled the golden age of my youth. Hearing Spanish then, I continued to be a careful, if sad, listener to sounds. Hearing a Spanish-speaking family walking behind me, I turned to look. I smiled for an instant, before my glance found the Hispanic-looking faces of strangers in the crowd going by.

Today I hear bilingual educators say that children lose a degree of "individuality" by becoming assimilated into public society. (Bilingual schooling was popularized in the seventies, that decade when middle-class ethnics began to resist the process of assimilation—the American melting pot.) But the bilingualists simplistically scorn the value and necessity of assimilation. They do not seem to realize that there are *two ways* a person is individualized. So they do not realize that while one suffers a diminished sense of *private* individuality by becoming assimilated into public society, such assimilation makes possible the achievement of *public* individuality.

40 The bilingualists insist that a student should be reminded of his difference from others in mass society, his heritage. But they equate mere separateness with individuality. The fact is that only in private—with intimates—is separateness from the crowd a prerequisite for individuality. (An intimate draws me apart, tells me that I am unique, unlike all others.) In public, by contrast, full individuality is achieved, paradoxically, by those who are able to consider themselves members of the crowd. Thus it happened for me: Only when I was able to think of myself as an American, no longer an alien in *gringo* society, could I seek the rights and opportunities necessary for full public individuality. The social and political advantages I enjoy as a man result from the day that I came to believe that my name, indeed, is *Rich-heard*

Road-ree-guess. It is true that my public society today is often impersonal. (My public society is usually mass society.) Yet despite the anonymity of the crowd and despite the fact that the individuality I achieve in public is often tenuous—because it depends on my being one in a crowd—I celebrate the day I acquired my new name. Those middle-class ethnics who scorn assimilation seem to me filled with decadent self-pity, obsessed by the burden of public life. Dangerously, they romanticize public separateness and they trivialize the dilemma of the socially disadvantaged.

Definition

Some Devil's Definitions

Ambrose Bierce

Ambrose Bierce (1842–c.1914) was born in Horse Cave Creek, Ohio, and grew up in Indiana. As a youth he worked for an antislavery newspaper. Bierce enrolled in the Kentucky Military Institute, but left after a year to enlist in the Ninth Indiana Volunteers. After the Civil War—an experience that impacts much of his writing—Bierce began a career as a writer, editor, and columnist in San Francisco, London, and Washington, D.C. His sharp-tongued journalistic style earned him the nickname "Bitter Bierce." His books include Tales of Soldiers and Civilians *(1891), Can Such Things Be? (1893), and* The Devil's Dictionary, *also known as* The Cynic's Word Book *(1906). In his early 70s, Bierce traveled to Mexico, ostensibly to find the legendary Mexican rebel Pancho Villa; he never returned. Keep Bierce's nickname in mind as you read these selections from* The Devil's Dictionary.

1 *Belladonna, n.* In Italian a beautiful lady; in English a deadly poison. A striking example of the essential identity of the two tongues.

Bigot, n. One who is obstinately and zealously attached to an opinion that you do not entertain.

Bore, n. A person who talks when you wish him to listen.

Brute, n. See HUSBAND.

5 *Cabbage, n.* A familiar kitchen-garden vegetable about as large and wise as a man's head.

Calamity, n. A more than commonly plain and unmistakable reminder that the affairs of this life are not of our own ordering. Calamities are of two kinds: misfortune to ourselves, and good fortune to others.

Cannibal, n. A gastronome of the old school who preserves the simple tastes and adheres to the natural diet of the pre-pork period.

Cannon, n. An instrument employed in the rectification of national boundaries.

Cat, n. A soft, indestructible automaton provided by nature to be kicked when things go wrong in the domestic circle.

Christian, n. One who believes that the New Testament is a divinely inspired book admirably suited to the spiritual needs of his neighbor. One who follows the teachings of Christ in so far as they are not inconsistent with a life of sin.

Clairvoyant, n. A person, commonly a woman, who has the power of seeing that which is invisible to her patron—namely, that he is a blockhead.

Commerce, n. A kind of transaction in which A plunders from B the goods of C, and for compensation B picks the pocket of D of money belonging to E.

Compromise, n. Such an adjustment of conflicting interests as gives each adversary the satisfaction of thinking he has got what he ought not to have, and is deprived of nothing except what was justly his due.

Compulsion, n. The eloquence of power.

Congratulation, n. The civility of envy.

Conservative, n. A statesman who is enamored of existing evils, as distinguished from the Liberal, who wishes to replace them with others.

Consul, n. In American politics, a person who having failed to secure an office from the people is given one by the Administration on condition that he leave the country.

Consult, v.t. To seek another's approval of a course already decided on.

Corsair, n. A politician of the seas.

Coward, n. One who in a perilous emergency thinks with his legs.

Curiosity, n. An objectionable quality of the female mind. The desire to know whether or not a woman is cursed with curiosity is one of the most active and insatiable passions of the masculine soul.

Cynic, n. A blackguard whose faulty vision sees things as they are, not as they ought to be. Hence the custom among the Scythians of plucking out a cynic's eyes to improve his vision.

Dance, v.i. To leap about to the sound of tittering music, preferably with arms about your neighbor's wife or daughter. There are many kinds of dances, but all those requiring the participation of the two sexes have two characteristics in common: they are conspicuously innocent, and warmly loved by the vicious.

Debauchee, n. One who has so earnestly pursued pleasure that he has had the misfortune to overtake it.

Decalogue, n. A series of commandments, ten in number—just enough to permit an intelligent selection for observance, but not enough to embarrass the choice.

Defame, v.t. To lie about another. To tell the truth about another.

Dentist, n. A prestidigitator who, putting metal in your mouth, pulls coins out of your pocket.

Die, n. The singular of "dice." We seldom hear the word, because there is a prohibitory proverb, "Never say die."

Discussion, n. A method of confirming others in their errors.

Distance, n. The only thing that the rich are willing for the poor to call theirs, and keep.

Duel, n. A formal ceremony preliminary to the reconciliation of two enemies. Great skill is necessary to its satisfactory observance; if awkwardly performed the most unexpected and deplorable consequences sometimes ensue. A long time ago a man lost his life in a duel.

Eccentricity, n. A method of distinction so cheap that fools employ it to accentuate their incapacity.

Edible, adj. Good to eat, and wholesome to digest, as a worm to a toad, a toad to a snake, a snake to a pig, a pig to a man, and a man to a worm.

Education, n. That which discloses to the wise and disguises from the foolish their lack of understanding.

Effect, n. The second of two phenomena which always occur together in the same order. The first, called a Cause, is said to generate the other—which is no more sensible than it would be for one who has never seen a dog except in pursuit of a rabbit to declare the rabbit the cause of the dog.

Egotist, n. A person of low taste, more interested in himself than in me.

Erudition, n. Dust shaken out of a book into an empty skull.

Eulogy, n. Praise of a person who has either the advantages of wealth and power, or the consideration to be dead.

Female, n. One of the opposing, or unfair, sex.

Fib, n. A lie that has not cut its teeth. A habitual liar's nearest approach to truth: the perigee of his eccentric orbit.

Fiddle, n. An instrument to tickle human ears by friction of a horse's tail on the entrails of a cat.

Friendship, n. A ship big enough to carry two in fair weather, but only one in foul.

Garter, n. An elastic band intended to keep a woman from coming out of her stockings and desolating the country.

Ghost, n. The outward and visible sign of an inward fear.

Glutton, n. A person who escapes the evils of moderation by committing dyspepsia.

Gout, n. A physician's name for the rheumatism of a rich patient.

Grammar, n. A system of pitfalls thoughtfully prepared for the feet of the self-made man, along the path by which he advances to distinction.

Guillotine, n. A machine which makes a Frenchman shrug his shoulders with good reason.

Anatomy of a Hangover

Donald G. Ross

In this article, readers who have not yet experienced the aftereffects of too much alcohol will be horrified, while readers who have experienced a hangover may be edifed to learn about the chemical causes of their misery. As you read, note particularly the way Ross uses cause and effect, description, and process analysis. Ross's techniques are familiar to readers and writers of scientific reports, but he has toned down the technicality of science and applied it to a well-known experience.

1 Fred awakens with a pounding headache. The room seems to be 1
spinning. Feeling nauseated and sweating profusely, he stumbles into the kitchen for a drink of water. As he glances around the room, he spots the empty bottles of red wine. "Did I really drink that much?" he asks himself. Shaking his head, he is overcome with another wave of piercing head pains and nausea. Fred is in the throws of a substantial hangover. But why do some people get hangovers while others seemingly are able to drink with abandon?

What Is a Hangover?

A hangover typically begins several hours after a person stops drinking, when the blood alcohol level is falling. Symptoms usually peak around the time it hits zero and persist for up to 24 hours. The unpleasant symptoms that commonly follow a heavy bout of drinking can range from a mild headache and upset stomach to a feeling of severe illness—raging headache, nausea, dizziness, and extreme sensitivity to light and sound (see Table 1). The specific symptoms and their intensity may vary widely—from person to person, from drinking bout to drinking bout, and with the type and amount of alcohol consumed.

In general, the more alcohol one consumes, the more likely that one will suffer a hangover. A 1993 survey found that 75 percent of the people who drank to intoxication had hangovers at least some of the time. A study of 2,160 Finnish men found that over 43.8 percent of the heaviest drinkers, those who drank about nine drinks per week, had one or more hangovers every month, compared to 6.6 percent for the rest of the study group. Yet individual differences are large. Some people have hangovers after drinking only one to three alcoholic drinks, while others drink heavily without any morning-after misery.

What Causes a Hangover?

Scientists blame hangover symptoms on several different factors. Alcohol directly affects the brain and other organs, and its withdrawal may be a culprit. Toxic compounds produced as the body processes alcohol may also be responsible. Alcoholic drinks often contain non-alcoholic, yet biologically active, components. Concurrent use of other drugs, restricted eating, and going to bed later than normal can contribute to the intensity of the hangover. Personal traits, such as temperament, personality, and family history of alcoholism, can also be cofactors. Evidence suggest that an interaction of more than one of these factors is responsible for the myriad of hangover symptoms.

Direct Effects of Alcohol

Since its diuretic properties increase urinary output and send drinkers on regular visits to the bathroom, alcohol commonly causes dehydration and electrolyte imbalance. Consumption of about four drinks of alcohol and water (about 250 milliliters) causes the excretion of 600 to 1,000 milliliters of urine! During a hangover, the sweating, vomiting, and diarrhea cause further fluid loss and electrolyte imbalance. Symptoms of dehydration—thirst, weakness, dryness of mucous membranes, dizziness, and lightheadedness—are also typical symptoms of a hangover.

Alcohol directly irritates and inflames the lining of the stomach and intestines. It also triggers increased production of gastric acid and increased pancreatic and intestinal secretions. Beverages with high alcohol content delay stomach emptying. And high alcohol consumption produces fatty acids in liver cells and can cause a fatty liver. An interplay of all these factors commonly causes the upper abdominal pain, nausea, and vomiting of a hangover.

Alcohol alters the body's normal metabolic processes and can cause low blood sugar levels (hypoglycemia). Alcohol-induced hypoglycemia usually occurs in diabetics, as well as alcoholics who binge drink for several days without eating. Hypoglycemia may or may not contribute to a hangover, but the two conditions have similar symptoms—headache, fatigue, weakness, and mood disturbances.

Alcohol has sedating effects that put one to sleep. But it is a disturbed sleep, and rebound effects can lead to insomnia. Drinking often takes place at night in competition with normal sleeping hours, so it reduces sleep time. Alcohol also decreases the amount of dreaming and deep sleep. You may have heard the sonorous sounds of someone snoring away the night after a bout of drinking. Alcohol relaxes the soft palate, increasing snoring and possibly causing sleep apnea.

Alcohol upsets circadian rhythms, and the effects persist into the hangover period. It alters the normal ebb and flow of body temperature, abnormally lowering it during intoxication and abnormally raising it during a hangover, thus promoting sweating the next morning. Alcohol also disrupts the nighttime release of growth hormone and the rise and fall of cortisol levels. The overall disruption of circadian rhythms is similar to "jet lag" and makes hangover symptoms worse.

Alcohol intoxication leads to the dilation of blood vessels, a possible cause of headaches. It also affects the activity of neurotransmitters and hormones, such as histamine, serotonin, and prostaglandins, which have been implicated in head pain.

Alcohol Withdrawal and Toxic Byproducts

A hangover may be a mild manifestation of alcohol withdrawal. Overlapping symptoms include nausea and vomiting, tremor, sweating, anxiety, agitation, and headache. Since consuming additional alcohol can alleviate the immediate unpleasantness of both alcohol withdrawal and hangover, they may share a common underlying mechanism. (Further alcohol use—the "hair of the dog that bit you" hangover remedy—should be avoided. Additional drinking only enhances the toxicity of the alcohol previously consumed and extends the recovery time.)

Your body gets rid of alcohol as fast as it can. The liver converts alcohol to acetaldehyde, which the enzyme aldehyde dehydrogenase (ALDH) quickly converts to a harmless substance that is used for energy or stored as fat. Acetaldehyde is highly toxic, and most people's bodies rapidly and efficiently convert it to avoid its accumulation. Despite this effort, small amounts of acetaldehyde are found in the bloodstream during intoxication.

The ability to convert acetaldehyde varies between women and men and has a strong genetic component. For nonalcoholics, the ALDH enzyme in the stomach lining of women is 40 percent less active than in men. About half the people of Asian descent have low levels of ALDH and experience flushing on the face and neck after drinking alcohol, probably due to high blood acetaldehyde levels. In alcohol aversion therapy, the medication disulfiram (Antabuse) deliberately blocks the conversion of acetaldehyde, allowing even small amounts of alcohol to trigger a highly unpleasant reaction, which includes a throbbing headache, breathing difficulties, nausea, copious vomiting, flushing, vertigo, confusion, and a drop in blood pressure.

Which Drinks Are More Likely To Cause a Hangover?

Gin and vodka are mostly pure ethanol, while brandy, whiskey, and red wine contain other biologically active compounds known as congeners. Congeners contribute to the distinctive taste, smell, and appearance of alcoholic beverages, but they have a dark side. Beverages containing congeners are more likely to cause a hangover than beverages of mostly pure ethanol. Congeners also may enhance the alcoholic beverage's intoxicating effects and worsen a subsequent hangover.

One congener, methanol, is a particularly vicious villain. Although it is a type of alcohol, its chemical structure differs slightly from ethanol's. When the body metabolizes methanol, it produces highly toxic compounds that in high concentrations cause blindness and even death.

The distilled spirits most frequently associated with hangovers, such as brandies and whiskeys, contain the highest concentrations of methanol. In addition, a study of red-wine consumption found that methanol persisted in the blood for several hours after ethanol was metabolized—a time period that matches the course of a hangover.

Some people suffer aftereffects from drinking red wine but not white wine or vodka. While red wine can increase serotonin and histamine levels, triggering pounding headaches in susceptible people, white wine and vodka do not affect the production of these substances.

Personal Factors

People with certain personality traits, such as neuroticism, anger, and defensiveness, seem to suffer hangovers more frequently than others. Hangovers also are associated with negative life events and feelings of guilt about drinking. People who have a personality risk for alcoholism tend to have more severe hangover symptoms and may drink in an attempt to find relief.

Treating a Hangover

So what can one do about a hangover? Innumerable folk remedies purport to prevent, shorten, or cure a hangover, but few have undergone rigorous, scientific investigation. Time is the most effective remedy—symptoms usually disappear within 8 to 24 hours. Consumption of fruits, fruit juices, or other fructose-containing foods has been reported to decrease a hangover's intensity, but this has not been well studied. Eating bland foods containing complex carbohydrates, such as toast or crackers, can combat low blood sugar levels and possibly nausea. Sleep can ease fatigue, and drinking nonalcoholic, noncaffeinated beverages can alleviate dehydration (caffeine is a diuretic and increases urine production).

Certain medications can provide symptom relief. Antacids may relieve nausea and stomach pains. Aspirin may reduce headache and muscle aches, but it could increase stomach irritation. Acetaminophen should be avoided because alcohol metabolism enhances its toxicity to the liver. People who drink three or more alcoholic beverages per day should avoid all over-the-counter pain relievers and fever reducers. These heavy drinkers may have an increased risk of liver damage and stomach bleeding from these medicines, which contain aspirin, other

salicylates, acetaminophen (Tylenol), ibuprofen (Advil), naproxen sodium (Aleve), or ketoprofen (Orudis KT and Actron).
Prevention

As the Old Adage Says, Prevention Is the Best Medicine

A person who drinks only small, nonintoxicating amounts of alcohol is less likely to suffer a hangover than a person who drinks to get drunk. Even among intoxicated people, the ones who drink the most are the most likely to wake up in misery.

TABLE 1: SYMPTOMS OF A HANGOVER

Class of Symptoms	**Type**
Constitutional	Fatigue, weakness, and thirst
Pain	Headache and muscle aches
Gastrointestinal	Nausea, vomiting, and stomach pain
Sleep and biological rhythms	Decreased duration and quality of sleep
Sensory	Vertigo and sensitivity to light and sound
Cognitive	Decreased attention and concentration
Mood	Depression, anxiety, and irritability
Sympathetic hyperactivity	Tremor, sweating, and increased pulse and systolic blood pressure

On Friendship

Margaret Mead and Rhoda Metraux

Margaret Mead (1901–1978), an anthropologist with the American Museum of Natural History in New York City, conducted many field studies in Pacific areas, including Bali, New Guinea, and Samoa. Mead wrote both academic and popular books, including Coming of Age in Samoa *(1928),* Growing Up in New Guinea *(1930), and* Sex and Temperament in Three Primitive Societies *(1935). Anthropologist Rhoda Metraux (1914–), who also worked at the American Museum of Natural History in New York City, performed field work in several Caribbean and South American countries. Mead and Metraux coauthored* Themes in French Culture *and collaborated on a series of articles written for* Redbook, *which were collected and published as* A Way of Seeing. *In this essay, an excerpt from* A Way of Seeing, *Mead and Metraux discuss how the concept of friendship varies from country to country.*

1 Few Americans stay put for a lifetime. We move from town to 1
city to suburb, from high school to college in a different state, from a job in one region to a better job elsewhere, from the home where we raise our children to the home where we plan to live in retirement. With each move we are forever making new friends, who become part of our new life at that time.

For many of us the summer is a special time for forming new friendships. Today millions of Americans vacation abroad, and they go not only to see new sights but also—in those places where they do not feel too strange—with the hope of meeting new people. No one really expects a vacation trip to produce a close friend. But surely the beginning of a friendship is possible? Surely in every country people value friendship?

They do. The difficulty when strangers from two countries meet is not a lack of appreciation of friendship, but different expectations about what constitutes friendship and how it comes into being. In those European countries that Americans are most likely to visit, friendship is quite sharply distinguished from other, more casual relations, and is differently related to family life. For a Frenchman, a German or an Englishman friendship is usually more particularized and carries a heavier burden of commitment.

But as we use the word, "friend" can be applied to a wide range of relationships—to someone one has known for a few weeks in a new place, to a close business associate, to a childhood playmate, to a man or woman, to a trusted confidant. There are real differences among these relations for Americans—a friendship may be superficial, casual, situational or deep and enduring. But to a European, who sees only our surface behavior, the differences are not clear.

5 As they see it, people known and accepted temporarily, casually, flow in and out of Americans' homes with little ceremony and often with little personal commitment. They may be parents of the children's friends, house guests of neighbors, members of a committee, business associates from another town or even another country. Coming as a guest into an American home, the European visitor finds no visible landmarks. The atmosphere is relaxed. Most people, old and young, are called by first names.

Who, then, is a friend?

Even simple translation from one language to another is difficult. "You see," a Frenchman explains, "if I were to say to you in France, 'This is my good friend,' that person would not be as close to me as someone about whom I said only, 'This is my friend.' Anyone about whom I have to say *more* is really less."

In France, as in many European countries, friends generally are of the same sex, and friendship is seen as basically a relationship between men. Frenchwomen laugh at the idea that "women can't be friends," but they also admit sometimes that for women "it's a different thing." And many French people doubt the possibility of a friendship between a man and a woman. There is also the kind of relationship within a group—men and women who have worked together for a long time, who may be very close, sharing great loyalty and warmth of feeling. They may call one another *copains*—a word that in English becomes "friends" but has more the feeling of "pals" or "buddies." In French eyes this is not friendship, although two members of such a group may well be friends.

For the French, friendship is a one-to-one relationship that demands a keen awareness of the other person's intellect, temperament and particular interests. A friend is someone who draws out your own best qualities, with whom you sparkle and become more of whatever the friendship draws upon. Your political philosophy assumes more depth, appreciation of a play becomes sharper, taste in food or wine is accentuated, enjoyment of a sport is intensified.

And French friendships are compartmentalized. A man may play chess with a friend for thirty years without knowing his political opinion, or he may talk politics with him for as long a time without knowing about his personal life. Different friends fill different niches in each person's life. These friendships are not made part of family life. A friend is not expected to spend evenings being nice to children or courteous to a deaf grandmother. These duties, also serious and enjoined, are primarily for relatives. Men who are friends may meet in a café. Intellectual friends may meet in larger groups for evenings of conversation. Working people may meet in the little *bistro* where they drink and talk, far from the family. Marriage does not affect such friendships; wives do not have to be taken into account.

In the past in France, friendships of this kind seldom were open to any but intellectual women. Since most women's lives centered on their homes, their warmest relations with other women often went back to their girlhood. The special relationship of friendship is based on what the French value most—on the mind, on compatibility of outlook, on vivid awareness of some chosen area of life.

Friendship heightens the sense of each person's individuality. Other relationships commanding as great loyalty and devotion have a different meaning. In World War II the first resistance groups formed in Paris were built on the foundation of *les copains.* But significantly, as time went on these little groups, whose lives rested in one another's hands, called themselves "families." Where each had a total responsibility for all, it was kinship ties that provided the model. And even today such ties, crossing every line of class and personal interest, remain binding on the survivors of these small, secret bands.

In Germany, in contrast with France, friendship is much more articulately a matter of feeling. Adolescents, boys and girls, form deeply sentimental attachments, walk and talk together—not so much to polish their wits as to share their hopes and fears and dreams, to form a common front against the world of schools and family and to join in a kind of mutual discovery of each other's and their own inner life. Within the family, the closest relationship over a lifetime is between brothers and sisters. Outside the family, men and women find in their closest friends of the same sex the devotion of a sister, the loyalty of a brother. Appropriately, in Germany friends usually are brought into the family. Children call their father's and their mother's friends "uncle" and "aunt." Between French friends, who have chosen each other for the congeniality of their point of view, lively disagreement and sharpness of argument are the breath of life. But for Germans, whose friendships are based on mutuality of feeling, deep disagreement on any subject that matters to both is regarded as a tragedy. Like ties of kinship, ties of friendship are meant to be irrevocably binding. Young Germans who come to the United States have a great difficulty in establishing such friendships with Americans. We view friendship more tentatively, subject to changes in intensity as people move, change their jobs, marry, or discover new interests.

English friendships follow still a different pattern. Their basis is shared activity. Activities at different stages of life may be of very different kinds—discovering a common interest in school, serving together in the armed forces, taking part in a foreign mission, staying in the same country house during a crisis. In the midst of the activity, whatever it may be, people fall into step—sometimes two men or two women, sometimes two couples, sometimes three people—and find that they walk or play a game or tell stories or serve on a tiresome and exacting committee with the same easy anticipation of what each will do day by day or in some critical situation. Americans who have made English friends comment that, even years later, "you can take up just where you left off." Meeting after a long interval, friends are like a couple who begin to dance again when the orchestra strikes up after a pause. English friendships are formed outside the family circle, but they are not, as in Germany, contrapuntal to the family nor are they, as in France, separated from the family. And a break in an English friendship comes not necessarily as a result of some irreconcilable difference of viewpoint or feeling but instead as a result of misjudgment, where one friend seriously misjudges how the other will think or feel or act, so that suddenly they are out of step.

What, then, is friendship? Looking at these different styles, including our own, each of which is related to a whole way of life, are there common elements? There is the recognition that friendship, in contrast with kinship, invokes freedom of choice. A friend is someone who chooses and is chosen. Related to this is the sense each friend gives the other of being a special individual, on whatever grounds this recognition is based. And between friends there is inevitably a kind of equality of give and take. These similarities make the bridge between societies possible, and the American's characteristic openness to different styles of relationships makes it possible for him to find new friends abroad with whom he feels at home.

The Tapestry of Friendship

Ellen Goodman

Ellen Goodman (1941–), was born in Newton, Massachusetts. A graduate of Radcliffe College (1963), Goodman worked for Newsweek *and* The Detroit Free Press *before joining* The Boston Globe *in 1967. In addition to writing a regular column for the* Globe, *"At Large," which has been syndicated since 1976, Goodman also is a frequent radio and television commentator. The recipient of a Pulitzer Prize for distinguished commentary in 1980, Goodman has published a number of collections of her columns—including* Close to Home *(1979) and* At Large *(1981)—as well as an interview-based review of the impact of the feminist movement—*Making Sense *(1989). Goodman's essays, which often probe very personal aspects of late 20th century America, generally are a twist of irony and satire. Originally published in* The Washington Post *(1978), this short essay explores female "friends" and male "buddies," while it also probes society's changing perspective on relationships.*

1 It was, in many ways, a slight movie. Nothing actually happened. There was no big-budget chase scene, no bloody shoot-out. The story ended without any cosmic conclusions.

Yet she found Claudia Weill's film *Girlfriends* gentle and affecting. Slowly, it panned across the tapestry of friendship—showing its fragility, its resiliency, its role as the connecting tissue between the lives of two young women.

When it was over, she thought about the movies she'd seen this year—*Julia, The Turning Point* and now *Girlfriends*. It seemed that the peculiar eye, the social lens of the cinema, had drastically shifted its focus. Suddenly the Male Buddy movies had been replaced by the Female Friendship flicks.

This wasn't just another binge of trendiness, but a kind of *cinéma vérité.* For once the movies were reflecting a shift, not just from men to women but from one definition of friendship to another.

Across millions of miles of celluloid, the ideal of friendship had always been male—a world of sidekicks and "pardners," of Butch Cassidys and Sundance Kids. There had been something almost atavistic about these visions of attachments—as if producers culled their plots from some pop anthropology book on male bonding. Movies portrayed the idea that only men, those direct descendants of hunters and Hemingways, inherited a primal capacity for friendship. In contrast, they portrayed women picking on each other, the way they once picked berries.

Well, that duality must have been mortally wounded in some shootout at the You're OK, I'm OK Corral. Now, on the screen, they were at least aware of the subtle distinction between men and women as buddies and friends.

About 150 years ago, Coleridge had written, "A woman's friendship borders more closely on love than man's. Men affect each other in the reflection of noble or friendly acts, whilst women ask fewer proofs and more signs and expressions of attachment."

Well, she thought, on the whole, men had buddies, while women had friends. Buddies bonded, but friends loved. Buddies faced adversity together, but friends faced each other. There was something palpably different in the way they spent their time. Buddies seemed to "do" things together; friends simply "were" together.

Buddies came linked, like accessories, to one activity or another. People have golf buddies and business buddies, college buddies and club buddies. Men often keep their buddies in these categories, while women keep a special category for friends.

A man once told her that men weren't real buddies until they'd been "through the wars" together—corporate or athletic or military. They had to soldier together, he said. Women, on the other hand, didn't count themselves as friends until they'd shared three loathsome confidences.

Buddies hang tough together; friends hang onto each other.

It probably had something to do with pride. You don't show off to a friend; you show need. Buddies try to keep the worst from each other; friends confess it.

A friend of hers once telephoned her lover, just to find out if he was home. She hung up without a hello when he picked up the phone. Later, wretched with embarrassment, the friend moaned, "Can you believe me? A thirty-five-year-old lawyer, making a chicken call?" Together they laughed and made it better.

Buddies seek approval. But friends seek acceptance.

She knew so many men who had been trained in restraint, afraid of each other's judgment or awkward with each other's affection. She wasn't sure which. Like buddies in the movies, they would die for each other, but never hug each other.

She'd reread *Babbitt* recently, that extraordinary catalogue of male grievances. The only relationship that gave meaning to the claustrophobic life of George Babbitt had been with Paul Riesling. But not once in the tragedy of their lives had one been able to say to the other: You make a difference.

Even now men shocked her at times with their description of friendship. Does this one have a best friend? "Why, of course, we see each other every February." Does that one call his most intimate pal long distance? "Why, certainly, whenever there's a real reason." Do those two old chums ever have dinner together? "You mean alone? Without our wives?"

Yet, things were changing. The ideal of intimacy wasn't this parallel playmate, this teammate, this trenchmate. Not even in Hollywood. In the double standard of friendship, for once the female version was becoming accepted as the general ideal.

After all, a buddy is a fine life-companion. But one's friends, as Santayana once wrote, "are that part of the race with which one can be human."

Friends, Good Friends—and Such Good Friends

Judith Viorst

Judith Viorst (1936–) has been an editor and columnist at Redbook *magazine, where the following essay originally appeared in 1977. In addition she has written a number of books, including* Alexander and the Terrible, Horrible, No Good, Very Bad Day *(1982) and* Sad Underwear and Other Complications *(1995), children's books;* It's Hard to Be Hip Over Thirty and Other Tragedies of Modern Life *(1970) and* How Did I Get to Be Forty and Other Atrocities *(1984), collections of light verse; and* Murdering Mr. Monti: A Merry Little Tale of Sex and Violence *(1994), a novel. Viorst's style typically combines her personal feelings and humor.*

1 Women are friends, I once would have said, when they totally love and support and trust each other, and bare to each other the secrets of their souls, and run—no questions asked—to help each other, and tell harsh truths to each other (no, you can't wear that dress unless you lose ten pounds first) when harsh truths must be told.

Women are friends, I once would have said, when they share the same affection for Ingmar Bergman, plus train rides, cats, warm rain, charades, Camus, and hate with equal ardor Newark and Brussels sprouts and Lawrence Welk and camping.

In other words, I once would have said that a friend is a friend all the way, but now I believe that's a narrow point of view. For the friendships I have and the friendships I see are conducted at many levels of intensity, serve many different functions, meet different needs and range from those as all-the-way as the friendship of the soul sisters mentioned above to that of the most nonchalant and casual playmates.

Consider these varieties of friendship:

5 1. Convenience friends. These are women with whom, if our paths weren't crossing all the time, we'd have no particular reason to be friends: a next-door neighbor, a woman in our car pool, the mother of one of our children's closest friends or maybe some mommy with whom we serve juice and cookies each week at the Glenwood Co-op Nursery.

Convenience friends are convenient indeed. They'll lend us their cups and silverware for a party. They'll drive our kids to soccer when we're sick. They'll take us to pick up our car when we need a lift to the garage. They'll even take our cats when we go on vacation. As we will for them.

But we don't, with convenience friends, ever come too close or tell too much; we maintain our public face and emotional distance. "Which means," says Elaine, "that I'll talk about being overweight but not about being depressed. Which means I'll admit being mad but not blind with rage. Which means that I might say that we're pinched this month but never that I'm worried sick over money."

But which doesn't mean that there isn't sufficient value to be found in these friendships of mutual aid, in convenience friends.

2. Special-interest friends. These friendships aren't intimate, and they needn't involve kids or silverware or cats. Their value lies in some interest jointly shared. And so we may have an office friend or a yoga friend or a tennis friend or a friend from the Women's Democratic Club.

10 "I've got one woman friend," says Joyce, "who likes, as I do, to take psychology courses. Which makes it nice for me—and nice for her. It's fun to go with someone you know and it's fun to discuss what you've learned, driving back from the classes." And for the most part, she says, that's all they discuss.

"I'd say that what we're doing is *doing* together, not being together," Suzanne says of her Tuesday-doubles friends. "It's mainly a tennis relationship, but we play together well. And I guess we all need to have a couple of playmates."

I agree.

My playmate is a shopping friend, a woman of marvelous taste, a woman who knows exactly *where* to buy *what,* and furthermore is a woman who always knows beyond a doubt what one ought to be buying. I don't have the time to keep up with what's new in eyeshadow, hemlines and shoes and whether the smock look is in or finished already. But since (oh, shame!) I care a lot about eyeshadow, hemlines and shoes, and since I don't *want* to wear smocks if the smock look is finished, I'm very glad to have a shopping friend.

3. Historical friends. We all have a friend who knew us when . . . maybe way back in Miss Meltzer's second grade, when our family lived in that three-room flat in Brooklyn, when our dad was out of work for seven months, when our brother Allie got in that fight where they had to call the police, when our sister married the endodontist from Yonkers and when, the morning after we lost our virginity, she was the first, the only, friend we told.

The years have gone by and we've gone separate ways and we've little in common now, but we're still an intimate part of each other's past. And so whenever we go to Detroit we always go to visit this friend of our girlhood. Who knows how we looked before our teeth were straightened. Who knows how we talked before our voice got un-Brooklyned. Who knows what we ate before we learned about artichokes. And who, by her presence, puts us in touch with an earlier part of ourself, a part of ourself it's important never to lose.

"What this friend means to me and what I mean to her," says Grace, "is having a sister without sibling rivalry. We know the texture of each other's lives. She remembers my grandmother's cabbage soup. I remember the way her uncle played the piano. There's simply no other friend who remembers those things."

4. Crossroads friends. Like historical friends, our crossroads friends are important for *what was*—for the friendship we shared at a crucial, now past, time of life. A time, perhaps, when we roomed in college together; or worked as eager young singles in the Big City together; or went together, as my friend Elizabeth and I did, through pregnancy, birth and that scary first year of new motherhood.

Crossroads friends forge powerful links, links strong enough to endure with not much more contact than once-a-year letters at Christmas. And out of respect for those crossroads years, for those dramas and dreams we once shared, we will always be friends.

5. Cross-generational friends. Historical friends and crossroads friends seem to maintain a special kind of intimacy—dormant but always ready to be revived—and though we may rarely meet, whenever

we do connect, it's personal and intense. Another kind of intimacy exists in the friendships that form across generations in what one woman calls her daughter-mother and her mother-daughter relationships.

20 Evelyn's friend is her mother's age—"but I share so much more than I ever could with my mother"—a woman she talks to of music, of books and of life. "What I get from her is the benefit of her experience. What she gets—and enjoys—from me is a youthful perspective. It's a pleasure for both of us."

I have in my own life a precious friend, a woman of 65 who has lived very hard, who is wise, who listens well; who has been where I am and can help me understand it; and who represents not only an ultimate ideal mother to me but also the person I'd like to be when I grow up.

In our daughter role we tend to do more than our share of self-revelation; in our mother role we tend to receive what's revealed. It's another kind of pleasure—playing wise mother to a questing younger person. It's another very lovely kind of friendship.

6. Part-of-a-couple friends. Some of the women we call our friends we never see alone—we see them as part of a couple at couples' parties. And though we share interests in many things and respect each other's views, we aren't moved to deepen the relationship. Whatever the reason, a lack of time or—and this is more likely—a lack of chemistry, our friendship remains in the context of a group. But the fact that our feeling on seeing each other is always, "I'm *so* glad she's here" and the fact that we spend half the evening talking together says that this too, in its own way, counts as a friendship.

(Other part-of-a-couple friends are the friends that came with the marriage, and some of these are friends we could live without. But sometimes, alas, she married our husband's best friend; and sometimes, alas, she *is* our husband's best friend. And so we find ourself dealing with her, somewhat against our will, in a spirit of what I'll call *reluctant* friendship.)

25 7. Men who are friends. I wanted to write just of women friends, but the women I've talked to won't let me—they say I must mention man-woman friendships too. For these friendships can be just as close and as dear as those that we form with women. Listen to Lucy's description of one such friendship:

"We've found we have things to talk about that are different from what he talks about with my husband and different from what I talk about with his wife. So sometimes we call on the phone or meet for lunch. There are similar intellectual interests—we always pass on to each other the books that we love—but there's also something tender and caring too."

In a couple of crises, Lucy says, "he offered himself for talking and for helping. And when someone died in his family he wanted me there. The sexual, flirty part of our friendship is very small, but *some*—just enough to make it fun and different." She thinks—and I agree—that the sexual part, though small, is always *some,* is always there when a man and a woman are friends.

It's only in the past few years that I've made friends with men, in the sense of a friendship that's *mine,* not just part of two couples. And achieving with them the ease and the trust I've found with women friends has value indeed. Under the dryer at home last week, putting on mascara and rouge, I comfortably sat and talked with a fellow named Peter. Peter, I finally decided, could handle the shock of me minus mascara under the dryer. Because we care for each other. Because we're friends.

8. There are medium friends, and pretty good friends, and very good friends indeed, and these friendships are defined by their level of intimacy. And what we'll reveal at each of these levels of intimacy is calibrated with care. We might tell a medium friend, for example, that yesterday we had a fight with our husband. And we might tell a pretty good friend that this fight with our husband made us so mad that we slept on the couch. And we might tell a very good friend that the reason we got so mad in that fight that we slept on the couch had something to do with that girl who works in his office. But it's only to our very best friends that we're willing to tell all, to tell what's going on with that girl in his office.

The best of friends, I still believe, totally love and support and trust each other, and bare to each other the secrets of their souls, and run—no questions asked—to help each other, and tell harsh truths to each other when they must be told.

But we needn't agree about everything (only 12-year-old girl friends agree about *everything*) to tolerate each other's point of view. To accept without judgment. To give and to take without ever keeping score. And to *be* there, as I am for them and as they are for me, to comfort our sorrows, to celebrate our joys.

On Dumpster Diving

Lars Eighner

Lars Eighner (1948–) became homeless in the 1980s after losing a job and being unable to find another immediately. He had been a student at the University of Texas at Austin before this, at which time he had been thrown out of his mother's house for being gay. While homeless he wrote stories and articles for magazines when he was able to find a typewriter to use and stay in one place long enough to write. He remained homeless for about three years, caring for and traveling with his dog, Lizbeth. In 1993 he published Travels with Lizbeth: Three Years on the Road and on the Streets, *an autobiographical account of that period which is in turns humorous, philosophical, and a good narrative. The following essay is an excerpted chapter from that book. Eighner's writing is successful because of the unabashedly honest and self-aware way he takes on his subject and opens his reader to a new world—here, the contents of trash dumpsters.*

This chapter was composed while the author was homeless. The present tense has been preserved.

1 Long before I began Dumpster diving I was impressed with 1
Dumpsters, enough so that I wrote the Merriam-Webster research service to discover what I could about the word *Dumpster*. I learned from them that it is a proprietary word belonging to the Dempsey Dumpster company. Since then I have dutifully capitalized the word, although it was lowercased in almost all the citations Merriam-Webster photocopied for me. Dempsey's word is too apt. I have never heard these things called anything but Dumpsters. I do not

know anyone who knows the generic name for these objects. From time to time I have heard a wino or hobo give some corrupted credit to the original and call them Dipsy Dumpsters.

I began Dumpster diving about a year before I became homeless.

I prefer the word *scavenging* and use the word *scrounging* when I mean to be obscure. I have heard people, evidently meaning to be polite, use the word *foraging,* but I prefer to reserve that word for gathering nuts and berries and such which I do also according to the season and the opportunity. *Dumpster diving* seems to me to be a little too cute and, in my case, inaccurate because I lack the athletic ability to lower myself into the Dumpsters as the true divers do, much as their increased profit.

I like the frankness of the word *scavenging,* which I can hardly think of without picturing a big black snail on an aquarium wall. I live from the refuse of others. I am a scavenger. I think it a sound and honorable niche, although if I could I would naturally prefer to live the comfortable consumer life, perhaps—and only perhaps—as a slightly less wasteful consumer, owing to what I have learned as a scavenger.

5 While Lizbeth and I were still living in the shack on Avenue B as my savings ran out, I put almost all my sporadic income into rent. The necessities of daily life I began to extract from Dumpsters. Yes, we ate from them. Except for jeans, all my clothes came from Dumpsters. Boom boxes, candles, bedding, toilet paper, a virgin male love doll, medicine, books, a typewriter, dishes, furnishings, and change, sometimes amounting to many dollars—I acquired many things from the Dumpsters.

I have learned much as a scavenger. I mean to put some of what I have learned down here, beginning with the practical art of Dumpster diving and proceeding to the abstract.

What is safe to eat?

After all, the finding of objects is becoming something of an urban art. Even respectable employed people will sometimes find something tempting sticking out of a Dumpster or standing beside one. Quite a number of people, not all of them of the bohemian type, are willing to brag that they found this or that piece in the trash. But eating from Dumpsters is what separates the dilettanti from the professionals. Eating safely from the Dumpsters involves three principles: using the senses and common sense to evaluate the conditions of the found materials, knowing the Dumpsters of a given area and checking them regularly, and seeking always to answer the question "Why was this discarded?"

Perhaps everyone who has a kitchen and a regular supply of groceries has, at one time or another, made a sandwich and eaten half of it before discovering mold on the bread or got a mouthful of milk before realizing the milk had turned. Nothing of the sort is likely to happen to a Dumpster diver because he is constantly reminded that most food is discarded for a reason. Yet a lot of perfectly good food can be found in Dumpsters.

Canned goods, for example, turn up fairly often in the Dumpsters I frequent. All except the most phobic people would be willing to eat from a can, even if it came from a Dumpster. Canned goods are among the safest of foods to be found in Dumpsters but are not utterly foolproof.

Although very rare with modern canning methods, botulism is a possibility. Most other forms of food poisoning seldom do lasting harm to a healthy person, but botulism is most certainly fatal and often the first symptom is death. Except for carbonated beverages, all canned goods should contain a slight vacuum and suck air when first punctured. Bulging, rusty, and dented cans and cans that spew when punctured should be avoided, especially when the contents are not very acidic or syrupy.

Heat can break down the botulin, but this requires much more cooking than most people do to canned goods. To the extent that botulism occurs at all, of course, it can occur in cans on pantry shelves as well as in cans from Dumpsters. Need I say that home-canned goods are simply too risky to be recommended

From time to time one of my companions, aware of the source of my provisions, will ask, "Do you think these crackers are really safe to eat?" For some reason it is most often the crackers they ask about.

This question has always made me angry. Of course I would not offer my companion anything I had doubts about. But more than that, I wonder why he cannot evaluate the condition of the crackers for himself. I have no special knowledge and I have been wrong before. Since he knows where the food comes from, it seems to me he ought to assume some of the responsibility for deciding what he will put in his mouth. For myself I have few qualms about dry foods such as crackers, cookies, cereal, chips, and pasta if they are free of visible contaminates and still dry and crisp. Most often such things are found in the original packaging, which is not so much a positive sign as it is the absence of a negative one.

15 Raw fruits and vegetables with intact skins seem perfectly safe to me, excluding of course the obviously rotten. Many are discarded for minor imperfections that can be pared away. Leafy vegetables, grapes, cauliflower, broccoli, and similar things may be contaminated by liquids and may be impractical to wash. 15

Candy, especially hard candy, is usually safe if it has not drawn ants. Chocolate is often discarded only because it has become discolored as the cocoa butter de-emulsified. Candying, after all, is one method of food preservation because pathogens do not like very sugary substances.

All of these foods might be found in any Dumpster and can be evaluated with some confidence largely on the basis of appearance. Beyond these are foods that cannot be correctly evaluated without additional information.

I began scavenging by pulling pizzas out of the Dumpster behind a pizza delivery shop. In general, prepared food requires caution, but in this case I knew when the shop closed and went to the Dumpster as soon as the last of the help left.

Such shops often get prank orders; both the orders and the products made to fill them are called *bogus.* Because help seldom stays long at these places, pizzas are often made with the wrong topping, refused on delivery for being cold, or baked incorrectly. The products to be discarded are boxed up because inventory is kept by counting boxes: A boxed pizza can be written off; an unboxed pizza does not exist.

20 I never placed a bogus order to increase the supply of pizzas and I believe no one else was scavenging in this Dumpster. But the people in the shop became suspicious and began to retain their garbage in the shop overnight. While it lasted I had a steady supply of fresh, sometimes warm pizza. Because I knew the Dumpster I knew the source of the pizza, and because I visited the Dumpster regularly I knew what was fresh and what was yesterday's. 20

The area I frequent is inhabited by many affluent college students. I am not here by chance; the Dumpsters in this area are very rich. Students throw out many good things, including food. In particular they tend to throw everything out when they move at the end of a semester, before and after breaks, and around midterm, when many of them despair of college. So I find it advantageous to keep an eye on the academic calendar.

Students throw food away around breaks because they do not know whether it has spoiled or will spoil before they return. A typical discard is a half jar of peanut butter. In fact, nonorganic peanut butter does not require refrigeration and is unlikely to spoil in any reasonable time. The student does not know that, and since it is Daddy's money, the student decides not to take a chance. Opened containers require caution and some attention to the question. "Why was this discarded?" But in the case of discards from student apartments, the answer may be that the item was thrown out through carelessness, ignorance, or wastefulness. This can sometimes be deduced when the item is found with many others, including some that are obviously perfectly good.

Some students, and others, approach defrosting a freezer by chucking out the whole lot. Not only do the circumstances of such a find tell the story, but also the mass of frozen goods stays cold for a long time and items may be found still frozen or freshly thawed.

Yogurt, cheese, and sour cream are items that are often thrown out while they are still good. Occasionally I find a cheese with a spot of mold, which of course I just pare off, and because it is obvious why such a cheese was discarded, I treat it with less suspicion than an apparently perfect cheese found in similar circumstances. Yogurt is often discarded, still sealed, only because the expiration date on the carton had passed. This is one of my favorite finds because yogurt will keep for several days, even in warm weather.

25 Students throw out canned goods and staples at the end of semesters and when they give up college at midterm. Drugs, pornography, spirits, and the like are often discarded when parents are expected—Dad's day, for example. And spirits also turn up after big party weekends, presumably discarded by the newly reformed. Wine and spirits, of course, keep perfectly well even once opened, but the same cannot be said of beer.

My test for carbonated soft drinks is whether they still fizz vigorously. Many juices or other beverages are too acidic or too syrupy to cause much concern, provided they are not visibly contaminated. I have discovered nasty molds in vegetable juices, even when the product was found under its original seal; I recommend that such products be decanted slowly into a clear glass. Liquids always require some care. One hot day I found a large jug of Pat O'Brien's Hurricane mix. The jug had been opened, but it was still ice cold. I drank three large glasses before it became apparent to me that someone had added the rum to the mix, and not a little rum. I never tasted the rum, and by the time I began to feel the effects I had already ingested a very large quantity of the beverage. Some divers would have considered this a boon, but being suddenly intoxicated in a public place in the early afternoon is not my idea of a good time.

I have heard of people maliciously contaminating discarded food and even handouts, but mostly I have heard of this from people with vivid imaginations who have had no experience with the Dumpsters themselves. Just before the pizza shop stopped discarding its garbage at night, jalapeños began showing up on most of the discarded pizzas. If indeed this was meant to discourage me it was a wasted effort because I am native Texan.

For myself, I avoid game, poultry, pork, and egg-based foods, whether I find them raw or cooked. I seldom have the means to cook what I find, but when I do I avail myself of plentiful supplies of beef, which is often in very good condition. I suppose fish becomes disagreeable before it becomes dangerous. Lizbeth is happy to have any such thing that is past its prime and, in fact, does not recognize fish as food until it is quite strong.

Home leftovers, as opposed to surpluses from restaurants, are very often bad. Evidently, especially among students, there is a common type of personality that carefully wraps up even the smallest leftover and shoves it into the back of the refrigerator for six months or so before discarding it. Characteristic of this type are the reused jars and margarine tubs to which the remains are committed. I avoid ethnic foods I am unfamiliar with. If I do not know what it is supposed to look like when it is good, I cannot be certain I will be able to tell if it is bad.

No matter how careful I am I still get dysentery at least once a month, oftener in warm weather. I do not want to paint too romantic a picture. Dumpster diving has serious drawbacks as a way of life.

I learned to scavenge gradually, on my own. Since then I have initiated several companions into the trade. I have learned that there is a predictable series of stages a person goes through in learning to scavenge.

At first the new scavenger is filled with disgust and self-loathing. He is ashamed of being seen and may lurk around, trying to duck behind things, or he may try to dive at night. (In fact, most people instinctively look away from a scavenger. By skulking around, the novice calls attention to himself and arouses suspicion. Diving at night is ineffective and needlessly messy.)

Every grain of rice seems to be a maggot. Everything seems to stink. He can wipe the egg yolk off the found can, but he cannot erase from his mind the stigma of eating garbage.

That stage passes with experience. The scavenger finds a pair of running shoes that fit and look and smell brand-new. He finds a pocket calculator in perfect working order. He finds pristine ice cream, still frozen, more than he can eat or keep. He begins to understand: People throw away perfectly good stuff, a lot of perfectly good stuff.

35 At this stage, Dumpster shyness begins to dissipate. The diver, after all, has the last laugh. He is finding all manner of good things that are his for the taking. Those who disparage his profession are the fools, not he.

He may begin to hang on to some perfectly good things for which he has neither a use nor a market. Then he begins to take note of the things that are not perfectly good but are nearly so. He mates a Walkman with broken earphones and one that is missing a battery cover. He picks up things that he can repair.

At this stage he may become lost and never recover. Dumpsters are full of things of some potential value to someone and also of things that never have much intrinsic value but are interesting. All the Dumpster divers I have known come to the point of trying to acquire everything they touch. Why not take it, they reason, since it is all free? This is, of course, hopeless. Most divers come to realize that they must restrict themselves to items of relatively immediate utility. But in some cases the diver simply cannot control himself. I have met several of these pack-rat types. Their ideas of the values of various pieces of junk verge on the psychotic. Every bit of glass may be a diamond, they think, and all that glisters, gold.

I tend to gain weight when I am scavenging. Partly this is because I always find far more pizza and doughnuts than water-packed tuna, nonfat yogurt, and fresh vegetables. Also I have not developed much faith in the reliability of Dumpsters as a food source, although it has been proven to me many times. I tend to eat as if I have no idea where my next meal is coming from. But mostly I just hate to see food go to waste and so I eat much more than I should. Something like this drives the obsession to collect junk.

As for collecting objects, I usually restrict myself to collecting one kind of small object at a time, such as pocket calculators, sunglasses, or campaign buttons. To live on the street I must anticipate my needs to a certain extent: I must pick up and save warm bedding I find in August because it will not be found in Dumpsters in November. As I have no access to health care, I often hoard essential drugs, such as antibiotics and antihistamines. (This course can be recommended only to those with some grounding in pharmacology. Antibiotics, for example, even when indicated are worse than useless if taken in insufficient amounts.) But even if I had a home with extensive storage space, I could not save everything that might be valuable in some contingency.

40 I have proprietary feelings about my Dumpsters. As I have mentioned, it is no accident that I scavenge from ones where good finds are common. But my limited experience with Dumpsters in other areas suggests to me that even in poorer areas, Dumpsters, if attended with sufficient diligence, can be made to yield a livelihood. The rich students discard perfectly good kiwifruit; poorer people discard perfectly good apples. Slacks and Polo shirts are found in the one place; jeans and T-shirts in the other. The population of competitors rather than the affluence of the dumpers most affects the feasibility of survival by scavenging. The large number of competitors is what puts me off the idea of trying to scavenge in places like Los Angeles.

Curiously, I do not mind my direct competition, other scavengers, so much as I hate the can scroungers.

People scrounge cans because they have to have a little cash. I have tried scrounging cans with an able-bodied companion. Afoot a can scrounger simply cannot make more than a few dollars a day. One can extract the necessities of life from the Dumpsters directly with far less effort than would be required to accumulate the equivalent value in cans. (These observations may not hold in places with container redemption laws.)

Can scroungers, then, are people who must have small amounts of cash. These are drug addicts and winos, mostly the latter because the amounts of cash are so small. Spirits and drugs do, like all other commodities, turn up in Dumpsters and the scavenger will from time to time have a half bottle of a rather good wine with his dinner. But the wino cannot survive on these occasional finds; he must have his daily dose to stave off the DTs. All the cans he can carry will buy about three bottles of Wild Irish Rose.

I do not begrudge them the cans, but can scroungers tend to tear up the Dumpsters, mixing the contents and littering the area. They become so specialized that they can see only cans. They earn my contempt by passing up change, canned goods, and readily hockable items.

45 There are precious few courtesies among scavengers. But it is common practice to set aside surplus items: pairs of shoes, clothing, canned goods, and such. A true scavenger hates to see good stuff go to waste, and what he cannot use he leaves in good condition in plain sight.

Can scroungers lay waste to everything in their path and will stir one of a pair of good shoes to the bottom of a Dumpster, to be lost or ruined in the muck. Can scroungers will even go through individual garbage cans, something I have never seen a scavenger do.

Individual garbage cans are set out on the public easement only on garbage days. On other days going through them requires trespassing close to a dwelling. Going through individual garbage cans without scattering litter is almost impossible. Litter is likely to reduce the public's tolerance of scavenging. Individual cans are simply not as productive as Dumpsters; people in houses and duplexes do not move so often and for some reason do not tend to discard as much useful material. Moreover, the time required to go through one garbage can that serves one household is not much less than the time required to go through a Dumpster that contains the refuse of twenty apartments.

But my strongest reservation about going through individual garbage cans is that this seems to me a very personal kind of invasion to which I would object if I were a householder. Although many things in Dumpsters are obviously meant never to come to light, a Dumpster is somehow less personal.

I avoid trying to draw conclusions about the people who dump in the Dumpsters I frequent. I think it would be unethical to do so, although I know many people will find the idea of scavenger ethics too funny for words.

50 Dumpsters contain bank statements, correspondence, and other documents, just as anyone might expect. But there are also less

obvious sources of information. Pill bottles, for example. The labels bear the name of the patient, the name of the doctor, and the name of the drug. AIDS drugs and antipsychotic medicines, to name but two groups, are specific and are seldom prescribed for any other disorders. The plastic compacts for birth-control pills usually have complete label information.

Despite all of this sensitive information, I have had only one apartment resident object to my going through the Dumpster. In that case it turned out the resident was a university athlete who was taking bets and who was afraid I would turn up his wager slips.

Occasionally a find tells a story. I once found a small paper bag containing some unused condoms, several partial tubes of flavored sexual lubricants, a partially used compact of birth-control pills, and the torn pieces of a picture of a young man. Clearly she was through with him and planning to give up sex altogether.

Dumpster things are often sad—abandoned teddy bears, shredded wedding books, despaired-of sales kits. I find many pets lying in state in Dumpsters. Although I hope to get off the streets so that Lizbeth can have a long and comfortable old age, I know this hope is not very realistic. So I suppose when her time comes she too will go into a Dumpster. I will have no better place for her. And after all, it is fitting, since for most of her life her livelihood has come from the Dumpster. When she finds something I think is safe that has been spilled from a Dumpster, I let her have it. She already knows the route around the best ones. I like to think that if she survives me she will have a chance of evading the dog catcher and of finding her sustenance on the route.

Silly vanities also come to rest in the Dumpsters. I am a rather accomplished needleworker. I get a lot of material from the Dumpsters. Evidently sorority girls, hoping to impress someone, perhaps themselves, with their mastery of a womanly art, buy a lot of embroider-by-number kits, work a few stitches horribly, and eventually discard the whole mess. I pull out their stitches, turn the canvas over, and work an original design. Do not think I refrain from chuckling as I make gifts from these kits.

55 I find diaries and journals. I have often thought of compiling a book of literary found objects. And perhaps I will one day. But what I find is hopelessly commonplace and bad without being, even unconsciously, camp. College students also discard their papers. I am

horrified to discover the kind of paper that now merits an A in an undergraduate course. I am grateful, however, for the number of good books and magazines the students throw out.

In the area I know best I have never discovered vermin in the Dumpsters, but there are two kinds of kitty surprise. One is alley cats whom I meet as they leap, claws first, out of Dumpsters. This is especially thrilling when I have Lizbeth in tow. The other kind of kitty surprise is a plastic garbage bag filled with some ponderous, amorphous mass. This always proves to be used cat litter.

City bees harvest doughnut glaze and this makes the Dumpster at the doughnut shop more interesting. My faith in the instinctive wisdom of animals is always shaken whenever I see Lizbeth attempt to catch a bee in her mouth, which she does whenever bees are present. Evidently some birds find Dumpsters profitable, for birdie surprise is almost as common as kitty surprise of the first kind. In hunting season all kinds of small game turn up in Dumpsters, some of it, sadly, not entirely dead. Curiously, summer and winter, maggots are uncommon.

The worst of the living and near-living hazards of the Dumpsters are the fire ants. The food they claim is not much of a loss, but they are vicious and aggressive. It is very easy to brush against some surface of the Dumpster and pick up half a dozen or more fire ants, usually in some sensitive area such as the underarm. One advantage of bringing Lizbeth along as I make Dumpster rounds is that, for obvious reasons, she is very alert to ground-based fire ants. When Lizbeth recognizes a fire-ant infestation around our feet, she does the Dance of the Zillion Fire Ants. I have learned not to ignore this warning from Lizbeth, whether I perceive the tiny ants or not, but to remove ourselves at Lizbeth's first pas de bourrée. All the more so because the ants are the worst in the summer months when I wear flip-flops if I have them. (Perhaps someone will misunderstand this. Lizbeth does the Dance of the Zillion Fire Ants when she recognizes more fire ants than she cares to eat, not when she is being bitten. Since I have learned to react promptly, she does not get bitten at all. It is the isolated patrol of fire ants that falls in Lizbeth's range that deserves pity. She finds them quite tasty.)

By far the best way to go through a Dumpster is to lower yourself into it. Most of the good stuff tends to settle at the bottom because it is usually weightier than the rubbish. My more athletic companions have often demonstrated to me that they can extract much good material from a Dumpster I have already been over.

60 To those psychologically or physically unprepared to enter a 60 Dumpster, I recommend a stout stick, preferably with some barb or hook at one end. The hook can be used to grab plastic garbage bags. When I find canned goods or other objects loose at the bottom of a Dumpster, I lower a bag into it, roll the desired object into the bag, and then hoist the bag out—a procedure more easily described than executed. Much Dumpster diving is a matter of experience for which nothing will do except practice.

Dumpster diving is outdoor work, often surprisingly pleasant. It is not entirely predictable; things of interest turn up every day and some days there are finds of great value. I am always very pleased when I can turn up exactly the thing I most wanted to find. Yet in spite of the element of chance, scavenging more than most other pursuits tends to yield returns in some proportion to the effort and intelligence brought to bear. It is very sweet to turn up a few dollars in change from a Dumpster that has just been gone over by a wino.

The land is now covered with cities. The cities are full of Dumpsters. If a member of the canine race is ever able to know what it is doing, then Lizbeth knows that when we go around to the Dumpsters, we are hunting. I think of scavenging as a modern form of self-reliance. In any event, after having survived nearly ten years of government service, where everything is geared to the lowest common denominator, I find it refreshing to have work that rewards initiative and effort. Certainly I would be happy to have a sinecure again, but I am no longer heartbroken that I left one.

I find from the experience of scavenging two rather deep lessons. The first is to take what you can use and let the rest go by. I have come to think that there is no value in the abstract. A thing I cannot use or make useful, perhaps by trading, has no value however rare or fine it may be. I mean useful in a broad sense—some art I would find useful and some otherwise.

I was shocked to realize that some things are not worth acquiring, but now I think it is so. Some material things are white elephants that eat up the possessor's substance. The second lesson is the transience of material being. This has not quite converted me to a dualist, but it has made some headway in that direction. I do not suppose that ideas are immortal, but certainly mental things are longer lived than other material things.

Once I was the sort of person who invests objects with sentimental value. Now I no longer have those objects, but I have the sentiments yet.

Many times in our travels I have lost everything but the clothes I was wearing and Lizbeth. The things I find in Dumpsters, the love letters and rag dolls of so many lives, remind me of this lesson. Now I hardly pick up a thing without envisioning the time I will cast it aside. This I think is a healthy state of mind. Almost everything I have now has already been cast out at least once, proving that what I own is valueless to someone.

Anyway, I find my desire to grab for the gaudy bauble has been largely sated. I think this is an attitude I share with the very wealthy—we both know there is plenty more where what we have came from. Between us are the rat-race millions who nightly scavenge the cable channels looking for they know not what.

I am sorry for them.

On Being a Cripple

Nancy Mairs

Nancy Mairs (1943–) was born in California, attended college in New England, and now lives in Tucson, Arizona. She earned her M. F. A. in creative writing and Ph.D. in literature from the University of Arizona and has taught writing and worked as an editor for many years. She has written a book of poetry, In All the Rooms of the Yellow House *(1984), and a number of collections of essays and autobiographical sketches, including* i*(1986),* Remembering the Bone House *(1989),* Carnal Acts *(1990),* Ordinary Time *(1993),* Voice Lessons *(1994),*Waist-High in the World: A Life Among the Nondisabled *(1996), and* A Troubled Guest: Life and Death Stories *(2001). As you'll see in the first few sentences of the following autobiographical essay, published in 1993, Mairs writes with an honest, outspoken style that immediately engages you in her subject.*

To escape is nothing. Not to escape is nothing.
—Louise Bogan

1 The other day I was thinking of writing an essay on being a cripple. I was thinking hard in one of the stalls of the women's room in my office building, as I was shoving my shirt into my jeans and tugging up my zipper. Preoccupied, I flushed, picked up my book bag, took my cane down from the hook, and unlatched the door. So many movements unbalanced me, and as I pulled the door open I fell over backward, landing fully clothed on the toilet seat with my legs splayed in front me: the old beetle-on-its-back routine. Saturday afternoon, the building deserted, I was free to laugh aloud as I wriggled back to my feet, my voice bouncing off the yellowish tiles from all 1

directions. Had anyone been there with me, I'd have been still and faint and hot with chagrin. I decided that it was high time to write the essay.

First, the matter of semantics. I am a cripple. I choose this word to name me. I choose from among several possibilities, the most common of which are "handicapped" and "disabled." I made the choice a number of years ago, without thinking, unaware of my motives for doing so. Even now, I'm not sure what those motives are, but I recognize that they are complex and not entirely flattering. People—crippled or not—wince at the word "cripple," as they do not at "handicapped" or "disabled." Perhaps I want them to wince. I want them to see me as a tough customer, one to whom the fates/gods/viruses have not been kind, but who can face the brutal truth of her existence squarely. As a cripple, I swagger.

But, to be fair to myself, a certain amount of honesty underlies my choice. "Cripple" seems to me a clean word, straightforward and precise. It has an honorable history, having made its first appearance in the Lindisfarne Gospel in the tenth century. As a lover of words, I like the accuracy with which it describes my condition: I have lost the full use of my limbs. "Disabled," by contrast, suggests an incapacity, physical or mental. And I certainly don't like "handicapped," which implies that I have deliberately been put at a disadvantage, by whom I can't imagine (my God is not a Handicapper General), in order to equalize chances in the great race of life. These words seem to me to be moving away from my condition, to be widening the gap between word and reality. Most remote is the recently coined euphemism "differently abled," which partakes of the same semantic hopefulness that transformed countries from "undeveloped" to "underdeveloped," then to "less developed," and finally to "developing" nations. People have continued to starve in those countries during the shift. Some realities do not obey the dictates of language.

Mine is one of them. Whatever you call me, I remain crippled. But I don't care what you call me, so long as it isn't "differently abled," which strikes me as pure verbal garbage designed, by its ability to describe anyone, to describe no one. I subscribe to George Orwell's thesis that "the slovenliness of our language makes it easier for us to have foolish thoughts." And I refuse to participate in the degeneration of the language to the extent that I deny that I have lost anything in the course of this calamitous disease; I refuse to pretend that the only differences between you and me are the various ordinary ones that distinguish any one person from another. But call me "disabled" or "handicapped" if you like. I have long since grown accustomed to them; and if they are vague, at least they hint at the truth. Moreover, I use them myself. Society is no readier to accept crippledness than to accept death, war, sex, sweat, or wrinkles. I would never refer to another person as a cripple. It is the word I use to name only myself.

5 I haven't always been crippled, a fact for which I am soundly grateful. To be whole of limb is, I know from experience, infinitely more pleasant and useful than to be crippled; and if that knowledge leaves me open to bitterness at my loss, the physical soundness I once enjoyed (though I did not enjoy it half enough) is well worth the occasional stab of regret. Though never any good at sports, I was a normally active child and young adult. I climbed trees, played hopscotch, jumped rope, skated, swam, rode my bicycle, sailed. I despised team sports, spending some of the wretchedest afternoons of my life sweaty and humiliated, behind a field-hockey stick and under a basketball hoop. I tramped alone for miles along the bridle paths that webbed the woods behind the house I grew up in. I swayed through countless dim hours in the arms of one man or another under the scattered shot of light from mirrored balls, and gyrated through countless more as Tab Hunter and Johnny Mathis gave way to the Rolling Stones, Creedence Clearwater Revival, Cream. I walked down the aisle. I pushed baby carriages, changed tires in the rain, marched for peace.

When I was twenty-eight I started to trip and drop things. What at first seemed my natural clumsiness soon became too pronounced to shrug off. I consulted a neurologist, who told me that I had a brain tumor. A battery of tests, increasingly disagreeable, revealed no tumor. About a year and a half later I developed a blurred spot in one eye. I had, at last, the episodes "disseminated in space and time" requisite for a diagnosis: multiple sclerosis. I have never been sorry for the doctor's initial misdiagnosis, however. For almost a week, until the negative results of the tests were in, I thought that I was going to die right away. Every day for the past nearly ten years, then, has been a kind of gift. I accept all gifts.

Multiple sclerosis is a chronic degenerative disease of the central nervous system, in which the myelin that sheathes the nerves is somehow eaten away and scar tissue forms in its place, interrupting the nerves' signals. During its course, which is unpredictable and uncontrollable, one may lose vision, hearing, speech, the ability to walk, control of bladder and/or bowels, strength in any or all extremities, sensitivity to touch, vibration, and/or pain, potency, coordination of movements—the list of possibilities is lengthy and yes, horrifying. One may also lose one's sense of humor. That's the easiest to lose and the hardest to survive without.

In the past ten years, I have sustained some of these losses. Characteristic of MS are sudden attacks, called exacerbations, followed by remissions, and these I have not had. Instead, my disease has been slowly progressive. My left leg is now so weak that I walk with the aid of a brace and a cane; and for distances I use an Amigo, a variation on the electric wheelchair that looks rather like an electrified kiddie car. I no longer have much use of my left hand. Now my right side is weakening as well. I still have the blurred spot in my right eye. Overall, though, I've been lucky so far. My world has, of necessity, been circumscribed by my losses, but the terrain left me has been ample enough for me to continue many of the activities that absorb me: writing, teaching, raising children and cats and plants and snakes, reading, speaking publicly about MS and depression, even playing bridge with people patient and honorable enough to let me scatter cards every which way without sneaking a peek.

Lest I begin to sound like Pollyanna, however, let me say that I don't like having MS. I hate it. My life holds realities—harsh ones, some of them—that no right-minded human being ought to accept without grumbling. One of them is fatigue. I know of no one with MS who does not complain of bone-weariness; in a disease that presents an astonishing variety of symptoms, fatigue seems to be a common factor. I wake up in the morning feeling the way most people do at the end of a bad day, and I take it from there. As a result, I spend a lot of time *in extremis* and, impatient with limitation, I tend to ignore my fatigue until my body breaks down in some way and forces rest. Then I miss picnics, dinner parties, poetry readings, the brief visits of old friends from out of town. The offspring of a puritanical tradition of exceptional venerability, I cannot view these lapses without shame. My life often seems a series of small failures to do as I ought.

10 I lead, on the whole, an ordinary life, probably rather like the one 10
I would have led had I not had MS. I am lucky that my predilections were already solitary, sedentary, and bookish—unlike the world-famous French cellist I have read about, or the young woman I talked with one long afternoon who wanted only to be a jockey. I had just begun graduate school when I found out something was wrong with me, and I have remained, interminably, a graduate student. Perhaps I

would not have if I'd thought I had the stamina to return to a full-time job as a technical editor; but I've enjoyed my studies.

In addition to studying, I teach writing courses. I also teach medical students how to give neurological examinations. I pick up freelance editing jobs here and there. I have raised a foster son and sent him into the world, where he has made me two grandbabies, and I am still escorting my daughter and son through adolescence. I go to Mass every Saturday. I am a superb, if messy, cook. I am also an enthusiastic laundress, capable of sorting a hamper full of clothes into five subtly differentiated piles, but a terrible housekeeper. I can do italic writing and, in an emergency, bathe an oil-soaked cat. I play a fiendish game of Scrabble. When I have the time and the money, I like to sit on my front steps with my husband, drinking Amaretto and smoking a cigar, as we imagine our counterparts in Leningrad and make sure that the sun gets down once more behind the sharp childish scrawl of the Tucson Mountains.

This lively plenty has its bleak complement, of course, in all the things I can no longer do. I will never run again, except in dreams, and one day I may have to write that I will never walk again. I like to go camping, but I can't follow George and the children along the trails that wander out of a campsite through the desert or into the mountains. In fact, even on the level I've learned never to check the weather or try to hold a coherent conversation: I need all my attention for my wayward feet. Of late, I have begun to catch myself wondering how people can propel themselves without canes. With only one usable hand, I have to select my clothing with care not so much for style as for ease of ingress and egress, and even so, dressing can be laborious. I can no longer do fine stitchery, pick up babies, play the piano, braid my hair. I am immobilized by acute attacks of depression, which may or may not be physiologically related to MS but are certainly its logical concomitant.

These two elements, the plenty and the privation, are never pure, nor are the delight and wretchedness that accompany them. Almost every pickle that I get into as a result of my weakness and clumsiness—and I get into plenty—is funny as well as maddening and sometimes painful. I recall one May afternoon when a friend and I were going out for a drink after finishing up at school. As we were climbing into opposite sides of my car, chatting, I tripped and fell, flat and hard, onto the asphalt parking lot, my abrupt departure interrupting him in mid-sentence. "Where'd you go?" he called as he came around the back of the car to find me hauling myself up by the door frame. "Are you all right?" Yes, I told him, I was fine, just a bit rattly, and we drove off to find a shady patio and some beer. When I got home an hour or so later, my daughter greeted me with "What have you done to yourself?" I looked down. One elbow of my white turtleneck with the green froggies, one knee of my white trousers, one white kneesock were bloodsoaked. We peeled off the clothes and inspected the damage, which was nasty enough but not alarming. That part wasn't funny: The abrasions took a long time to heal, and one got a little infected. Even so, when I think of my friend talking earnestly, suddenly, to the hot thin air while I dropped from his view as though through a trap door, I find the image as silly as something from a Marx Brothers movie.

I may find it easier than other cripples to amuse myself because I live propped by the acceptance and the assistance and, sometimes, the amusement of those around me. Grocery clerks tear my checks out of my checkbook for me, and sales clerks find chairs to put into dressing rooms when I want to try on clothes. The people I work with make sure I teach at times when I am least likely to be fatigued, in places I can get to, with the materials I need. My students, with one anonymous exception (in an end-of-the-semester evaluation) have been unperturbed by my disability. Some even like it. One was immensely cheered by the information that I paint my own fingernails; she decided, she told me, that if I could go to such trouble over fine details, she could keep on writing essays. I suppose I became some sort of bright-fingered muse. She wrote good essays, too.

15 The most important struts in the framework of my existence, of course, are my husband and children. Dismayingly few marriages survive the MS test, and why should they? Most twenty-two- and nineteen-year-olds, like George and me, can vow in clear conscience, after a childhood of chickenpox and summer colds, to keep one another in sickness and in health so long as they both shall live. Not many are equipped for catastrophe: the dismay, the depression, the extra work, the boredom that a degenerative disease can insinuate into a relationship. And our society, with its emphasis on fun and its association of fun with physical performance, offers little encouragement for a whole spouse to stay with a crippled partner. Children experience similar stresses when faced with a crippled parent, and they are more helpless, since parents and children can't usually get divorced. They hate, of

course, to be different from their peers, and the child whose mother is tacking down the aisle of a school auditorium packed with proud parents like a Cape Cod dinghy in a stiff breeze jolly well stands out in a crowd. Deprived of legal divorce, the child can at least deny the mother's disability, even her existence, forgetting to tell her about recitals and PTA meetings, refusing to accompany her to stores or church or the movies, never inviting friends to the house. Many do.

But I've been limping along for ten years now, and so far George and the children are still at my left elbow, holding tight. Anne and Matthew vacuum floors and dust furniture and haul trash and rake up dog droppings and button my cuffs and bake lasagne and Toll House cookies with just enough grumbling so I know that they don't have brain fever. And far from hiding me, they're forever dragging me by racks of fancy clothes or through teeming school corridors, or welcoming gaggles of friends while I'm wandering through the house in Anne's filmy pink babydoll pajamas. George generally calls before he brings someone home, but he does just as many dumb thankless chores as the children. And they all yell at me, laugh at some of my jokes, write me funny letters when we're apart—in short, treat me as an ordinary human being for whom they have some use. I think they like me. Unless they're faking. . . .

Faking. There's the rub. Tugging at the fringes of my consciousness always is the terror that people are kind to me only because I'm a cripple. My mother almost shattered me once, with that instinct mothers have—blind, I think, in this case, but unerring nonetheless—for striking blows along the fault-lines of their children's hearts, by telling me, in an attack on my selfishness, "We all have to make allowances for you, of course, because of the way you are." From the distance of a couple of years, I have to admit that I haven't any idea just what she meant, and I'm not sure that she knew either. She was awfully angry. But at the time, as the words thudded home, I felt my worst fear, suddenly realized. I could bear being called selfish: I am. But I couldn't bear the corroboration that those around me were doing in fact what I'd always suspected them of doing, professing fondness while silently putting up with me because of the way I am. A cripple. I've been a little cracked ever since.

Along with this fear that people are secretly accepting shoddy goods comes a relentless pressure to please—to prove myself worth the burdens I impose, I guess, or to build a substantial account of goodwill against which I may write drafts in times of need. Part of the pressure arises from social expectations. In our society, anyone who deviates from the norm had better find some way to compensate. Like fat people, who are expected to be jolly, cripples must bear their lot meekly and cheerfully. A grumpy cripple isn't playing by the rules. And much of the pressure is self-generated. Early on I vowed that, if I had to have MS, by God I was going to do it well. This is a class act, ladies and gentlemen. No tears, no recriminations, no faint-heartedness.

One way and another, then, I wind up feeling like Tiny Tim, peering over the edge of the table at the Christmas goose, waving my crutch, piping down God's blessing on us all. Only sometimes I don't want to play Tiny Tim. I'd rather be Caliban, a most scurvy monster. Fortunately, at home no one much cares whether I'm a good cripple or a bad cripple as long as I make vichyssoise with fair regularity. One evening several years ago, Anne was reading at the dining-room table while I cooked dinner. As I opened a can of tomatoes, the can slipped in my left hand and juice spattered me and the counter with bloody spots. Fatigued and infuriated, I bellowed, "I'm so sick of being crippled!" Anne glanced at me over the top of her book. "There now," she said, "do you feel better?" "Yes," I said, "yes, I do." She went back to her reading. I felt better. That's about all the attention my scurviness ever gets.

20 Because I hate being crippled, I sometimes hate myself for being 20 a cripple. Over the years I have come to expect—even accept—attacks of violent self-loathing. Luckily, in general our society no longer connects deformity and disease directly with evil (though a charismatic once told me that I have MS because a devil is in me) and so I'm allowed to move largely at will, even among small children. But I'm not sure that this revision of attitude has been particularly helpful. Physical imperfection, even freed of moral disapprobation, still defies and violates the ideal, especially for women, whose confinement in their bodies as objects of desire is far from over. Each age, of course, has its ideal, and I doubt that ours is any better or worse than any other. Today's ideal woman, who lives on the glossy pages of dozens of magazines, seems to be between the ages of eighteen and twenty-five; her hair has body, her teeth flash white, her breath smells minty, her underarms are dry; she has a career but is still a fabulous cook, especially of meals that take less than twenty minutes to prepare; she does not ordinarily appear to have a husband or children; she is trim and deeply tanned; she jogs, swims, plays tennis, rides a bicycle, sails, but does not

bowl; she travels widely, even to out-of-the-way places like Finland and Samoa, always in the company of the ideal man, who possesses a nearly identical set of characteristics. There are a few exceptions. Though usually white and often blonde, she may be black, Hispanic, Asian, or Native American, so long as she is unusually sleek. She may be old, provided she is selling a laxative or is Lauren Bacall. If she is selling a detergent, she may be married and have a flock of strikingly messy children. But she is never a cripple.

Like many women I know, I have always had an uneasy relationship with my body. I was not a popular child, largely, I think now, because I was peculiar: intelligent, intense, moody, shy, given to unexpected actions and inexplicable notions and emotions. But as I entered adolescence, I believed myself unpopular because I was homely: my breasts too flat, my mouth too wide, my hips too narrow, my clothing never quite right in fit or style. I was not, in fact, particularly ugly, old photographs inform me, though I was well off the ideal; but I carried this sense of self-alienation with me into adulthood, where it regenerated in response to the depredations of MS. Even with my brace I walk with a limp so pronounced that, seeing myself on the videotape of a television program on the disabled, I couldn't believe that anything but an inchworm could make progress humping along like that. My shoulders droop and my pelvis thrusts forward as I try to balance myself upright, throwing my frame into a bony S. As a result of contractures, one shoulder is higher than the other and I carry one arm bent in front of me, the fingers curled into a claw. My left arm and leg have wasted into pipe-stems, and I try always to keep them covered. When I think about how my body must look to others, especially to men, to whom I have been trained to display myself, I feel ludicrous, even loathsome.

At my age, however, I don't spend much time thinking about my appearance. The burning egocentricity of adolescence, which assures one that all the world is looking all the time, has passed, thank God, and I'm generally too caught up in what I'm doing to step back, as I used to, and watch myself as though upon a stage. I'm also too old to believe in the accuracy of self-image. I know that I'm not a hideous crone, that in fact, when I'm rested, well dressed, and well made up, I look fine. The self-loathing I feel is neither physically nor intellectually substantial. What I hate is not me but a disease.

I am not a disease.

And a disease is not—at least not singlehandedly—going to determine who I am, though at first it seemed to be going to. Adjusting to a chronic incurable illness, I have moved through a process similar to that outlined by Elizabeth Kübler-Ross in *On Death and Dying.* The major difference—and it is far more significant than most people recognize—is that I can't be sure of the outcome, as the terminally ill cancer patient can. Research studies indicate that, with proper medical care, I may achieve a "normal" life span. And in our society, with its vision of death as the ultimate evil, worse even than decrepitude, the response to such news is, "Oh well, at least you're not going to *die.*" Are there worse things than dying? I think that there may be.

I think of two women I know, both with MS, both enough older than I to have served as models. One took to her bed several years ago and has been there ever since. Although she can sit in a high-backed wheelchair, because she is incontinent she refuses to go out at all, even though incontinence pants, which are readily available at any pharmacy, could protect her from embarrassment. Instead, she stays at home and insists that her husband, a small quiet man, a retired civil servant, stay there with her except for a quick weekly foray to the supermarket. The other woman, whose illness was diagnosed when she was eighteen, a nursing student engaged to a young doctor, finished her training, married her doctor, accompanied him to Germany when he was in the service, bore three sons and a daughter, now grown and gone. When she can, she travels with her husband; she plays bridge, embroiders, swims regularly; she works, like me, as a symptomatic-patient instructor of medical students in neurology. Guess which woman I hope to be.

At the beginning, I thought about having MS almost incessantly. And because of the unpredictable course of the disease, my thoughts were always terrified. Each night I'd get into bed wondering whether I'd get out again the next morning, whether I'd be able to see, to speak, to hold a pen between my fingers. Knowing that the day might come when I'd be physically incapable of killing myself, I thought perhaps I ought to do so right away, while I still had the strength. Gradually I came to understand that the Nancy who might one day lie inert under a bedsheet, arms and legs paralyzed, unable to feed or bathe herself, unable to reach out for a gun, a bottle of pills, was not the Nancy I was at present, and that I could not presume to make decisions for that future Nancy, who might well not want in the least to die. Now the only provision I've made for the future Nancy is that when the time comes—and it is likely to come in the form of pneumonia, friend to the weak and the old—I am not to be treated with machines and medications. If she is unable to communicate by then, I hope she will be satisfied with these terms.

Thinking all the time about having MS grew tiresome and intrusive, especially in the large and tragic mode in which I was accustomed to considering my plight. Months and even years went by without catastrophe (at least without one related to MS), and really I was awfully busy, what with George and children and snakes and students and poems, and I hadn't the time, let alone the inclination, to devote myself to being a disease. Too, the richer my life became, the funnier it seemed, as though there were some connection between largesse and laughter, and so my tragic stance began to waver until, even with the aid of a brace and cane, I couldn't hold it for very long at a time.

After several years I was satisfied with my adjustment. I had suffered my grief and fury and terror, I thought, but now I was at ease with my lot. Then one summer day I set out with George and the children across the desert for a vacation in California. Part way to Yuma I became aware that my right leg felt funny. "I think I've had an exacerbation," I told George. "What shall we do?" he asked. "I think we'd better get the hell to California," I said, "because I don't know whether I'll ever make it again." So we went on to San Diego and then to Orange, and up the Pacific Coast Highway to Santa Cruz, across to Yosemite, down to Sequoia and Joshua Tree, and so back over the desert to home. It was a fine two-week trip, filled with friends and fair weather, and I wouldn't have missed it for the world, though I did in fact make it back to California two years later. Nor would there have been any point in missing it, since in MS, once the symptoms have appeared, the neurological damage has been done, and there's no way to predict or prevent that damage.

The incident spoiled my self-satisfaction, however. It renewed my grief and fury and terror, and I learned that one never finishes adjusting to MS. I don't know now why I thought one would. One does not, after all, finish adjusting to life, and MS is simply a fact of my life—not my favorite fact, of course—but as ordinary as my nose and my tropical fish and my yellow Mazda station wagon. It may at any time get worse, but no amount of worry or anticipation can prepare me for a new loss. My life is a lesson in losses. I learn one at a time.

30 And I had best be patient in the learning, since I'll have to do it 30
like it or not. As any rock fan knows, you can't always get what you want. Particularly when you have MS. You can't, for example, get cured. In recent years researchers and the organizations that fund research have started to pay MS some attention even though it isn't fatal; perhaps they have begun to see that life is something other than a quantitative phenomenon, that one may be very much alive for a very long time in a life that isn't worth living. The researchers have made some progress toward understanding the mechanism of the disease: It may well be an autoimmune reaction triggered by a slow-acting virus. But they are nowhere near its prevention, control, or cure. And most of us want to be cured. Some, unable to accept incurability, grasp at one treatment after another, no matter how bizarre: megavitamin therapy, gluten-free diet, injections of cobra venom, hypothermal suits, lymphocytopharesis, hyperbaric chambers. Many treatments are probably harmless enough, but none are curative.

The absence of a cure often makes MS patients bitter toward their doctors. Doctors are, after all, the priests of modern society, the new shamans, whose business is to heal, and many an MS patient roves from one to another, searching for the "good" doctor who will make him well. Doctors too think of themselves as healers, and for this reason many have trouble dealing with MS patients, whose disease in its intransigence defeats their aims and mocks their skills. Too few doctors, it is true, treat their patients as whole human beings, but the reverse is also true. I have always tried to be gentle with my doctors, who often have more at stake in terms of ego than I do. I may be frustrated, maddened, depressed by the incurability of my disease, but I am not diminished by it, and they are. When I push myself up from my seat in the waiting room and stumble toward them, I incarnate the limitation of their powers. The least I can do is refuse to press on their tenderest spots.

This gentleness is part of the reason that I'm not sorry to be a cripple. I didn't have it before. Perhaps I'd have developed it anyway—how could I know such a thing?—and I wish I had more of it, but I'm glad of what I have. It has opened and enriched my life enormously, this sense that my frailty and need must be mirrored in others, that in searching for and shaping a stable core in a life wrenched by change and loss, change and loss, I must recognize the same process, under individual conditions, in the lives around me. I do not deprecate such knowledge, however I've come by it.

All the same, if a cure were found, would I take it? In a minute. I may be a cripple, but I'm only occasionally a loony and never a saint. Anyway, in my brand of theology God doesn't give bonus points for a limp. I'd take a cure; I just don't need one. A friend who also has MS startled me once by asking, "Do you ever say to yourself, 'Why me, Lord?' " "No, Michael, I don't," I told him, "because whenever I try, the only response I can think of is 'Why not?' " If I could make a cosmic deal, who would I put in my place? What in my life would I give up in exchange for sound limbs and a thrilling rush of energy? No one. Nothing. I might as well do the job myself. Now that I'm getting the hang of it.

The Right Stuff

Tom Wolfe

Tom Wolfe (1931–), born in Virginia, received his Ph.D. in American Studies from Yale University. He has worked as a newspaper reporter in New York and Washington and has published essays in magazines such as Esquire *and* Rolling Stone. *His publications include* The Bonfire of the Vanities *(1987),* The Electric Kool-Aid Acid Test *(1968),* Radical Chic and Mau Mauing the Flak Catchers *(1970),* A Man in Full *(1998),* Hooking Up *(2000), and* I Am Charlotte Simmons *(2005), The essay excerpted here is from one of his most acclaimed books,* The Right Stuff *(1979), which describes the American space program and the development of astronauts from military test pilots. In these nonfiction books Wolfe writes in what is often called the "new journalism," a style of writing in which a true story is written with techniques of fiction, including characterization, scene building, dialogue, and narration. Wolfe is also known for his polished, clever, often exuberant style as well as a satiric tone. Readers are sometimes not quite sure what to take seriously, or how seriously to take it. You may find yourself wondering the same at times about this quality of "the right stuff" in this passage describing the beginning of flight training.*

1 A young man might go into military flight training believing 1
that he was entering some sort of technical school in which he was simply going to acquire a certain set of skills. Instead, he found himself all at once enclosed in a fraternity. And in this fraternity, even though it was military, men were not rated by their outward

---

rank as ensigns, lieutenants, commanders, or whatever. No, herein the world was divided into those who had it and those who did not. This quality, this *it,* was never named, however, nor was it talked about in any way.

As to just what this ineffable quality was . . . well, it obviously involved bravery. But it was not bravery in the simple sense of being willing to risk your life. The idea seemed to be that any fool could do that, if that was all that was required, just as any fool could throw away his life in the process. No, the idea here (in the all-enclosing fraternity) seemed to be that a man should have the ability to go up in a hurtling piece of machinery and put his hide on the line and then have the moxie, the reflexes, the experience, the coolness, to pull it back in the last yawning moment—and then go up again *the next day,* and the next day, and every next day, even if the series should prove infinite and, ultimately, in its best expression, do so in a cause that means something to thousands, to a people, a nation, to humanity, to God. Nor was there a test to show whether or not a pilot had this righteous quality. There was, instead, a seemingly infinite series of tests. A career in flying was like climbing one of those ancient Babylonian pyramids made up of a dizzy progression of steps and ledges, a ziggurat, a pyramid extraordinarily high and steep; and the idea was to prove at every foot of the way up that pyramid that you were one of the elected and anointed ones who had *the right stuff* and could move higher and higher and even—ultimately, God willing, one day—that you might be able to join that special few at the very top, that elite who had the capacity to bring tears to men's eyes, the very Brotherhood of the Right Stuff itself.

None of this was to be mentioned, and yet it was acted out in a way that a young man could not fail to understand. When a new flight (i.e., a class) of trainees arrived at Pensacola, they were brought into an auditorium for a little lecture. An officer would tell them: "Take a look at the man on either side of you." Quite a few actually swiveled their heads this way and that in the interest of appearing diligent. Then the officer would say: "One of the three of you is not going to make it!"—meaning, not get his wings. That was the opening theme, the *motif* of primary training. We already know that one-third of you do not have the right stuff—it only remains to find out who.

Furthermore, that was the way it turned out. At every level in one's progress up that staggeringly high pyramid, the world was once more divided into those men who had the right stuff to continue the climb and those who had to be *left behind* in the most obvious way. Some were eliminated in the course of the opening classroom work, as either not smart enough or not hardworking enough, and were left behind. Then came the basic flight instruction, in single-engine, propeller-driven trainers, and a few more—even though the military tried to make this stage easy—were washed out and left behind. Then came more demanding levels, one after the other, formation flying, instrument flying, jet training, all-weather flying, gunnery, and at each level more were washed out and left behind. By this point easily a third of the original candidates had been, indeed, eliminated . . . from the ranks of those who might prove to have the right stuff.

5 In the Navy, in addition to the stages that Air Force trainees went through, the neophyte always had waiting for him, out in the ocean, a certain grim gray slab; namely, the deck of an aircraft carrier; and with it perhaps the most difficult routine in military flying, carrier landings. He was shown films about it, he heard lectures about it, and he knew that carrier landings were hazardous. He first practiced touching down on the shape of a flight deck painted on an airfield. He was instructed to touch down and gun right off. This was safe enough—the shape didn't move, at least—but it could do terrible things to, let us say, the gyroscope of the soul. *That shape!—It's so damned small!* And more candidates were washed out and left behind. Then came the day, without warning, when those who remained were sent out over the ocean for the first of many days of reckoning with the slab. The first day was always a clear day with little wind and a calm sea. The carrier was so steady that it seemed, from up there in the air, to be resting on pilings, and the candidate usually made his first carrier landing successfully, with relief and even *élan.* Many young candidates looked like terrific aviators up to that very point—and it was not until they were actually standing on the carrier deck that they first began to wonder if they had the proper stuff, after all. In the training film the flight deck was a grand piece of gray geometry, perilous, to be sure, but an amazing abstract shape as one looks down upon it on the screen. And yet once the newcomer's two feet were on it . . . *Geometry*—my God, man, this is a . . . skillet! It *heaved,* it moved up and down underneath his feet, it pitched up, it pitched down, it rolled to port (this great beast *rolled!*) and it rolled to starboard, as the ship moved into the wind and, therefore, into the waves,

and the wind kept sweeping across, sixty feet up in the air out in the open sea, and there were no railings whatsoever. This was a *skillet!*—a frying pan!—a short-order grill!—not gray but black, smeared with skid marks from one end to the other and glistening with pools of hydraulic fluid and the occasional jet-fuel slick, all of it still hot, sticky, greasy, runny, virulent from God knows what traumas—still ablaze!—consumed in detonations, explosions, flames, combustion, roars, shrieks, whines, blasts, horrible shudders, fracturing impacts, as little men in screaming red and yellow and purple and green shirts with black Mickey Mouse helmets over their ears skittered about on the surface as if for their very lives (you've said it now!), hooking fighter planes onto the catapult shuttles so that they can explode their afterburners and be slung off the deck in a red-mad fury with a *kaboom*! that pounds through the entire deck—a procedure that seems absolutely controlled, orderly, sublime, however, compared to what he is about to watch as aircraft return to the ship for what is known in the engineering stoicisms of the military as "recovery and arrest." To say that an F-4 was coming back onto this heaving barbecue from out of the sky at a speed of 135 knots . . . that might have been the truth in the training lecture, but it did not begin to get across the idea of what the newcomer saw from the deck itself, because it created the notion that perhaps the plane was gliding in. On the deck one knew differently! As the aircraft came closer and the carrier heaved on into the waves and the plane's speed did not diminish and the deck did not grow steady—indeed, it pitched up and down five or ten feet per greasy heave—one experienced a neural alarm that no lecture could have prepared him for: This is not an *airplane* coming toward me, it is a brick with some poor sonofabitch riding it (*someone much like myself!*), and it is not *gliding,* it is *falling,* a thirty-thousand-pound brick, headed not for a stripe on the deck but for *me*—and with a horrible *smash*! it hits the skillet, and with a blur of momentum as big as a freight train's it hurtles toward the far end of the deck—another blinding storm!—another roar as the pilot pushes the throttle up to full military power and another smear of rubber screams out over the skillet—and this is nominal!—quite okay!—for a wire stretched across the deck has grabbed the hook on the end of the plane as it hit the deck tail down, and the smash was the rest of the fifteen-ton brute slamming onto the deck, as it tripped up, so that it is now straining against the wire at full throttle, in case it hadn't held and the plane had "boltered" off the end of the deck and had to struggle up into the air again. And already the Mickey Mouse helmets are running toward the fiery monster. . . .

And the candidate, looking on, begins to *feel* that great heaving sun-blazing deathboard of a deck wallowing in his own vestibular system—and suddenly he finds himself backed up against his own limits. He ends up going to the flight surgeon with so-called conversion symptoms. Overnight he develops blurred vision or numbness in his hands and feet or sinusitis so severe that he cannot tolerate changes in altitude. On one level the symptom is real. He really cannot see too well or use his fingers or stand the pain. But somewhere in his subconscious he knows it is a plea and a beg-off; he shows not the slightest concern (the flight surgeon notes) that the condition might be permanent and affect him in whatever life awaits him outside the arena of the right stuff.

Those who remained, those who qualified for carrier duty—and even more so those who later on qualified for *night* carrier duty—began to feel a bit like Gideon's warriors. *So many have been left behind!* The young warriors were now treated to a deathly sweet and quite unmentionable sight. They could gaze at length upon the crushed and wilted pariahs who had washed out. They could inspect those who did not have that righteous stuff.

The military did not have very merciful instincts. Rather than packing up these poor souls and sending them home, the Navy, like the Air Force and the Marines, would try to make use of them in some other role such as flight controller. So the washout has to keep taking classes with the rest of his group, even though he can no longer touch an airplane. He sits there in the classes staring at sheets of paper with cataracts of sheer human mortification over his eyes while the rest steal looks at him . . . this man reduced to an ant, this untouchable, this poor sonofabitch. And in what test had he been found wanting? Why, it seemed to be nothing less than *manhood* itself. Naturally, this was never mentioned, either.Yet there it was. *Manliness, manhood, manly courage* . . . there was something ancient, primordial, irresistible about the challenge of this stuff, no matter what a sophisticated and rational age one might think he lived in.

Notes on Class

Paul Fussell

Paul Fussell (1924-) was born in California, the son of a millionaire. After completing a degree at Pomona College, he served as an infantry officer in World War II and returned to take a Ph.D. in literature at Harvard. His book, Poetic Meter and Poetic Form *(1965, revised 1979), is used widely in literature courses; and his* The Great War and Modern Memory *(1975), written about the British experience of World War I, won the National Book Award in 1976. He has taught at Rutgers and currently occupies a chair in English literature at the University of Pennsylvania. In his delightful book,* Class, *he ironically describes the fascination of an allegedly democratic American society with the details of social class. In the essay reprinted here, taken from* The Boy Scout Handbook and Other Observations *(1982), he is particularly merciless with the middle class.*

1 If the dirty little secret used to be sex, now it is the facts about social class. No subject today is more likely to offend. Over thirty years ago Dr. Kinsey generated considerable alarm by disclosing that despite appearances one-quarter of the male population had enjoyed at least one homosexual orgasm. A similar alarm can be occasioned today by asserting that despite the much-discussed mechanism of "social mobility" and the constant redistribution of income in this country, it is virtually impossible to break out of the social class in which one has been nurtured. Bad news for the ambitious as well as the bogus, but there it is.

Defining class is difficult, as sociologists and anthropologists have learned. The more data we feed into the machines, the less likely it is that significant formulations will emerge. What follows here is based not on interviews, questionnaires, or any kind of quantitative technique but on perhaps a more trustworthy method—perception. Theory may inform us that there are three classes in America, high, middle, and low. Perception will tell us that there are at least nine, which I would designate and arrange like this:

Top Out-of-Sight
Upper
Upper Middle

Middle
High-Proletarian
Mid-Proletarian
Low-Proletarian

Destitute
Bottom Out-of-Sight

In addition, there is a floating, class with no permanent location in this hierarchy. We can call it Class X. It consists of well-to-do hippies, "artist," "writers" (who write nothing), floating bohemians, politicians out of office, disgraced athletic coaches, residers abroad, rock stars, "celebrities," and the shrewder sort of spies.

The quasi-official division of the population into three economic classes called high-, middle-, and low-income groups rather misses the point, because as a class indicator the amount of money is not as important as the source. Important distinctions at both the top and bottom of the class scale arise less from degree of affluence than from the people or institutions to whom one is beholden for support. For example, the main thing distinguishing the top three classes from each other is the amount of money inherited in relation to the amount currently earned. The Top Out-of-Sight Class (Rockefellers, du Ponts, Melons, Fords, Whitneys) lives on inherited capital entirely. Its money is like the hats of the Boston ladies who, asked where they got them, answer, "Oh, we *have* our hats." No one whose money, no matter how ample, comes from his own work, like film stars, can be a member of the Top Out-of-Sights, even if the size of his income and the extravagance of his expenditure permit him temporary social access to it.

Since we expect extremes to meet, we are not surprised to find the very lowest class, Bottom Out-of-Sight, similar to the highest in one crucial respect: It is given its money and kept sort of afloat not by its own efforts but by the welfare machinery or the prison system. Members of the Top Out-of-Sight Class sometimes earn some money, as directors or board members of philanthropic or even profitable enterprises, but the amount earned is laughable in relation to the amount already possessed. Membership in the Top Out-of-Sight Class depends on the ability to flourish without working at all, and it is this that suggests a curious brotherhood between those at the top and the bottom of the scale.

5 It is this also that distinguishes the Upper Class from its betters. It lives on both inherited money and a salary from attractive, if usually slight, work, without which, even if it could survive and even flourish, it would feel bored and a little ashamed. The next class down, the Upper Middle, may possess virtually as much as the two above it. The difference is that it has earned most of it, in law, medicine, oil, real-estate, or even the more honorific forms of trade. The Upper Middles are afflicted with a bourgeois sense of shame, a conviction that to live on the earnings of others, even forebears, is not entirely nice.

The Out-of-Sight Classes at top and bottom have something else in common: They are literally all but invisible (hence their name). The façades of Top Out-of-Sight houses are never seen from the street, and such residences (like Rockefeller's upstate New York premises) are often hidden away deep in the hills, safe from envy and its ultimate attendants, confiscatory taxation and finally expropriation. The Bottom Out-of-Sight Class is equally invisible. When not hidden away in institutions or claustrated in monasteries, lamaseries, or communes, it is hiding from creditors, deceived bail-bondsmen, and merchants intent on repossessing cars and furniture. (This class is visible briefly in one place, in the spring on the streets of New York City, but after this ritual yearly show of itself it disappears again.) When you pass a house with a would-be impressive façade addressing the street, you know it is occupied by a mere member of the Upper or Upper Middle Class. The White House is an example. Its residents, even on those occasions when they are Kennedys, can never be classified as Top Out-of-Sight but only Upper Class. The house is simply too conspicuous, and temporary residence there usually constitutes a come-down for most of its occupants. It is a hopelessly Upper- or Upper-Middle-Class place.

Another feature of both Top and Bottom Out-of-Sight Classes is their anxiety to keep their names out of the papers, and this too suggests that socially the President is always rather vulgar. All the classes in between Top and Bottom Out-of-Sight slaver for personal publicity (monograms on shirts, inscribing one's name on lawn-mowers and power tools, etc.), and it is this lust to be known almost as much as income that distinguishes them from their Top and Bottom neighbors. The High- and Mid-Prole Classes can be recognized immediately by their pride in advertising their physical presence, a way of saying, "Look! We pay our bills and have a known place in the community, and you can find us there any time." Thus hypertrophied house numbers on the front, or house numbers written "Two Hundred Five" ("Two Hundred and Five" is worse) instead of 205, or flamboyant house or family names blazoned on façades, like "The Willows" or "The Polnickis."

(If you go behind the façade into the house itself, you will find a fairly trustworthy class indicator in the kind of wood visible there. The top three classes invariably go in for hardwoods for doors and panelling; the Middle and High-Prole Classes, pine, either plain or "knotty." The knotty-pine "den" is an absolute stigma of the Middle Class, one never to be overcome or disguised by temporarily affected higher usages. Below knotty pine there is plywood.)

Façade study is a badly neglected anthropological field. As we work down from the (largely white-painted) bank-like façades of the Upper and Upper Middle Classes, we encounter such Middle and Prole conventions as these, which I rank in order of social status:

Middle

1. A potted tree on either side of the front door, and the more pointy and symmetrical the better.
2. A large rectangular picture-window in a split-level "ranch" house, displaying a table-lamp between two side curtains. The cellophane on the lampshade must be visibly inviolate.
3. Two chairs, usually metal with pipe arms, disposed on the front porch as a "conversation group," in stubborn defiance of the traffic thundering past.

High-Prole 4. Religious shrines in the garden, which if small and understated, are slightly higher class than

Mid-Prole 5. Plaster gnomes and flamingoes, and blue or lavender shiny spheres supported by fluted cast-concrete pedestals.

Low-Prole 6. Defunct truck tires painted white and enclosing flower beds. (Auto tires are a grade higher.)

7. Flower-bed designs worked in dead light bulbs or the butts of disused beer bottles.

The Destitute have no façades to decorate, and of course the Bottom Out-of-Sights, being invisible, have none either, although both these classes can occasionally help others decorate theirs–painting tires white on an hourly basis, for example, or even watering and fertilizing the potted trees of the Middle Class. Class X also does not decorate its façades, hoping to stay loose and unidentifiable, ready to re-locate and shape-change the moment it sees that its cover has been penetrated.

10 In this list of façade conventions an important principle emerges. Organic materials have higher status than metal or plastic. We should take warning from Sophie Portnoy's aluminum venetian blinds, which are also lower than wood because the slats are curved, as if "improved," instead of classically flat. The same principle applies, as *The Preppy Handbook* has shown so effectively, to clothing fabrics, which must be cotton or wool, never Dacron or anything of that prole kind. In the same way, yachts with wood hulls, because they must be repaired or replaced (at high cost) more often, are classier than yachts with fiberglass hulls, no matter how shrewdly merchandised. Plastic hulls are cheaper and more practical, which is precisely why they lack class.

As we move down the scale, income of course decreases, but income is less important to class than other seldom-invoked measurements: for example, the degree to which one's work is supervised by an omnipresent immediate superior. The more free from supervision, the higher the class, which is why a dentist ranks higher than a mechanic working under a foreman in a large auto shop, even if he makes considerably more money than the dentist. The two trades may be thought equally dirty: It is the dentist's freedom from supervision that helps confer class upon him. Likewise, a high-school teacher obliged to file weekly "lesson plans" with a principal or "curriculum coordinator" thereby occupies a class position lower than a tenured professor, who reports to no one, even though the high-school teacher may be richer, smarter, and nicer. (Supervisors and Inspectors are titles that go with public schools, post offices, and police departments: The student of class will need to know no more.) It is largely because they must report that even the highest members of the naval and military services lack social status: They all have designated supervisors—even the Chairman of the Joint Chiefs of Staff has to report to the President.

Class is thus defined less by bare income than by constraints and insecurities. It is defined also by habits and attitudes. Take television watching. The Top Out-of-Sight Class doesn't watch at all. It owns the companies and pays others to monitor the thing. It is also entirely devoid of intellectual or even emotional curiosity: It has its ideas the way it has its money. The Upper Class does look at television but it prefers Camp offerings, like the films of Jean Harlow or Jon Hall. The Upper Middle Class regards TV as vulgar except for the highminded emissions of National Educational Television, which it watches avidly, especially when, like the Shakespeare series, they are the most incompetently directed and boring. Upper Middles make a point of forbidding children to watch more than an hour a day and worry a lot about violence in society and sugar in cereal. The Middle-Class watches, preferring the more "beautiful" kinds of non-body-contact sports like tennis or gymnastics or figure-skating (the music is a redeeming feature here). With High-, Mid-, and Low-Proles we find heavy viewing of the soaps in the daytime and rugged body-contact sports (football, hockey, boxing) in the evening. The lower one is located in the Prole classes the more likely one is to watch "Bowling for Dollars" and "Wonder Woman" and "The Hulk" and when choosing a game show to prefer "Joker's Wild" to "The Family Feud," whose jokes are sometimes incomprehensible. Destitutes and Bottom Out-of-Sights have in common a problem involving choice. Destitutes usually "own" about three color sets, and the problem is which three programs to run at once. Bottom Out-of-Sights exercise no choice at all, the decisions being made for them by correctional or institutional personnel.

The time when the evening meal is consumed defines class better than, say, the presence or absence on the table of ketchup bottles and ashtrays shaped like little toilets enjoining the diners to "Put Your Butts Here." Destitutes and Bottom Out-of-Sights eat dinner at 5:30, for the Prole staff on which they depend must clean up and be out roller-skating or bowling early in the evening. Thus Proles eat at 6:00 or 6:30. The Middles eat at 7:00, the Upper Middles at 7:30 or, if very ambitious, at 8:00. The Uppers and Top Out-of-Sights dine at 8:30 or 9:00 or even later, after nightly protracted "cocktail" sessions lasting usually around two hours. Sometimes they forget to eat at all.

Similarly, the physical appearance of the various classes defines them fairly accurately. Among the top four classes thin is good, and the bottom two classes appear to ape this usage, although down there thin is seldom a matter of choice. It is the three Prole classes that tend to fat, partly as a result of their use of convenience foods and plenty of beer. These are the classes too where anxiety about slipping down a rung causes nervous overeating, resulting in fat that can be rationalized as advertising the security of steady wages and the ability to "eat out" often. Even "Going Out for Breakfast" is not unthinkable for Proles, if we are to believe that they respond to the McDonald's TV ads as they're supposed to. A recent magazine ad for a diet book aimed at Proles stigmatizes a number of erroneous assumptions about body weight, proclaiming with some inelegance that "They're all a crock." Among such vulgar errors is the proposition that "All Social Classes Are Equally Over-weight." This the ad rejects by noting quite accurately,

> *Your weight is an advertisement of your social standing. A century ago, corpulence was a sign of success. But no more. Today it is the badge of the lower-middle-class, where obesity is four times more prevalent than it is among the upper-middle and middle classes.*

It is not just four times more prevalent. It is at least four times more visible, as any observer can testify who has witnessed Prole women perambulating shopping malls in their bright, very tight jersey trousers. Not just obesity but the flaunting of obesity is the Prole sign, as if the object were to give maximum aesthetic offense to the higher classes and thus achieve a form of revenge.

15 Another physical feature with powerful class meaning is the wearing of plaster casts on legs and ankles by members of the top three classes. These casts, a sort of white badge of honor, betoken stylish mishaps with frivolous but costly toys like horses, skis, snowmobiles, and mopeds. They signify a high level of conspicuous waste in a social

world where questions of unpayable medical bills or missed working days do not apply. But in the matter of clothes, the Top Out-of-Sight is different from both Upper and Upper Middle Classes. It prefers to appear in new clothes, whereas the class just below it prefers old clothes. Likewise, all three Prole classes make much of new garments, with the highest possible polyester content. The question does not arise in the same form with Destitutes and Bottom Out-of-Sights. They wear used clothes, the thrift shop and prison supply room serving as their Bonwit's and Korvette's.

This American class system is very hard for foreigners to master, partly because most foreigners imagine that since America was founded by the British it must retain something of British institutions. But our class system is more subtle than the British, more a matter of gradations than of blunt divisions, like the binary distinction between a gentleman and a cad. This seems to lack plausibility here. One seldom encounters in the United States the sort of absolute prohibitions which (half-comically, to be sure) one is asked to believe define the gentleman in England. Like these:

> *A gentleman never wears brown shoes in the city, or*
> *A gentleman never wears a green suit, or*
> *A gentleman never has soup at lunch, or*
> *A gentleman never uses a comb, or*
> *A gentleman never smells of anything but tar, or*
> *"No gentleman can fail to admire Bellini."*
>
> W. H. Auden

In America it seems to matter much less the way you present yourself—green, brown, neat, sloppy, scented—than what your backing is—that is, where your money comes from. What the upper orders display here is no special uniform but the kind of psychological security they derive from knowing that others recognize their freedom from petty anxieties and trivial prohibitions.

She: Portrait of the Essay as a Warm Body

Cynthia Ozick

Cynthia Ozick (1928-) was born in New York City and received degrees from New York University and Ohio State University. She has published numerous works of stories, novels, plays, and essays. More recently, her works include Portrait of the Artist as Bad Character and Other Essays on Writing *(1994),* Fame and Folly *(1996), and* The Puttermesser Papers *(1997). She has been the recipient of many literary accolades, among them a Guggenheim Fellowship and awards from the American Academy and the National Institute of Arts and Letters. She has said that "What is fictitious about the essay is that it is pretending not to be made up—so that reading an essay may be more dangerous than reading a story." In the following essay from the September 1998 issue of* The Atlantic Monthly, *Ozick talks about the relationship between the essay and the imagination.*

1 An essay is a thing of the imagination. If there is information in an essay, it is by-the-by, and if there is an opinion, one need not trust it for the long run. A genuine essay rarely has an educational, polemical, or sociopolitical use: it is the movement of a free mind at play. Though it is written in prose, it is closer in kind to poetry than to any other form. Like a poem, a genuine essay is made of language and character and mood and temperament and pluck and chance.

"She: Portrait of the Essay as a Warm Body" by Cynthia Ozick, published in *The Atlantic Monthly*, September 1998. Reprinted by permission of the author.

I speak of a "genuine" essay because fakes abound. Here the old-fashioned term *poetaster* may apply, if only obliquely. As the poetaster is to the poet—a lesser aspirant—so the average article is to the essay: a look-alike knockoff guaranteed not to wear well. An article is often gossip. An essay is reflection and insight. An article often has the temporary advantage of social heat—what's hot out there right now. An essay's heat is interior. An article can be timely, topical, engaged in the issues and personalities of the moment; it is likely to be stale within the month. In five years it may have acquired the quaint aura of a rotary phone. An article is usually Siamese-twinned to its date of birth. An essay defies its date of birth—and ours, too. (A necessary caveat: some genuine essays are popularly called "articles"—but this is no more than an idle, though persistent, habit of speech. What's in a name? The ephemeral is the ephemeral. The enduring is the enduring.)

A small historical experiment. Who are the classic essayists who come at once to mind? Montaigne, obviously. Among the nineteenth-century English masters, the long row of Hazlitt, Lamb, De Quincey, Stevenson, Carlyle, Ruskin, Newman, Martineau, Arnold. Of the Americans, Emerson. Nowadays, admittedly, these are read only by specialists and literature majors, and by the latter only under compulsion. However accurate this observation, it is irrelevant to the experiment, which has to do with beginnings and their disclosures. Here, then, are some introductory passages:

> One of the pleasantest things in the world is going a journey; but I like to go by myself. I can enjoy society in a room; but out of doors, nature is company enough for me. I am then never less alone than when alone.
>
> —William Hazlitt, "On Going a Journey"

> To go into solitude, a man needs to retire as much from his chamber as from society. I am not solitary whilst I read and write, though nobody is with me. But if a man would be alone, let him look at the stars.
>
> —Ralph Waldo Emerson, "Nature"

> . . . I have often been asked, how I first came to be a regular opium-eater; and have suffered, very unjustly, in the opinion of my acquaintance, from being reputed to have brought upon myself all the sufferings which I shall have to record, by a long course of indulgence in this practice purely for the sake

of creating an artificial state of pleasurable excitement. This, however, is a misrepresentation of my case.

—Thomas De Quincey,
"Confessions of an English Opium-Eater"

The human species, according to the best theory I can form of it, is composed of two distinct races, *the men who borrow, and the men who lend.*

—Charles Lamb, "The Two Races of Men"

I saw two hareems in the East; and it would be wrong to pass them over in an account of my travels; though the subject is as little agreeable as any I can have to treat. I cannot now think of the two mornings thus employed without a heaviness of heart greater than I have ever brought away from Deaf and Dumb Schools, Lunatic Asylums, or even Prisons.

—Harriet Martineau, "The Hareem"

The future of poetry is immense, because in poetry, where it is worthy of its high destinies, our race, as time goes on, will find an ever surer and surer stay. There is not a creed which is not shaken, not an accredited dogma which is not shown to be questionable, not a received tradition which does not threaten to dissolve. . . . But for poetry the idea is everything; the rest is a world of illusion, of divine illusion.

—Matthew Arnold, "The Study of Poetry"

10 The changes wrought by death are in themselves so sharp and final, and so terrible and melancholy in their consequences, that the thing stands alone in man's experience, and has no parallel upon earth. It outdoes all other accidents because it is the last of them. Sometimes it leaps suddenly upon its victims, like a Thug; sometimes it lays a regular siege and creeps upon their citadel during a score of years. And when the business is done, there is sore havoc made in other people's lives, and a pin knocked out by which many subsidiary friendships hung together.

—Robert Louis Stevenson, "*Aes Triplex*"

It is recorded of some people, as of Alexander the Great, that their sweat, in consequence of some rare and extraordinary constitution, emitted a sweet odour, the cause of which Plutarch and others investigated. But the nature of most bodies is the opposite, and at their best they are free from smell. Even the purest breath has nothing more excellent than to be without offensive odour, like that of very healthy children.

—Michel de Montaigne, "Of Smells"

What might such a little anthology of beginnings reveal? First, that language differs from one era to the next: archaism intrudes, if only in punctuation and cadence. Second, that splendid minds may contradict each other (outdoors, Hazlitt never feels alone; Emerson urges others to go outdoors in order to feel alone). Third, that the theme of an essay can be anything under the sun, however trivial (the smell of sweat) or crushing (the thought that we must die). Fourth, that the essay is a consistently recognizable and venerable—or call it ancient—form. In English, Addison and Steele in the eighteenth century, Bacon and Browne in the seventeenth, Lyly in the sixteenth, Bede in the eighth. And what of the biblical Koheleth (Ecclesiastes), who may be the oldest essayist reflecting on one of the oldest subjects—world-weariness?

So the essay is ancient and various; but this is a commonplace. Something else, more striking yet, catches our attention—the essay's power. By "power" I mean precisely the capacity to do what force always does: coerce assent. Never mind that the shape and inclination of any essay is against coercion or suasion, or that the essay neither proposes nor purposes to get us to think like its author—at least not overtly. If an essay has a "motive," it is linked more to happenstance and opportunity than to the driven will. A genuine essay is not a doctrinaire tract or a propaganda effort or a broadside. Thomas Paine's "Common Sense" and Emile Zola's "*J'Accuse. . . !*" are heroic landmark writings; but to call them essays, though they may resemble the form, is to misunderstand. The essay is not meant for the barricades; it is a stroll through someone's mazy mind. This is not to say that no essayist has ever been intent on making a moral argument, however, obliquely—George Orwell is a case in point. At the end of the day the essay turns out to be a force for agreement. It co-opts agreement; it courts agreement; it seduces agreement. For the brief hour we give to it, we are sure to fall into surrender and conviction. And this will occur even if we are intrinsically roused to resistance.

To illustrate: I may not be persuaded by Emersonianism as an ideology, but Emerson—his voice, his language, his music—persuades me. When we look for words of praise, not for nothing do we speak of "commanding" or "compelling" prose. If I am a skeptical rationalist or an advanced biochemist, I may regard (or discard) the idea of the soul as no better than a puff of warm vapor. But here is Emerson on the soul: “When it breathes through [man’s] intellect, it is genius; when it breathes through his will, it is virtue; when it flows through his affection, it is love.” And then—well, I am in thrall; I am possessed; I believe.

The novel has its own claims on surrender. It suspends our participation in the society we ordinarily live in, so that for the time we are reading, we forget it utterly. But the essay does not allow us to forget our usual sensations and opinions. It does something even more potent; it makes us deny them. The authority of a masterly essayist—the authority of sublime language and intimate observation—is absolute. When I am with Hazlitt, I know no greater companion than nature. When I am with Emerson, I know no greater solitude than nature.

And what is oddest about the essay’s power to lure us into its lair is how it goes about this work. We feel it when a political journalist comes after us with a point of view—we feel it the way the cat is wary of the dog. A polemic is a herald, complete with feathered hat and trumpet. A tract can be a trap. Certain magazine articles have the scent of so much per word. What is indisputable is that all of these are more or less in the position of a lepidopterist with his net: they mean to catch and skewer. They are focused on prey—us. The genuine essay, in contrast, never thinks of us; the genuine essay may be the most self-centered (the politer word would be subjective) arena for human thought ever devised.

Or else, though still not having us in mind (unless as an embodiment of common folly), it is not self-centered at all. When I was a child, I discovered in the public library a book that enchanted me then, and the idea of which has enchanted me for life. I have no recollection of either the title or the writer—and anyhow, very young readers rarely take note of authors; stories are simply and magically *there*. The characters include, as I remember them, three or four children and a delightful relation who is a storyteller, and the scheme is this: each child calls out a story element, most often an object, and the storyteller gathers up whatever is supplied (blue boots, a river, a fairy, a pencil box) and makes out of these random, unlikely, and disparate offerings a tale both logical and surprising. An essay, it seems to me, may be similarly constructed—if so deliberate a term applies. The essayist, let us say, unexpectedly stumbles over a pair of old blue boots in a corner of the garage, and this reminds her of when she last wore them—twenty years ago, on a trip to Paris, where on the bank of the Seine she stopped to watch an old fellow sketching, with a box of colored pencils at his side. The pencil wiggling over his sheet is a grayish pink, which reflects the threads of sunset pulling westward in the sky, like the reins of a fairy cart . . . and so on. The mind meanders, slipping from one impression to another, from reality to memory to dreamscape and back again.

In the same way Montaigne, when contemplating the unpleasantness of sweat, ends with the pure breath of children. Stevenson, starting out with mortality, speaks first of ambush, then of war, and finally of a displaced pin. No one is freer than the essayist—free to leap out in any direction, to hop from thought to thought, to begin with the finish and finish with the middle, or to eschew beginning and end and keep only a middle. The marvel is that out of this apparent causelessness, out of this scattering of idiosyncratic seeing and telling, a coherent world is made. It is coherent because, after all, an essayist must be an artist, and every artist, whatever the means, arrives at a sound and singular imaginative frame—call it, on a minor scale, a cosmogony.

Into this frame, this work of art, we tumble like tar babies, and are held fast. What holds us there? The authority of a voice, yes; the pleasure—sometimes the anxiety—of a new idea, an untried angle, a snatch of reminiscence, bliss displayed or shock conveyed. An essay can be the product of intellect or memory, lightheartedness or gloom, well-being or disgruntlement. But always we sense a certain quietude, on occasion a kind of detachment. Rage and revenge, I think, belong to fiction. The essay is cooler than that. Because it so often engages in acts of memory, and despite its gladder or more antic incarnations, the essay is by and large a serene or melancholic form. It mimics that low electric hum, which sometimes rises to resemble actual speech, that all human beings carry inside their heads—a vibration, garrulous if somewhat indistinct, that never leaves us while we are awake. It is the hum of perpetual noticing: the configuration of someone's eyelid or tooth, the veins on a hand, a wisp of string caught on a twig; some words your fourth-grade teacher said, so long ago, about the rain; the look of an awning, a sidewalk, a bit of cheese left on a plate. All day long this inescapable hum drums on, recalling one thing and another, and pointing out this and this and this. Legend has it that Titus, Emperor of Rome, went mad because of the buzzing of a gnat that made her home in his ear; and presumably the gnat, flying out into the great world and then returning to her nest, whispered what she had seen and felt and learned there. But an essayist is more resourceful than an Emperor, and can be relieved of this interior noise, if only for the time required to record its murmurings. To seize the hum and set it down for others to hear is the essayist's genius.

It is a genius bound to leisure, and even to luxury, if luxury is measured in hours. The essay's limits can be found in its own reflective nature. Poems have been wrested from the inferno of catastrophe or war, and battlefield letters, too; these are the spontaneous bursts and burnings that danger excites. But the meditative temperateness of an essay requires a desk and a chair, a musing and a mooning, a connection to a civilized surround; even when the subject itself is a wilderness of lions and tigers, mulling is the way of it. An essay is a fireside thing, not a conflagration or a safari.

This may be why, when we ask who the essayists are, we discover that though novelists may now and then write essays, true essayists rarely write novels. Essayists are a species of metaphysician: they are inquisitive, and analytic, about the least grain of being. Novelists go about the strenuous business of marrying and burying their people, or else they send them to sea, or to Africa, or at the least out of town. Essayists in their stillness ponder love and death. It is probably an illusion that men are essayists more often than women, especially since women's essays have in the past frequently assumed the form of unpublished correspondence. (Here I should, I suppose, add a note about maleness and femaleness as a literary issue—what is popularly termed "gender," as if men and women were French or German tables and sofas. I *should* add such a note—it is the fashion, or, rather, the current expectation or obligation—but nothing useful can be said about any of it.) Essays are written by men. Essays are written by women. That is the long and the short of it. John Updike, in a genially confident discourse on maleness ("The Disposable Rocket"), takes the view—though he admits to admixture—that the "male sense of space must differ from that of the female, who has such interesting, active, and significant inner space. The space that interests men is outer." Except, let it be observed, when men write essays, since it is only inner space—interesting, active, and significant—that can conceive and nourish the contemplative essay. The "ideal female body," Updike adds, "curves around centers of repose," and no phrase could better describe the shape of the ideal essay—yet women are no fitter as essayists than men. In promoting the felt salience of sex, Updike nevertheless drives home an essayist's point. Essays, unlike novels, emerge from the sensations of the self. Fiction creeps into foreign bodies: the novelist can inhabit not only a sex not his own but also beetles and noses and hunger artists and nomads and beasts. The essay is, as we say, personal.

And here is an irony. Though I have been intent on distinguishing the marrow of the essay from the marrow of fiction, I confess that I have been trying all along, in a subliminal way, to speak of the essay as if it—or she—were a character in a novel or a play; moody, fickle, given to changing her clothes, or the subject, on a whim; sometimes obstinate, with a mind of her own, or hazy and light; never predictable. I mean for her to be dressed—and addressed—as we would Becky Sharp, or Ophelia, or Elizabeth Bennet, or Mrs. Ramsay, or Mrs. Wilcox, or even Hester Prynne. Put it that it is pointless to say (as I have done repeatedly, disliking it every time) "the essay," or "an essay." The essay—an essay—is not an abstraction; she may have recognizable contours, but she is highly colored and individuated; she is not a type. She is too fluid, too elusive, to be a category. She may be bold, she may be diffident, she may rely on beauty or cleverness, on eros or exotica. Whatever her story, she is the protagonist, the secret self's personification. When we knock on her door, she opens to us; she is a presence in the doorway; she leads us from room to room. Then why should we not call her "she"? She may be privately indifferent to us, but she is anything but unwelcoming. Above all, she is not a hidden principle or a thesis or a construct: she is *there*, a living voice. She takes us in.

Argument

The Declaration of Independence

Thomas Jefferson

Thomas Jefferson (1743–1826) was born in Virginia in a well-to-do land-owning family. He graduated from the College of William and Mary and then studied law. When he was elected at age 26 to the Virginia legislature, he had already begun forming his revolutionary views. As a delegate to the Second Continental Congress in 1775, he was the principal writer of the Declaration of Independence, which was adopted on July 4, 1776. After the Revolution he was Governor of Virginia from 1775 to 1777. From then until 1801, when he was elected the third President of the United States, Jefferson served in various federal positions, including secretary of state and ambassador to France. Jefferson was influential as an advocate of democracy in the early years of the United States, although his ideas were more typical of the eighteenth century "enlightened man" than original. The Declaration of Independence shows his ideas and style as well as those of the times and remains not merely an important historical document but also an eloquent statement of the founding principles of this country.

1 When in the course of human events, it becomes necessary for one people to dissolve the political bands which have connected them with another, and to assume among the powers of the earth, the separate and equal station to which the Laws of Nature and of Nature's God entitle them, a decent respect to the opinions of mankind requires that they should declare the causes which impel them to the separation.

We hold these truths to be self-evident, that all men are created equal, that they are endowed by their Creator with certain inalienable rights, that among these are life, liberty, and the pursuit of happiness. That to secure these rights, governments are instituted among men, deriving their just powers from the consent of the governed. That whenever any form of government becomes destructive of these ends, it is the right of the people to alter or to abolish it, and to institute new government, laying its foundation on such principles and organizing its powers in such form, as to them shall seem most likely to effect their safety and happiness. Prudence, indeed, will dictate that governments long established should not be changed for light and transient causes; and accordingly all experience hath shown, that mankind are more disposed to suffer, while evils are sufferable, than to right themselves by abolishing the forms to which they are accustomed. But when a long train of abuses and usurpations, pursuing invariably the same object, evinces a design to reduce them under absolute despotism, it is their right, it is their duty, to throw off such government, and to provide new guards for their future security. Such has been the patient sufferance of these Colonies; and such is now the necessity which constrains them to alter their former systems of government. The history of the present King of Great Britain is a history of repeated injuries and usurpations, all having in direct object the establishment of an absolute tyranny over these States. To prove this, let facts be submitted to a candid world.

He has refused his assent to laws, the most wholesome and necessary for the public good.

He has forbidden his Governors to pass laws of immediate and pressing importance, unless suspended in their operation till his assent should be obtained; and when so suspended, he has utterly neglected to attend to them.

5 He has refused to pass other laws for the accommodation of large districts of people, unless those people would relinquish the right of representation in the legislature, a right inestimable to them and formidable to tyrants only.

He has called together legislative bodies at places unusual, uncomfortable, and distant from the depository of their public records, for the sole purpose of fatiguing them into compliance with his measures.

He has dissolved representative houses repeatedly, for opposing with manly firmness his invasions on the rights of the people.

He has refused for a long time, after such dissolutions, to cause others to be elected; whereby the legislative powers, incapable of annihilation, have returned to the people at large for their exercise; the State remaining in the meantime exposed to all the dangers of invasion from without and convulsions within.

He has endeavoured to prevent the population of these states; for that purpose obstructing the laws for naturalization of foreigners; refusing to pass others to encourage their migration hither, and raising the conditions of new appropriations of lands.

He has obstructed the administration of justice, by refusing his assent to laws for establishing judiciary powers.

He has made judges dependent on his will alone, for the tenure of their offices, and the amount and payment of their salaries.

He has erected a multitude of new offices, and sent hither swarms of officers to harass our people, and eat out their substance.

He has kept among us, in times of peace, standing armies without the consent of our legislatures.

He has affected to render the military independent of and superior to the civil power.

He has combined with others to subject us to a jurisdiction foreign of our constitution, and unacknowledged by our laws; giving his assent to their acts of pretended legislation:

For quartering large bodies of armed troops among us:

For protecting them, by a mock trial, from punishment for any murders which they should commit on the inhabitants of these States:

For cutting off our trade with all parts of the world:

For imposing taxes on us without our consent:

For depriving us in many cases of the benefits of trial by jury:

For transporting us beyond seas to be tried for pretended offences:

For abolishing the free system of English laws in a neighbouring Province, establishing therein an arbitrary government, and enlarging its boundaries so as to render it at once an example and fit instrument for introducing the same absolute rule into these Colonies:

For taking away our Charters, abolishing our most valuable laws, and altering fundamentally the forms of our governments:

For suspending our own legislatures, and declaring themselves invested with power to legislate for us in all cases whatsoever.

He has abdicated government here, by declaring us out of his protection and waging war against us.

He has plundered our seas, ravaged our coasts, burnt our towns, and destroyed the lives of our people.

He is at this time transporting large armies of foreign mercenaries to complete the works of death, desolation, and tyranny, already begun with circumstances of cruelty and perfidy scarcely paralleled in the most barbarous ages, and totally unworthy the head of a civilized nation.

He has constrained our fellow citizens taken captive on the high seas to bear arms against their country, to become the executioners of their friends and brethren, or to fall themselves by their hands.

He has excited domestic insurrections amongst us, and has endeavoured to bring on the inhabitants of our frontiers, the merciless Indian savages, whose known rule of warfare, is an undistinguished destruction of all ages, sexes, and conditions.

In every stage of these oppressions we have petitioned for redress in the most humble terms: our repeated petitions have been answered only by repeated injury. A prince whose character is thus marked by every act which may define a tyrant is unfit to be the ruler of a free people.

Nor have we been wanting in attention to our British brethren. We have warned them from time to time of attempts by their legislature to extend an unwarrantable jurisdiction over us. We have reminded them of the circumstances of our emigration and settlement here. We have appealed to their native justice and magnanimity, and we have conjured them by the ties of our common kindred to disavow these usurpations, which would inevitably interrupt our connections and correspondence. They too have been deaf to the voice of justice and of consanguinity. We must, therefore, acquiesce in the necessity, which denounces our separation, and hold them, as we hold the rest of mankind, enemies in war, in peace friends.

We, therefore, the Representatives of the United States of America, in General Congress assembled, appealing to the Supreme Judge of the world for the rectitude of our intentions, do, in the name, and by authority of the good people of these Colonies, solemnly publish and declare, That these United Colonies are, and of right ought to be, Free and Independent States; that they are absolved from all allegiance to the British Crown, and that all political connection between them and the state of Great Britain, is and ought to be totally dissolved; and that as Free and Independent States, they have full power to levy war, conclude peace, contract alliances, establish commerce, and to do all other acts and things which Independent States may of right do. And for the support of this declaration, with a firm reliance on the protection of Divine Providence, we mutually pledge to each other our lives, our fortunes, and our sacred honor.

The Case Against College

Caroline Bird

Caroline Bird (1915-) was born in New York City. In addition to writing about business issues affecting women, she has taught at Vassar College and worked in public relations. Her books include Born Female *(1968),* What Women Want *(1979),* The Two-Paycheck Marriage *(1982),* The Good Years: Your Life in the 21st Century *(1983), and* Lives of Our Own: Secrets of Salty Old Women *(1995). In this essay, which was excerpted from* The Case Against College *(1975), Bird questions the value of college and a college education.*

1 The case *for* college has been accepted without question for more than a generation. All high school graduates ought to go, says Conventional Wisdom and statistical evidence, because college will help them earn more money, become "better" people, and learn to be more responsible citizens than those who don't go.

But college has never been able to work its magic for everyone. And now that close to half our high school graduates are attending, those who don't fit the pattern are becoming more numerous, and more obvious. College graduates are selling shoes and driving taxis; college students sabotage each other's experiments and forge letters of recommendation in the intense competition for admission to graduate school. Others find no stimulation in their studies, and drop out—often encouraged by college administrators.

Some observers say the fault is with the young people themselves—they are spoiled, stoned, overindulged, and expecting too much. But that's mass character assassination, and doesn't explain all campus unhappiness. Others blame the state of the world, and they are partly right. We've been told that young people have to go to college because our economy can't absorb an army of untrained eighteen-year-olds. But disillusioned graduates are learning that it can no longer absorb an army of trained twenty-two-year-olds, either. . . .

The ultimate defense of college has always been that while it may not teach you anything vocationally useful, it will somehow make you a better person, able to do anything better, and those who make it through the process are initiated into the "fellowship of educated men and women." In a study intended to probe what graduates seven years out of college thought their colleges should have done for them, the Carnegie Commission found that most alumni expected the "development of my abilities to think and express myself." But if such respected educational psychologists as Bruner and Piaget are right, specific learning skills have to be acquired very early in life, perhaps even before formal schooling begins.

5 So, when pressed, liberal-arts defenders speak instead about something more encompassing, and more elusive. "College changed me inside," one graduate told us fervently. The authors of a Carnegie Commission report, who obviously struggled for a definition, concluded that one of the common threads in the perceptions of a liberal education is that it provides "an integrated view of the world which can serve as an inner guide." More simply, alumni say that college should have "helped me to formulate the values and goals of my life,"

In theory, a student is taught to develop these values and goals himself, but in practice, it doesn't work quite that way. All but the wayward and the saintly take their sense of the good, the true, and the beautiful from the people around them. When we speak of students acquiring "values" in college, we often mean that they will acquire the values—and sometimes that means only the tastes—of their professors. The values of professors may be "higher" than many students will encounter elsewhere, but they may not be relevant to situations in which students find themselves in college and later.

Of all the forms in which ideas are disseminated, the college professor lecturing a class is the slowest and most expensive. You don't have to go to college to read the great books or learn about the great ideas of Western Man. Today you can find them everywhere—in paperbacks, in the public libraries, in museums, in public lectures, in adult-education courses, in abridged, summarized, or adapted form in magazines, films, and television. The problem is no longer one of access to broadening ideas; the problem is the other way around: how to choose among the many courses of action proposed to us, how to edit the stimulations that pour into our eyes and ears every waking hour. A college experience that piles option on option and stimulation on stimulation merely adds to the contemporary nightmare.

What students and graduates say that they did learn on campus comes under the heading of personal, rather than intellectual, development. Again and again I was told that the real value of college is learning to get along with others, to practice social skills, to "sort out my head," and these have nothing to do with curriculum.

For whatever impact the academic experience used to have on college students, the sheer size of many undergraduate classes . . . dilutes faculty-student dialogue, and, more often than not, they are taught by teachers who were hired when colleges were faced with a shortage of qualified instructors, during their years of expansion and when the big rise in academic pay attracted the mediocre and the less than dedicated.

10 On the social side, colleges are withdrawing from responsibility for feeding, housing, policing, and protecting students at a time when the environment of college may be the most important service it could render. College officials are reluctant to "intervene" in the personal lives of the students. They no longer expect to take over from parents, but often insist that students—who have, most often, never lived away from home before—take full adult responsibility for their plans, achievements, and behavior.

Most college students do not live in the plush, comfortable countryclublike surroundings their parents envisage, or, in some cases, remember. Open dorms, particularly when they are coeducational, are noisy, usually overcrowded, and often messy. Some students desert the institutional "zoos" (their own word for dorms) and move into run-down, overpriced apartments. Bulletin boards in student centers are littered with notices of apartments to share and the drift of conversation suggests that a lot of money is dissipated in scrounging for food and shelter.

Taxpayers now provide more than half of the astronomical sums that are spent on higher education. But less than half of today's high school graduates go on, raising a new question of equity: Is it fair to make all the taxpayers pay for the minority who actually go to college? We decided long ago that it is fair for childless adults to pay school taxes because everyone, parents and nonparents alike, profits by a literate population. Does the same reasoning hold true for state-supported higher education? There is no conclusive evidence on either side.

Young people cannot be expected to go to college for the general good of mankind. They may be more altruistic than their elders, but no great numbers are going to spend four years at hard intellectual labor, let alone tens of thousands of family dollars, for "the advancement of human capability in society at large," one of the many purposes invoked by the Carnegie Commission report. Nor do any considerable number of them want to go to college to beat the Russians to Jupiter, improve the national defense, increase the Gross National Product, lower the crime rate, improve automobile safety, or create a market for the arts—all of which have been suggested at one time or other as benefits taxpayers get for supporting higher education.

One sociologist said that you don't have to have a reason for going to college because it's an institution. His definition of an institution is something everyone subscribes to without question. The burden of proof is not on why you should go to college, but why anyone thinks there might be a reason for not going. The implication—and some educators express it quite frankly—is that an eighteen-year-old high school graduate is still too young and confused to know what he wants to do, let alone what is good for him.

Mother knows best, in other words.

It had always been comfortable for students to believe that authorities, like Mother, or outside specialists, like educators, could determine what was best for them. However, specialists and authorities no longer enjoy the credibility former generations accorded them. Patients talk back to doctors and are not struck suddenly dead. Clients question the lawyer's bills and sometimes get them reduced. It is no longer self-evident that all adolescents must study a fixed curriculum that was constructed at a time when all educated men could agree on precisely what it was that made them educated.

The same with college. If high school graduates don't want to continue their education, or don't want to continue it right away, they may perceive more clearly than their elders that college is not for them.

College is an ideal place for those young adults who love learning for its own sake, who would rather read than eat, and who like nothing better than writing research papers. But they are a minority, even at the prestigious colleges, which recruit and attract the intellectually oriented.

The rest of our high school graduates need to look at college more closely and critically, to examine it as a consumer product, and decide if the cost in dollars, in time, in continued dependency, and in future returns, is worth the very large investment each student—and his family—must make.

Why Don't We Complain?

William F. Buckley, Jr.

William F. Buckley, Jr. (1925–) was born in New York. One of ten children of a lawyer who had earned great wealth from Texas oil, Buckley was educated as a youth at St. Thomas More School in London and Millbrook School in New York. After a stint in the Navy during World War II, he attended Yale University, where he wrote for The Yale Daily News *and was a member of the debating team. Shortly after his graduation from Yale, he published* God and Man at Yale *(1951), a memoir in which he discusses his conservative political philosophy and basic Christian principles. An erudite and articulate spokesman for American conservatives, Buckley has published a number of books on politics and government, including* Happy Days Were Here Again: Reflections of a Libertarian Journalist *(1993); written a syndicated newspaper column; founded and edited a magazine expounding conservative viewpoints,* The National Review; *and hosted a weekly television program,* Firing Line. *He has also written novels and books on sailing, another passion. Buckley received the Presidential Medal of Freedom in 1991 from President Bush. Although liberals disagree vociferously with some of his viewpoints, they just as strongly respect his intelligence and forthrightness. The following essay, written in 1961, reflects not only Buckley's verbal precision, but also his trademark wry sense of humor.*

1 It was the very last coach and the only empty seat on the entire train, 1
so there was no turning back. The problem was to breathe. Outside, the temperature was below freezing. Inside the railroad car the temperature must have been about 85 degrees. I took off my overcoat,

and a few minutes later my jacket, and noticed that the car was flecked with the white shirts of the passengers. I soon found my hand moving to loosen my tie. From one end of the car to the other, as we rattled through Westchester County, we sweated; but we did not moan.

I watched the train conductor appear at the head of the car. "Tickets, all tickets, please!" In a more virile age, I thought, the passengers would seize the conductor and strap him down on a seat over the radiator to share the fate of his patrons. He shuffled down the aisle, picking up tickets, punching commutation cards. *No one addressed a word to him.* He approached my seat, and I drew a deep breath of resolution. "Conductor," I began with a considerable edge to my voice. . . . Instantly the doleful eyes of my seatmate turned tiredly from his newspaper to fix me with a resentful stare: what question could be so important as to justify my sibilant intrusion into his stupor? I was shaken by those eyes. I am incapable of making a discreet fuss, so I mumbled a question about what time were we due in Stamford (I didn't even ask whether it would be before or after dehydration could be expected to set in), got my reply, and went back to my newspaper and to wiping my brow.

The conductor had nonchalantly walked down the gauntlet of eighty sweating American freemen, and not one of them had asked him to explain why the passengers in that car had been consigned to suffer. There is nothing to be done when the temperature *outdoors* is 85 degrees, and indoors the air conditioner has broken down; obviously when that happens there is nothing to do, except perhaps curse the day that one was born. But when the temperature outdoors is below freezing, it takes a positive act of will on somebody's part to set the temperature *indoors* at 85. Somewhere a valve was turned too far, a furnace overstocked, a thermostat maladjusted: something that could easily be remedied by turning off the heat and allowing the great outdoors to come indoors. All this is so obvious. What is not obvious is what has happened to the American people.

It isn't just the commuters, whom we have come to visualize as a supine breed who have got on to the trick of suspending their sensory faculties twice a day while they submit to the creeping dissolution of the railroad industry. It isn't just they who have given up trying to rectify irrational vexations. It is the American people everywhere.

5 A few weeks ago at a large movie theatre I turned to my wife and said, "The picture is out of focus." "Be quiet," she answered. I obeyed.

But a few minutes later I raised the point again, with mounting impatience. "It will be all right in a minute," she said apprehensively. (She would rather lose her eyesight than be around when I make one of my infrequent scenes.) I waited, it was *just* out of focus—not glaringly out, but out. My vision is 20–20, and I assume that is the vision, adjusted, of most people in the movie house. So, after hectoring my wife throughout the first reel, I finally prevailed upon her to admit that it *was* off, and very annoying. We then settled down, coming to rest on the presumption that: a) someone connected with the management of the theatre must soon notice the blur and make the correction; or b) that someone seated near the rear of the house would make the complaint in behalf of those of us up front; or c) that—any minute now—the entire house would explode into catcalls and foot stamping, calling dramatic attention to the irksome distortion.

What happened was nothing. The movie ended, as it had begun, *just* out of focus, and as we trooped out, we stretched our faces in a variety of contortions to accustom the eye to the shock of normal focus.

I think it is safe to say that everybody suffered on that occasion. And I think it is safe to assume that everyone was expecting someone else to take the initiative in going back to speak to the manager. And it is probably true even that if we had supposed the movie would run right through the blurred image, someone surely would have summoned up the purposive indignation to get up out of his seat and file his complaint.

But notice that no one did. And the reason no one did is because we are all increasingly anxious in America to be unobtrusive, we are reluctant to make our voices heard, hesitant about claiming our rights; we are afraid that our cause is unjust, or that if it is not unjust, that it is ambiguous; or if not even that, that it is too trivial to justify the horrors of a confrontation with Authority; we will sit in an oven or endure a racking headache before undertaking a head-on, I'm-here-to-tell-you complaint. That tendency to passive compliance, to a heedless endurance, is something to keep one's eyes on—in sharp focus.

I myself can occasionally summon the courage to complain, but I cannot, as I have intimated, complain softly. My own instinct is so strong to let the thing ride, to forget about it—to expect that someone will take the matter up, when the grievance is collective, in my behalf—that it is only when the provocation is at a very special key, whose vibrations touch simultaneously a complexus of nerves, allergies, and passions, that I catch fire and find the reserves of courage and assertiveness to speak up. When that happens, I get quite carried away. My blood gets hot, my brow wet, I become unbearably and unconscionably sarcastic and bellicose; I am girded for a total showdown.

Why should that be? Why could not I (or anyone else) on that railroad coach have said simply to the conductor, "Sir"—I take that back: that sounds sarcastic—"Conductor, would you be good enough to turn down the heat? I am extremely hot. In fact I tend to get hot every time the temperature reaches 85 degr—" Strike that last sentence. Just end it with the simple statement that you are extremely hot, and let the conductor infer the cause.

Every New Year's Eve I resolve to do something about the Milquetoast in me and vow to speak up, calmly, for my rights, and for the betterment of our society, on every appropriate occasion. Entering last New Year's Eve I was fortified in my resolve because that morning at breakfast I had had to ask the waitress three times for a glass of milk. She finally brought it—after I had finished my eggs, which is when I don't want it any more. I did not have the manliness to order her to take the milk back, but settled instead for a cowardly sulk, and ostentatiously refused to drink the milk—though I later paid for it—rather than state plainly to the hostess, as I should have, why I had not drunk it, and would not pay for it.

So by the time the New Year ushered out the Old, riding in on my morning's indignation and stimulated by the gastric juices of resolution that flow so faithfully on New Year's Eve, I rendered my vow. Henceforward I would conquer my shyness, my despicable disposition to supineness. I would speak out like a man against the unnecessary annoyances of our time.

Forty-eight hours later, I was standing in line at the ski repair store in Pico Peak, Vermont. All I needed, to get on with my skiing, was the loan, for one minute, of a small screwdriver, to tighten a loose binding. Behind the counter in the workshop were two men. One was industriously engaged in serving the complicated requirements of a young lady at the head of the line, and obviously he would be tied up for quite a while. The other—"Jiggs," his workmate called him—was a middle-aged man, who sat in a chair puffing a pipe, exchanging small talk with his working partner. My pulse began its telltale acceleration. The minutes ticked on. I stared at the idle shopkeeper, hoping to shame him into action, but he was impervious to my telepathic reproof and continued his small talk with his friend, brazenly insensitive to the nervous demands of six good men who were raring to ski.

Suddenly my New Year's Eve resolution struck me. It was now or never. I broke from my place in line and marched to the counter. I was going to control myself. I dug my nails into my palms. My effort was only partially successful:

"If you are not too busy," I said icily, "would you mind handing me a screwdriver?"

Work stopped and everyone turned his eyes on me, and I experienced the mortification I always feel when I am the center of centripetal shafts of curiosity, resentment, perplexity.

But the worst was yet to come. "I am sorry, sir," said Jiggs defensively, moving the pipe from his mouth. "I am not supposed to move. I have just had a heart attack." That was the signal for a great whirring noise that descended from heaven. We looked, stricken, out the window, and it appeared as though a cyclone had suddenly focused on the snowy courtyard between the shop and the ski lift. Suddenly a gigantic army helicopter materialized, and hovered down to a landing. Two men jumped out of the plane carrying a stretcher, tore into the ski shop, and lifted the shopkeeper onto the stretcher. Jiggs bade his companion good-by, was whisked out the door, into the plane, up to the heavens, down—we learned—to a near-by army hospital. I looked up manfully—into a score of man-eating eyes. I put the experience down as a reversal.

As I write this, on an airplane, I have run out of paper and need to reach into my briefcase under my legs for more. I cannot do this until my empty lunch tray is removed from my lap. I arrested the stewardess as she passed empty-handed down the aisle on the way to the kitchen to fetch the lunch trays for the passengers up forward who haven't been served yet. "Would you please take my tray?" "Just a *moment, sir!*" she said, and marched on sternly. Shall I tell her that since she is headed for the kitchen *anyway,* it could not delay the feeding of the other passengers by more than two seconds necessary to stash away my empty tray? Or remind her that not fifteen minutes ago she spoke unctuously into the loudspeaker the words undoubtedly devised by the airline's highly paid public relations counselor: "If there is anything I or Miss French can do for you to make your trip more enjoyable, *please* let us—" I have run out of paper.

I think the observable reluctance of the majority of Americans to assert themselves in minor matters is related to our increased sense of helplessness in an age of technology and centralized political and economic power. For generations, Americans who were too hot, or too cold, got up and did something about it. Now we call the plumber, or the electrician, or the furnace man. The habit of looking after our own needs obviously had something to do with the assertiveness that characterized the American family familiar to readers of American literature. With the technification of life goes our direct responsibility for our material environment, and we are conditioned to adopt a position of helplessness not only as regards the broken air conditioner, but as regards the overheated train. It takes an expert to fix the former, but not the latter; yet these distinctions, as we withdraw into helplessness, tend to fade away.

Our notorious political apathy is a related phenomenon. Every year, whether the Republican or the Democratic Party is in office, more and more power drains away from the individual to feed vast reservoirs in far-off places; and we have less and less say about the shape of events which shape our future. From this alienation of personal power comes the sense of resignation with which we accept the political dispensations of a powerful government whose hold upon us continues to increase.

An editor of a national weekly news magazine told me a few years ago that as few as a dozen letters of protest against an editorial stance of his magazine was enough to convene a plenipotentiary meeting of the board of editors to review policy. "So few people complain, or make their voices heard," he explained to me, "that we assume a dozen letters represent the inarticulated views of thousands of readers." In the past ten years, he said, the volume of mail has noticeably decreased, even though the circulation of his magazine has risen.

When our voices are finally mute, when we have finally suppressed the natural instinct to complain, whether the vexation is trivial or grave, we shall have become automatons, incapable of feeling. When Premier Khrushchev first came to this country late in 1959 he was primed, we are informed, to experience the bitter resentment of the American people against his tyranny, against his persecutions, against the movement which is responsible for the great number of American deaths in Korea, for billions in taxes every year, and for life everlasting on the brink of disaster; but Khrushchev was pleasantly surprised, and reported back to the Russian people that he had been met with overwhelming cordiality (read: apathy), except, to be sure, for "a few fascists who followed me around with their wretched posters, and should be horsewhipped."

I may be crazy, but I say there would have been lots more posters in a society where train temperatures in the dead of winter are not allowed to climb to 85 degrees without complaint.

Today's Kids Are, Like, Killing the English Language. Yeah, Right.

Kirk Johnson

Every generation, it seems, has some comment about the younger generation and the butchery it performs on the English language. Adults point to the speech of teenagers and see it as a sign of civilization in decline. School becomes the place where the problem is addressed and teenagers learn to use "proper" language, the language of grownups. In spite of these efforts, the language of youth persists, forcing us to ask the question, "What is language, anyway?" In this article from the August 9, 1998 issue of the New York Times, *Kirk Johnson offers a dynamic view of language, one in which language may be viewed as a logical and creative response to shifting social conditions, the cultural climate, and technological developments.*

1 As a father of two pre-teen boys, I have in the last year or so be- 1
come a huge fan of the word "duh." This is a word much maligned by educators, linguistic brahmins and purists, but they are all quite wrong.

Duh has elegance. Duh has shades of meaning, even sophistication. Duh and its perfectly paired linguistic partner, "yeah right," are the ideal terms to usher in the millennium and the information age, and to highlight the differences from the stolid old 20th century.

Even my sons might stop me at this point and quash my hyperbole with a quickly dispensed, "Yeah, right, Dad." But hear me out:

"Today's Kids Are, Like, Killing the English Language. Yeah, Right." by Kirk Johnson, reprinted from the *New York Times*, August 9, 1998.

I have become convinced that duh and yeah right have arisen to fill a void in the language because the world has changed. Fewer questions these days can effectively be answered with yes or no, while at the same time, a tidal surge of hype and mindless blather threatens to overwhelm old-fashioned conversation. Duh and yeah right are the cure.

Good old yes and no were fine for their time—the archaic, black and white era of late industrialism that I was born into in the 1950's. The yes-or-no combo was hard and fast and most of all simple: It belonged to the Manichean red-or-dead mentality of the cold war, to manufacturing, to "Father Knows Best" and "It's a Wonderful Life."

5 The information-age future that my 11-year-old twins own is more complicated than yes or no. It's more subtle and supple, more loaded with content and hype and media manipulation than my childhood—or any adult's, living or dead—ever was.

And duh, whatever else it may be, is drenched with content. Between them, duh and yeah-right are capable of dividing all language and thought into an exquisitely differentiated universe. Every statement and every question can be positioned on a gray scale of understatement or overstatement, stupidity or insightfulness, information saturation or yawning emptiness.

And in an era when plain speech has become endangered by the pressures of political correctness, duh and yeah right are matchless tools of savvy, winking sarcasm and skepticism: caustic without being confrontational, incisive without being quite specific.

With duh, you can convey a response, throw in a whole basket full of auxiliary commentary about the question or the statement you're responding to, and insult the speaker all at once! As in this hypothetical exchange:

Parent: "Good morning, son, it's a beautiful day."

10 *Eleven-year-old boy: "Duh."*

And there is a kind of esthetic balance as well. Yeah—right is the yin to duh's yang, the antithesis to duh's empathetic thesis. Where duh is assertive and edgy, a perfect tool for undercutting mindless understatement or insulting repetition, yeah right is laid back, a surfer's cool kind of response to anything overwrought or oversold.

New York, for example, is duh territory, while Los Angeles is yeah—right. Television commercials can be rendered harmless and inert by simply saying, "yeah, right," upon their conclusion. Local television news reports are helped out with a sprinkling of well-placed duhs, at moments of stunning obviousness. And almost any politician's speech cries out for heaping helpings of both at various moments.

Adolescent terms like "like," by contrast, scare me to death. While I have become convinced through observation and personal experimentation that just about any adult of even modest intelligence can figure out how to use duh and yeah right properly, like is different. Like is hard. Like is, like, dangerous.

Marcel Danesi, a professor of linguistics and semiotics at the University of Toronto who has studied the language of youth and who coined the term "pubilect" to describe the dialect of pubescence, said he believes like is in fact altering the structure of the English language, making it more fluid in construction, more like Italian or some other Romance language than good old hard-and-fast Anglo-Saxon. Insert like in the middle of a sentence, he said, and a statement can be turned into a question, a question into an exclamation, an exclamation into a quiet meditation.

15 Consider these hypothetical expressions: "If you're having broccoli for dinner, Mr. Johnson, I'm, like, out of here!" and "I was, like, no way!" and perhaps most startlingly, "He was, like, duh!" 15

In the broccoli case, like softens the sentence. It's less harsh and confrontational than saying flatly that the serving of an unpalatable vegetable would require a fleeing of the premises.

In the second instance, like functions as a kind of a verbal quotation mark, an announcement that what follows, "no way," is to be heard differently. The quote itself can then be loaded up with any variety of intonation—irony, sarcasm, even self-deprecation—all depending on the delivery.

In the third example—"He was, like, duh!"—like becomes a crucial helping verb for duh, a verbal springboard. (Try saying the sentence without like and it becomes almost incomprehensible.)

But like and duh and yeah right, aside from their purely linguistic virtues, are also in many ways the perfect words to convey the sense of reflected reality that is part of the age we live in. Image manipulation, superficiality, and shallow media culture are, for better or worse, the backdrop of adolescent life.

20 Adults of the yes-or-no era could perhaps grow up firm in their knowledge of what things "are," but in the Age of Duh, with images reflected back from every angle at every waking moment, kids swim 20

in a sea of what things are "like." Distinguishing what is from what merely seems to be is a required skill of an 11-year-old today; like reflects modern life, and duh and yeah right are the tools with which such a life can be negotiated and mastered.

But there is a concealed paradox in the Age of Duh. The information overload on which it is based is built around the computer, and the computer is, of course, built around—that's right—the good old yes-or-no binary code: Billions of microcircuits all blinking on or off, black or white, current in or current out. Those computers were designed by minds schooled and steeped in the world of yes or no, and perhaps it is not too much of a stretch to imagine my sons' generation, shaped by the broader view of duh, finding another path: binary code with attitude. Besides, most computers I know already seem to have an attitude. Incorporating a little duh would at least give them a sense of humor.

The Triumph of the Yell

Deborah Tannen

Deborah Tannen (1945–), born in Brooklyn, New York, received her Ph.D. in linguistics from the University of California, Berkeley and teaches at Georgetown University. Her research into how people communicate has brought her critical and popular acclaim, and she has appeared on several television programs and has written for The New York Times, The Washington Post, *and* Vogue. *Her book* That's Not what I Meant *(1987) analyzes the effects of conversational styles on relationships.* You Just Don't Understand *(1990) examines differences in how men and women converse.* Talking From 9 to 5 *(1994) resulted from her research into conversational styles in work settings and their impact on how work is performed and who gets ahead. The following essay, which first appeared in* The New York Times *in 1994, discusses what happens when public discourse takes on the characteristics of having an argument. As you read it, think about current issues in the press and how some journalists turn complex issues into a simple battle of sound bytes between two sides.*

1 I put the question to a journalist who had written a vitriolic attack 1
on a leading feminist researcher: "Why do you need to make others wrong for you to be right?" Her response: "It's an argument!"

That's the problem. More and more these days, journalists, politicians and academics treat public discourse as an argument—not in the sense of *making* an argument, but in the sense of *having* one, of having a fight.

When people have arguments in private life, they're not trying to understand what the other person is saying. They're listening for weaknesses in logic to leap on, points they can distort to make the other look bad. We all do this when we're angry, but is it the best model for public intellectual interchange? This breakdown of the boundary between public and private is contributing to what I have come to think of as a culture of critique.

Fights have winners and losers. If you're fighting to win, the temptation is great to deny facts that support your opponent's views and present only those facts that support your own.

5 At worst, there's a temptation to lie. We accept this style of arguing because we believe we can tell when someone is lying. But we can't. Paul Ekman, a psychologist at the University of California at San Francisco, has found that even when people are very sure they can tell whether or not someone is dissembling, their judgments are as likely as not to be wrong.

If public discourse is a fight, every issue must have two sides—no more, no less. And it's crucial to show "the other side," even if one has to scour the margins of science or the fringes of lunacy to find it.

The culture of critique is based on the belief that opposition leads to truth: when both sides argue, the truth will emerge. And because people are presumed to enjoy watching a fight, the most extreme views are presented, since they make the best show. But it is a myth that opposition leads to truth when truth does not reside on one side or the other but is rather a crystal of many sides. Truth is more likely to be found in the complex middle than in the simplified extremes, but the spectacles that result when extremes clash are thought to get higher ratings or larger readership.

Because the culture of critique encourages people to attack and often misrepresent others, those others must waste their creativity and time correcting the misrepresentations and defending themselves. Serious scholars have had to spend years of their lives writing books proving that the Holocaust happened, because a few fanatics who claim it didn't have been given a public forum. Those who provide the platform know that what these people say is, simply put, not true, but rationalize the dissemination of lies as showing "the other side." The determination to find another side can spread disinformation rather than lead to truth.

The culture of critique has given rise to the journalistic practice of confronting prominent people with criticism couched as others' views. Meanwhile, the interviewer has planted an accusation in readers' or viewers' minds. The theory seems to be that when provoked, people are spurred to eloquence and self-revelation. Perhaps some are. But others are unable to say what they know because they are hurt, and begin to sputter when their sense of fairness is outraged. In those cases, opposition is not the path to truth.

When people in power know that what they say will be scrutinized for weaknesses and probably distorted, they become more guarded. As an acquaintance recently explained about himself, public figures who once gave long, free-wheeling press conferences now limit themselves to reading brief statements. When less information gets communicated, opposition does not lead to truth.

Opposition also limits information when only those who are adept at verbal sparring take part in public discourse, and those who cannot handle it, or do not like it, decline to participate. This winnowing process is evident in graduate schools, where many talented students drop out because what they expected to be a community of intellectual inquiry turned out to be a ritual game of attack and counterattack.

One such casualty graduated from a small liberal arts college, where she "luxuriated in the endless discussions." At the urging of her professors, she decided to make academia her profession. But she changed her mind after a year in an art history program at a major university. She felt she had fallen into a "den of wolves." "I wasn't cut out for academia," she concluded. But does academia have to be so combative that it cuts people like her out?

In many university classrooms, "critical thinking" means reading someone's life work, then ripping it to shreds. Though critique is surely one form of critical thinking, so are integrating ideas from disparate fields and examining the context out of which they grew. Opposition does not lead to truth when we ask only "What's wrong with this argument?" and never "What can we use from this in building a new theory, and a new understanding?"

Several years ago I was on a television talk show with a representative of the men's movement. I didn't foresee any problem, since there is nothing in my work that is anti-male. But in the room where guests gather before the show I found a man wearing a shirt and tie and a floor-length skirt, with waist-length red hair. He politely introduced himself and told me he liked my book. Then he added: "When I get out there, I'm going to attack you. But don't take it personally. That's why they invite me on, so that's what I'm going to do."

When the show began, I spoke only a sentence or two before this man nearly jumped out of his chair, threw his arms before him in gestures of anger and began shrieking—first attacking me, but soon moving on to rail against women. The most disturbing thing about his hysterical ranting was what it sparked in the studio audience: they too became vicious, attacking not me (I hadn't had a chance to say anything) and not him (who wants to tangle with someone who will scream at you?) but the other guests: unsuspecting women who had agreed to come on the show to talk about their problems communicating with their spouses.

This is the most dangerous aspect of modeling intellectual interchange as a fight: it contributes to an atmosphere of animosity that spreads like a fever. In a society where people express their anger by shooting, the result of demonizing those with whom we disagree can be truly demonic.

I am not suggesting that journalists stop asking tough questions necessary to get at the facts, even if those questions may appear challenging. And of course it is the responsibility of the media to represent serious opposition when it exists, and of intellectuals everywhere to explore potential weaknesses in others' arguments. But when opposition becomes the overwhelming avenue of inquiry, when the lust for opposition exalts extreme views and obscures complexity, when our eagerness to find weaknesses blinds us to strengths, when the atmosphere of animosity precludes respect and poisons our relations with one another, then the culture of critique is stifling us. If we could move beyond it, we would move closer to the truth.

What I've Learned from Men

Barbara Ehrenreich

Barbara Ehrenreich (1941–) was born in Montana and earned her Ph.D. from Rockefeller University. She is known as—and speaks of herself as—an independent and outspoken feminist, liberal, and democratic socialist. Most of her non-fiction writing could be classified as social criticism, including a number of books: The Hearts of Men *(1983),* Fear of Falling *(1989),* The Worst Years of Our Lives *(1990), and* Bait and Switch: The (Futile) Pursuit of the American Dream *(2005). Her* New York Times *best seller* Nickel and Dimed: on (Not) Getting By in America *(2001) exposed the reality of the working poor. Her novel,* Kipper's Game *was published in 1993. She is a regular essayist for* Time *and other magazines. "What I've Learned from Men" was first printed in* Ms. *magazine in 1985. Ehrenreich has the ability to make us laugh at things—including herself—as we see the deeper truths. Her use of detail to exemplify her ideas is particularly strong in this essay.*

1 For many years I believed that women had only one thing to learn 1
from men: how to get the attention of a waiter by some means short of kicking over the table and shrieking. Never in my life have I gotten the attention of a waiter, unless it was an off-duty waiter whose car I'd accidentally scraped in a parking lot somewhere. Men, however, can summon a maître d' just by thinking the word "coffee," and this is a power women would be well-advised to study. What else would we possibly want to learn from them? How to interrupt someone in mid-sentence as if you were performing an act of conversational euthanasia? How to drop a pair of socks three feet from an open

From *Ms. Magazine,* 1985.

hamper and keep right on walking? How to make those weird guttural gargling sounds in the bathroom?

But now, at mid-life, I am willing to admit that there are some real and useful things to learn from men. Not from all men—in fact, we may have the most to learn from some of the men we like the least. This realization does not mean that my feminist principles have gone soft with age: what I think women could learn from men is how to get *tough*. After more than a decade of consciousness-raising, assertiveness training, and hand-to-hand combat in the battle of the sexes, we're still too ladylike. Let me try that again—we're just too *damn* ladylike.

Here is an example from my own experience, a story that I blush to recount. A few years ago, at an international conference held in an exotic and luxurious setting, a prestigious professor invited me to his room for what he said would be an intellectual discussion on matters of theoretical importance. So far, so good. I showed up promptly. But only minutes into the conversation—held in all-too-adjacent chairs—it emerged that he was interested in something more substantial than a meeting of minds. I was disgusted, but not enough to overcome 30-odd years of programming in ladylikeness. Every time his comments took a lecherous turn, I chattered distractingly; every time his hand found its way to my knee, I returned it as if it were something he had misplaced. This went on for an unconscionable period (as much as 20 minutes); then there was a minor scuffle, a dash for the door, and I was out—with nothing violated but my self-esteem. I, a full-grown feminist, conversant with such matters as rape crisis counseling and sexual harassment at the workplace, had behaved like a ninny—or, as I now understand it, like a lady.

The essence of ladylikeness is a persistent servility masked as "niceness." For example, we (women) tend to assume that it is our responsibility to keep everything "nice" even when the person we are with is rude, aggressive, or emotionally AWOL. (In the above example, I was so busy taking responsibility for preserving the veneer of "niceness" that I almost forgot to take responsibility for myself.) In conversations with men, we do almost all the work: sociologists have observed that in male-female social interactions it's the woman who throws out leading questions and verbal encouragements ("So how did you *feel* about that?" and so on) while the man, typically, says "Hmmmm." Wherever we go, we're perpetually smiling—the on-cue smile, like the now-outmoded curtsy, being one of our culture's little rituals of submission.

We're trained to feel embarrassed if we're praised, but if we see a criticism coming at us from miles down the road, we rush to acknowledge it. And when we're feeling aggressive or angry or resentful, we just tighten up our smiles or turn them into rueful little moues. In short, we spend a great deal of time acting like wimps.

5 For contrast, think of the macho stars we love to watch. Think, for example, of Mel Gibson facing down punk marauders in "The Road Warrior" . . . John Travolta swaggering his way through the early scenes of "Saturday Night Fever" . . . or Marlon Brando shrugging off the local law in "The Wild One." Would they simper their way through tight spots? Chatter aimlessly to keep the conversation going? Get all clutched up whenever they think they might—just might—have hurt someone's feelings? No, of course not, and therein, I think, lies their fascination for us.

The attraction of the "tough guy" is that he has—or at least seems to have—what most of us lack, and that is an aura of power and control. In an article, feminist psychiatrist Jean Baker Miller writes that "a woman's using self-determined power for herself is equivalent to selfishness [and] destructiveness"—an equation that makes us want to avoid even the appearance of power. Miller cites cases of women who get depressed just when they're on the verge of success—and of women who do succeed and then bury their achievement in self-deprecation. As an example, she describes one company's periodic meetings to recognize outstanding salespeople: when a woman is asked to say a few words about her achievement, she tends to say something like, "Well, I really don't know how it happened. I guess I was just lucky this time." In contrast, the men will cheerfully own up to the hard work, intelligence, and so on, to which they owe their success. By putting herself down, a woman avoids feeling brazenly powerful and potentially "selfish"; she also does the traditional lady's work of trying to make everyone else feel better ("She's not really so smart, after all, just lucky").

So we might as well get a little tougher. And a good place to start is by cutting back on the small acts of deference that we've been programmed to perform since girlhood. Like unnecessary smiling. For many women—waitresses, flight attendants, receptionists—smiling is an occupational requirement, but there's no reason for anyone to go around grinning when she's not being paid for it. I'd suggest that we save our off-duty smiles for when we truly feel like sharing them, and if you're not sure what to do with your face in the meantime, study Clint Eastwood's expressions—both of them.

Along the same lines, I think women should stop taking responsibility for every human interaction we engage in. In a social encounter with a woman, the average man can go 25 minutes saying nothing more than "You don't say?" "Izzat so?" and, of course, "Hmmmm." Why should we do all the work? By taking so much responsibility for making conversations go well, we act as if we had much more at stake in the encounter than the other party—and that gives him (or her) the power advantage. Every now and then, we deserve to get more out of a conversation than we put into it: I'd suggest not offering information you'd rather not share ("I'm really terrified that my sales plan won't work") and not, out of sheer politeness, soliciting information you don't really want ("Wherever did you get that lovely tie?"). There will be pauses, but they don't have to be awkward for *you.*

It is true that some, perhaps most, men will interpret any decrease in female deference as a deliberate act of hostility. Omit the free smiles and perky conversation-boosters and someone is bound to ask, "Well, what's come over *you* today?" For most of us, the first impulse is to stare at our feet and make vague references to a terminally ill aunt in Atlanta, but we should have as much right to be taciturn as the average (male) taxi driver. If you're taking a vacation from smiles and small talk and some fellow is moved to inquire about what's "bothering" you, just stare back levelly and say, the international debt crisis, the arms race, or the death of God.

10 There are all kinds of ways to toughen up—and potentially move up—at work, and I leave the details to the purveyors of assertiveness training. But Jean Baker Miller's study underscores a fundamental principle that anyone can master on her own. We can stop acting less capable than we actually are. For example, in the matter of taking credit when credit is due, there's a key difference between saying "I was just lucky" and saying "I had a plan and it worked." If you take the credit you deserve, you're letting people know that you were confident you'd succeed all along, and that you fully intend to do so again.

Finally, we may be able to learn something from men about what to do with anger. As a general rule, women get irritated: men get *mad.* We make tight little smiles of ladylike exasperation; they pound on desks and roar. I wouldn't recommend emulating the full basso profundo male tantrum, but women do need ways of expressing justified anger clearly, colorfully, and, when necessary, crudely. If you're not just irritated, but *pissed off,* it might help to say so.

I, for example, have rerun the scene with the prestigious professor many times in my mind. And in my mind, I play it like Bogart. I start by moving my chair over to where I can look the professor full in the face. I let him do the chattering, and when it becomes evident that he has nothing serious to say, I lean back and cross my arms, just to let him know that he's wasting my time. I do not smile, neither do I nod encouragement. Nor, of course, do I respond to his blandishments with apologetic shrugs and blushes. Then, at the first flicker of lechery, I stand up and announce coolly, "All right, I've had enough of this crap." Then I walk out—slowly, deliberately, confidently. Just like a man.

Or—now that I think of it—just like a woman.

Motherhood: Who Needs It?

Betty Rollin

Betty Rollin (1936–) was born in New York City. A graduate of Sarah Lawrence College (B.A., 1957), Rollin has worked for Vogue, Look, *NBC News, and ABC Nightline. Her books include* I Thee Wed *(1958),* Mothers are Funnier than Children *(1964),* The Non-Drinker's Drink Book *(1966),* First You Cry *(1976), and* Last Wish *(1985). This essay, published in* Look *in 1970, debunks what Rollin calls the "motherhood myth."*

1 Motherhood is in trouble, and it ought to be. A rude question is long overdue: Who needs it? The answer used to be (1) society and (2) women. But now, with the impending horrors of overpopulation, society desperately *doesn't* need it. And women don't need it either. Thanks to the Motherhood Myth—the idea that having babies is something that all normal women instinctively want and need and will enjoy doing—they just *think* they do. 1

The notion that the maternal wish and the activity of mothering are instinctive or biologically predestined is baloney. Try asking most sociologists, psychologists, psychoanalysts, biologists—many of whom are mothers—about motherhood being instinctive: it's like asking department store presidents if their Santa Clauses are real. "Motherhood—instinctive?" shouts distinguished sociologist/author Dr. Jessie Bernard. "Biological destiny? Forget biology! If it were biology, people would die from not doing it."

"Women don't need to be mothers any more than they need spaghetti," says Dr. Richard Rabkin, a New York psychiatrist. "But if you're in a world where everyone is eating spaghetti, thinking they need it and want it, you will think so too. Romance has really contaminated science. So-called instincts have to do with stimulation. They are not things that well up inside of you."

"When a woman says with feeling that she craved her baby from within, she is putting into biological language what is psychological," says University of Michigan psychoanalyst and motherhood-researcher Dr. Frederick Wyatt. "There are no instincts," says Dr. William Goode, president-elect of the American Sociological Association. "There are reflexes, like eye-blinking, and drives, like sex. There is no innate drive for children. Otherwise, the enormous cultural pressures that there are to reproduce wouldn't exist. There are no cultural pressures to sell you on getting your hand out of the fire."

5 There are, to be sure, biologists and others who go on about biological destiny, that is, the innate or instinctive goal of motherhood. (At the turn of the century, even good old capitalism was explained by a theorist as "the *instinct* of acquisitiveness.") And many psychoanalysts will hold the Freudian view that women feel so rotten about not having a penis that they are necessarily propelled into the child-wish to replace the missing organ. Psychoanalysts also make much of the psychological need to repeat what one's parent of the same sex has done. Since every woman has a mother, it is considered normal to wish to imitate one's mother by being a mother.

There is, surely, a wish to pass on love if one has received it, but to insist women must pass it on in the same way is like insisting that every man whose father is a gardener has to be a gardener. One dissenting psychoanalyst says, simply, "There is a wish to comply with one's biology, yes, but we needn't and sometimes we shouldn't." (Interestingly, the woman who has been the greatest contributor to child therapy and who has probably given more to children than anyone alive is Dr. Anna Freud, Freud's magnificent daughter, who is not a mother.)

Anyway, what an expert cast of hundreds is telling us is, simply, that biological *possibility* and desire are not the same as biological *need.* Women have childbearing equipment. To choose not to use the equipment is no more blocking what is instinctive than it is for a man who, muscles or no, chooses not to be a weight lifter.

So much for the wish. What about the "instinctive" *activity* of mothering? One animal study shows that when a young member of a species is put in a cage, say, with an older member of the same species, the latter will act in a protective, "maternal" way. But that goes for both males and females who have been "mothered" themselves. And studies indicate that a human baby will also respond to whoever is around playing mother—even if it's father. Margaret Mead and many others frequently point out that mothering can be a fine occupation, if you want it, for either sex. Another experiment with monkeys who were brought up without mothers found them lacking in maternal behavior toward their own offspring. A similar study showed that monkeys brought up without other monkeys of the opposite sex had no interest in mating—all of which suggests that both mothering and mating behavior are learned, not instinctual. And, to turn the cart (or the baby carriage) around, baby ducks who lovingly follow their mothers seemed, in the mother's absence, to just as lovingly follow wooden ducks or even vacuum cleaners.

If motherhood isn't instinctive, when and why, then, was the Motherhood Myth born? Until recently, the entire question of maternal motivation was academic. Sex, like it or not, meant babies. Not that there haven't always been a lot of interesting contraceptive tries. But until the creation of the diaphragm in the 1880's, the birth of babies was largely unavoidable. And, generally speaking, nobody really seemed to mind. For one thing, people tend to be sort of good sports about what seems to be inevitable. For another, in the past, the population needed beefing up. Mortality rates were high, and agricultural cultures, particularly, have always needed children to help out. So because it "just happened" and because it was needed, motherhood was assumed to be innate.

10 Originally, it was the word of God that got the ball rolling with "Be fruitful and multiply," a practical suggestion, since the only people around then were Adam and Eve. But in no time, supermoralists like St. Augustine changed the tone of the message: "Intercourse, even with one's legitimate wife, is unlawful and wicked where the conception of the offspring is prevented," he, we assume, thundered. And the Roman Catholic position was thus cemented. So then and now, procreation took on a curious value among people who viewed (and view) the pleasures of sex as sinful. One could partake in the sinful pleasure, but feel vindicated by the ensuing birth. Motherhood cleaned up sex. Also, it cleaned up women, who have always been considered somewhat evil, because of Eve's transgression (". . . but the woman was deceived and became a transgressor. Yet woman will be saved through

bearing children . . . ," I Timothy, 2:14–15), and somewhat dirty because of menstruation.

And so, based on need, inevitability, and pragmatic fantasy—the Myth *worked,* from society's point of view—the Myth grew like corn in Kansas. And society reinforced it with both laws and propaganda—laws that made woman a chattel, denied her education and personal mobility, and madonna propaganda that she was beautiful and wonderful doing it and it was all beautiful and wonderful to do. (One rarely sees a madonna washing dishes.)

In fact, the Myth persisted—breaking some kind of record for long-lasting fallacies—until something like yesterday. For as the truth about the Myth trickled in—as women's rights increased, as women gradually got the message that it was certainly possible for them to do most things that men did, that they live longer, that their brains were not tinier—then, finally, when the really big news rolled in, that they could choose whether or not to be mothers—what happened? The Motherhood Myth soared higher than ever. As Betty Friedan made oh-so-clear in *The Feminine Mystique,* the '40's and '50's produced a group of ladies who not only had babies as if they were going out of style (maybe they were) but, as never before, they turned motherhood into a cult. First, they wallowed in the aesthetics of it all—natural childbirth and nursing became maternal musts. Like heavy-bellied ostriches, they grounded their heads in the sands of motherhood, only coming up for air to say how utterly happy and fulfilled they were. But, as Mrs. Friedan says only too plainly, they weren't. The Myth galloped on, moreover, long after making babies had turned from practical asset to liability for both individual parents and society. With the average cost of a middle-class child figured conservatively at $30,000 (not including college), any parent knows that the only people who benefit economically from children are manufacturers of consumer goods. Hence all those gooey motherhood commercials. And the Myth gathered momentum long after sheer numbers, while not yet extinguishing us, have made us intensely uncomfortable. Almost all of our societal problems, from minor discomforts like traffic to major ones like hunger, the population people keep reminding us, have to do with there being too many people. And who suffers most? The kids who have been so mindlessly brought into the world, that's who. They are the ones who have to cope with all of the difficult and dehumanizing conditions brought on by overpopulation. They are the ones who have to cope with the psychological nausea of feeling unneeded by society. That's not the only reason for drugs, but, surely, it's a leading contender,

Unfortunately, the population curbers are tripped up by a romantic, stubborn, ideological hurdle. How can birth-control programs really be effective as long as the concept of glorious motherhood remains unchanged? (Even poor old Planned Parenthood has to euphemize—why not Planned Unparenthood?) Particularly among the poor, motherhood is one of the few inherently positive institutions that are accessible. As Berkeley demographer Judith Blake points out, "Poverty-oriented birth control programs do not make sense as a welfare measure . . . as long as existing pronatalist policies . . . encourage mating, pregnancy, and the care, support, and rearing of children." Or, she might have added, as long as the less-than-idyllic child-rearing part of motherhood remains "in small print."

Sure, motherhood gets dumped on sometimes: Philip Wylie's Momism got going in the '40's and Philip Roth's *Portnoy's Complaint* did its best to turn rancid the chicken-soup concept of Jewish motherhood. But these are viewed as the sour cries of a black humorist here, a malcontent there. Everyone shudders, laughs, but it's like the mouse and the elephant joke. Still, the Myth persists. Last April, a Brooklyn woman was indicted on charges of manslaughter and negligent homicide—eleven children died in a fire in a building she owned and criminally neglected—"But," sputtered her lawyer, "my client, Mrs. Breslow, is a mother, a grandmother, and a great grandmother!"

15 Most remarkably, the Motherhood Myth persists in the face of the most overwhelming maternal unhappiness and incompetence. If reproduction were merely superfluous and expensive, if the experience were as rich and rewarding as the cliché would have us believe, if it were a predominantly joyous trip for everyone riding—mother, father, child—then the going everybody-should-have-two-children plan would suffice. Certainly, there are a lot of joyous mothers, and their children and (sometimes, not necessarily) their husbands reflect their joy. But a lot of evidence suggests that for more women than anyone wants to admit, motherhood can be miserable. ("If it weren't," says one psychiatrist wryly, "the world wouldn't be in the mess it's in.")

There is a remarkable statistical finding from a recent study of Dr. Bernard's, comparing the mental illness and unhappiness of married mothers and single women. The latter group, it turned out, was both markedly less sick and overtly more happy. Of course, it's not easy to measure slippery attitudes like happiness. "Many women have achieved a kind of reconciliation—a conformity," says Dr. Bernard,

> *that they interpret as happiness. Since feminine happiness is supposed to lie in devoting one's life to one's husband and children, they do that; so* ipso facto, *they assume they are happy. And for many women, untrained for independence and "processed" for motherhood, they find their state far preferable to the alternatives, which don't really exist.*

Also, unhappy mothers are often loath to admit it. For one thing, if in society's view not to be a mother is to be a freak, not to be a *blissful* mother is to be a witch. Besides, unlike a disappointing marriage, disappointing motherhood cannot be terminated by divorce. Of course, none of that stops such a woman from expressing her dissatisfaction in a variety of ways. Again, it is not only she who suffers but her husband and children as well. Enter the harridan housewife, the carping shrew. The realities of motherhood can turn women into terrible people. And, judging from the 50,000 cases of child abuse in the U.S. each year, some are worse than terrible.

In some cases, the unpleasing realities of motherhood begin even before the beginning. In *Her Infinite Variety,* Morton Hunt describes young married women pregnant for the first time as "very likely to be frightened and depressed, masking these feelings in order not to be considered contemptible. The arrival of pregnancy interrupts a pleasant dream of motherhood and awakens them to the realization that they have too little money, or not enough space, or unresolved marital problems. . . ."

The following are random quotes from interviews with some mothers in Ann Arbor, Mich., who described themselves as reasonably happy. They all had positive things to say about their children, although when asked about the best moment of their day, they all confessed it was when the children were in bed. Here is the rest:

> *Suddenly I had to devote myself to the child totally. I was under the illusion that the baby was going to fit into my life, and I found that I had to switch my life and my schedule to fit him. You think, "I'm in love, I'll get married, and we'll have a baby." First there's two, then three, it's simple and romantic. You don't even think about the work. . . .*

> *You never get away from the responsibility. Even when you leave the children with a sitter, you are not out from under the pressure of the responsibility. . . .*
>
> *I hate ironing their pants and doing their underwear, and they never put their clothes in the laundry basket. . . . As they get older, they make less demands on our time because they're in school, but the demands are greater in forming their values. . . . Best moment of the day is when all the children are in bed. . . . The worst time of the day is 4* P.M., *when you have to get dinner started, the kids are tired, hungry and crabby—everybody wants to talk to you about their day . . . your day is only half over.*
>
> *Once a mother, the responsibility and concern for my children became so encompassing. . . . It took me a great deal of will to keep up other parts of my personality. . . . To me, motherhood gets harder as they get older because you have less control. . . . In an abstract sense, I'd have, several. . . . In the nonabstract, I would not have any. . . .*
>
> *I had anticipated that the baby would sleep and eat, sleep and eat. Instead, the experience was overwhelming. I really had not thought particularly about what motherhood would mean in a realistic sense. I want to do* other *things, like to become involved in things that are worthwhile—I don't mean women's clubs—but I don't have the physical energy to go out in the evenings. I feel like I'm missing something . . . the experience of being somewhere with people and having them talking about something—something that's going on in the world.*

Every grownup person expects to pay a price for his pleasures, but seldom is the price as vast as the one endured "however happily" by most mothers. We have mentioned the literal cost factor. But what does that mean? For middle-class American women, it means a life style with severe and usually unimagined limitations; i.e., life in the suburbs, because who can afford three bedrooms in the city? And what do suburbs mean? For women, suburbs mean other women and children and leftover peanut-butter sandwiches and car pools and seldom-seen husbands. Even the Feminine Mystiqueniks—the housewives who finally admitted that their lives behind brooms (OK, electric brooms) were driving them crazy—were loath to trace their predicament to their children. But it is simply a fact that a childless married woman has no child-work and little housework. She can live in a city, or, if she still chooses the suburbs or the country, she can leave on the commuter train with her husband if she wants to. Even the most ardent job-seeking mother will find little in the way of great opportunities in Scarsdale. Besides, by the time she wakes up, she usually lacks both the preparation for the outside world and the self-confidence to get it. You will say there are plenty of city-dwelling working mothers. But most of those women do additional-funds-for-the-family kind of work, not the interesting career kind that takes plugging during child-bearing years.

20 Nor is it a bed of petunias for the mother who does make it professionally. Says writer-critic Marya Mannes:

> *If the creative woman has children, she must pay for this indulgence with a long burden of guilt, for her life will be split three ways between them and her husband and her work. . . . No woman with any heart can compose a paragraph when her child is in trouble. . . . The creative woman has no wife to protect her from intrusion. A man at his desk in a room with closed door is a man at work. A woman at a desk in any room is available.*

Speaking of jobs, do remember that mothering, salary or not, is a job. Even those who can afford nurses to handle the nitty-gritty still need to put out emotionally. "Well-cared-for" neurotic rich kids are not exactly unknown in our society. One of the more absurd aspects of the Myth is the underlying assumption that, since most women are biologically equipped to bear children, they are psychologically, mentally, emotionally, and technically equipped (or interested) to rear them. Never mind happiness. To assume that such an exacting, consuming, and important task is something almost all women are equipped to do is far more dangerous and ridiculous than assuming that everyone with vocal chords should seek a career in the opera.

A major expectation of the Myth is that children make a not-so-hot marriage hotter, or a hot marriage, hotter still. Yet almost every available study indicates that childless marriages are far happier. One of the biggest, of 850 couples, was conducted by Dr. Harold Feldman of Cornell University, who states his finding in no uncertain terms: "Those couples with children had a significantly lower level of marital satisfaction than did those without children." Some of the reasons are obvious. Even the most adorable children make for additional demands, complications, and hardships in the lives of even the most loving parents. If a woman feels disappointed and trapped in her mother role, it is bound to affect her marriage in any number of ways: she may take out her frustrations directly on her husband, or she may count on him too heavily for what she feels she is missing in her daily life.

". . . You begin to grow away from your husband," says one of the Michigan ladies. "He's working on his career and you're working on your family. But you both must gear your lives to the children. You do things the children enjoy, more than things you might enjoy." More subtle and possibly more serious is what motherhood may do to a woman's sexuality. Often when the stork flies in, sexuality flies out. Both in the emotional minds of some women and in the minds of their husbands, when a woman becomes a mother, she stops being a woman. It's not only that motherhood may destroy her physical attractiveness, but its madonna concept may destroy her *feelings* of sexuality.

And what of the payoff? Usually, even the most self-sacrificing of maternal self-sacrificers expects a little something back. Gratified parents are not unknown to the Western world, but there are probably at least just as many who feel, to put it crudely, shortchanged. The experiment mentioned earlier—where the baby ducks followed vacuum cleaners instead of their mothers—indicates that what passes for love from baby to mother is merely a rudimentary kind of object attachment. Without necessarily feeling like a Hoover, a lot of women become disheartened because babies and children are not only not interesting to talk to (not everyone thrills at the wonders of da-da-mama talk) but they are generally not empathetic, considerate people. Even the nicest children are not capable of empathy, surely a major ingredient of love, until they are much older. Sometimes they're never capable of it. Dr. Wyatt says that often, in later years particularly, when most of the "returns" are in, it is the "good mother" who suffers most of all. It is then she must face a reality: The child—the appendage with her genes—is not an appendage, but a separate person. What's more, he or she may be a separate person who doesn't even like her—or whom she doesn't really like.

25 So if the music is lousy, how come everyone's dancing? Because the motherhood minuet is taught freely from birth, and whether or not she has rhythm or likes the music, every woman is expected to do it. Indeed, she *wants* to do it. Little girls start learning what to want—and what to be—when they are still in their cribs. Dr. Miriam Keiffer, a

young social psychologist at Bensalem, the Experimental College of Fordham University, points to studies showing that

> *at six months of age, mothers are already treating their baby girls and boys quite differently. For instance, mothers have been found to touch, comfort, and talk to their females more. If these differences can be found at such an early stage, it's not surprising that the end product is as different as it is. What is surprising is that men and women are, in so many ways, similar.*

Some people point to the way little girls play with dolls as proof of their innate motherliness. But remember, little girls are *given* dolls. When Margaret Mead presented some dolls to New Guinea children, it was the boys, not the girls, who wanted to play with them, which they did by crooning lullabies and rocking them in the most maternal fashion.

By the time they reach adolescence, most girls, unconsciously or not, have learned enough about role definition to qualify for a master's degree. In general, the lesson has been that no matter what kind of career thoughts one may entertain, one must, first and foremost, be a wife and mother. A girl's mother is usually her first teacher. As Dr. Goode says, "A woman is not only taught by society to have a child; she is taught to have a child who will have a child." A woman who has hung her life on the Motherhood Myth will almost always reinforce her young married daughter's early training by pushing for grandchildren. Prospective grandmothers are not the only ones. Husbands, too, can be effective sellers. After all, they have the Fatherhood Myth to cope with. A married man is *supposed* to have children. Often, particularly among Latins, children are a sign of potency. They help him assure the world—and himself—that he is the big man he is supposed to be. Plus, children give him both immortality (whatever that means) and possibly the chance to become more in his lifetime through the accomplishments of his children, particularly his son. (Sometimes it's important, however, for the son to do better, but not *too* much better.)

Friends, too, can be counted on as myth-pushers. Naturally one wants to do what one's friends do. One study, by the way, found a correlation between a woman's fertility and that of her three closest friends. The negative sell comes into play here, too. We have seen what the concept of non-mother means (cold, selfish, unwomanly, abnormal). In practice, particularly in the suburbs, it can mean, simply, exclusion—both from child-centered activities (that is, most activities) and child-centered conversations (that is, most conversations). It can also mean being the butt of a lot of unfunny jokes. ("Whaddya waiting for? An immaculate conception? Ha ha.") Worst of all, it can mean being an object of pity.

In case she's escaped all those pressures (that is, if she was brought up in a cave), a young married woman often wants a baby just so that she'll (1) have something to do (motherhood is better than clerk/typist, which is often the only kind of job she can get, since little more has been expected of her and, besides, her boss also expects her to leave and be a mother); (2) have something to hug and possess, to be needed by and have power over; and (3) have something to *be*—e.g., a baby's mother. Motherhood affords an instant identity. First, through wifehood, you are somebody's wife; then you are somebody's mother. Both give not only identity and activity, but status and stardom of a kind. During pregnancy, a woman can look forward to the kind of attention and pampering she may not ever have gotten or may never otherwise get. Some women consider birth the biggest accomplishment of their lives, which may be interpreted as saying not much for the rest of their lives. As Dr. Goode says, "It's like the gambler who may know the roulette wheel is crooked, but it's the only game in town." Also, with motherhood, the feeling of accomplishment is immediate. It is really much faster and easier to make a baby than paint a painting, or write a book, or get to the point of accomplishment in a job. It is also easier in a way to shift focus from self-development to child development—particularly since, for women, self-development is considered selfish. Even unwed mothers may achieve a feeling of this kind. (As we have seen, little thought is given to the aftermath.) And, again, since so many women are underdeveloped as people, they feel that, besides children, they have little else to give—to themselves, their husbands, to their world.

You may ask why then, when the realities do start pouring in, does a woman want to have a second, third, even fourth child? OK, (1) just because reality is pouring in doesn't mean she wants to *face* it. A new baby can help bring back some of the old illusions. Says psychoanalyst Dr. Natalie Shainess, "She may view each successive child as a knight in armor that will rescue her from being a 'bad unhappy mother.' " (2) Next on the horror list of having no children, is having one. It suffices to say that only children are not only OK, they even have a high rate of exceptionality. (3) Both parents usually want at least one child of each sex. The husband, for reasons discussed earlier, probably wants a son. (4) The more children one has, the more of an excuse one has not to develop in any other way.

30 What's the point? A world without children? Of course not. Nothing could be worse or more unlikely. No matter what anyone says in *Look* or anywhere else, motherhood isn't about to go out like a blown bulb, and who says it should? Only the Myth must go out, and now it seems to be dimming.

The younger-generation females who have been reared on the Myth have not rejected it totally, but at least they recognize it can be more loving to children not to have them. And at least they speak of adopting children instead of bearing them. Moreover, since the new nonbreeders are "less hung-up" on ownership, they seem to recognize that if you dig loving children, you don't necessarily have to own one. The end of the Motherhood Myth might make available more loving women (and men!) for those children who already exist.

When motherhood is no longer culturally compulsory, there will, certainly, be less of it. Women are now beginning to think and do more about development of self, of their individual resources. Far from being selfish, such development is probably our only hope. That means more alternatives for women. And more alternatives means more selective, better, happier, motherhood—and childhood and husbandhood (or manhood) and peoplehood. It is not a question of whether or not children are sweet and marvelous to have and rear; the question is, even if that's so, whether or not one wants to pay the price for it. It doesn't make sense any more to pretend that women need babies, when what they really need is themselves. If God were still speaking to us in a voice we could hear, even He would probably say, "Be fruitful. Don't multiply."

Is There a There in Cyberspace?

John Perry Barlow

John Perry Barlow, former Wyoming rancher, one-time songwriter for the Grateful Dead, cofounder of the Electronic Frontier Foundation, and board member of the WELL (Whole Earth 'Lectronic Link), often speaks and writes about computer communication. This essay, which appeared in the Utne Reader *(March/April 1995), explores the differences and similarities between a small town in Wyoming, the "nomadic City of the Deadheads," and cyberspace.*

1 I am often asked how I went from pushing cows around a remote Wyoming ranch to my present occupation (which *The Wall Street Journal* recently described as "cyber-space cadet"). I haven't got a short answer, but I suppose I came to the virtual world looking for community.

Unlike most modern Americans, I grew up in an actual place, an entirely nonintentional community called Pinedale, Wyoming. As I struggled for nearly a generation to keep my ranch in the family, I was motivated by the belief that such places were the spiritual home of humanity. But I knew their future was not promising.

At the dawn of the 20th century, over 40 percent of the American workforce lived off the land. The majority of us lived in towns like Pinedale. Now fewer than 1 percent of us extract a living from the soil. We just became too productive for our own good.

Of course, the population followed the jobs. Farming and ranching communities are now home to a demographically insignificant percentage of Americans, the vast majority of whom live not in ranch houses but in more or less identical split-level "ranch homes" in more or less identical suburban "communities." Generica.

From John Perry Barlow, "Is There a There in Cyberspace?"

In my view, these are neither communities nor homes. I believe the combination of television and suburban population patterns is simply toxic to the soul. I see much evidence in contemporary America to support this view.

Meanwhile, back at the ranch, doom impended. And, as I watched community in Pinedale growing ill from the same economic forces that were killing my family's ranch, the Bar Cross, satellite dishes brought the cultural infection of television. I started looking around for evidence that community in America would not perish altogether.

I took some heart in the mysterious nomadic City of the Deadheads, the virtually physical town that follows the Grateful Dead around the country. The Deadheads lacked place, touching down briefly wherever the band happened to be playing, and they lacked continuity in time, since they had to suffer a new diaspora every time the band moved on or went home. But they had many of the other necessary elements of community, including a culture, a religion of sorts (which, though it lacked dogma, had most of the other, more nurturing aspects of spiritual practice), a sense of necessity, and, most importantly, shared adversity.

I wanted to know more about the flavor of their interaction, what they thought and felt, but since I wrote Dead songs (including "Estimated Prophet" and "Cassidy"), I was a minor icon to the Deadheads, and was thus inhibited, in some socially Heisenbergian way, from getting a clear view of what really went on among them.

Then, in 1987, I heard about a "place" where Deadheads gathered where I could move among them without distorting too much the field of observation. Better, this was a place I could visit without leaving Wyoming. It was a shared computer in Sausalito, California, called the Whole Earth 'Lectronic Link, or WELL. After a lot of struggling with modems, serial cables, init strings, and other computer arcana that seemed utterly out of phase with such notions as Deadheads and small towns, I found myself looking at the glowing yellow word "Login:" beyond which lay my future.

"Inside" the WELL were Deadheads in community. There were thousands of them there, gossiping, complaining (mostly about the Grateful Dead), comforting and harassing each other, bartering, engaging in religion (or at least exchanging their totemic set lists), beginning and ending love affairs, praying for one another's sick kids.

There was, it seemed, everything one might find going on in a small town, save dragging Main Street and making out on the back roads.

I was delighted. I felt I had found the new locale of human community—never mind that the whole thing was being conducted in mere words by minds from whom the bodies had been amputated. Never mind that all these people were deaf, dumb, and blind as paramecia or that their town had neither seasons nor sunsets nor smells.

Surely all these deficiencies would be remedied by richer, faster communications media. The featureless log-in handles would gradually acquire video faces (and thus expressions), shaded 3-D body puppets (and thus body language). This "space," which I recognized at once to be a primitive form of the cyberspace William Gibson predicted in his sci-fi novel *Neuromancer,* was still without apparent dimensions or vistas. But virtual reality would change all that in time.

Meanwhile, the commons, or something like it, had been rediscovered. Once again, people from the 'burbs had a place where they could encounter their friends as my fellow Pinedalians did at the post office and the Wrangler Cafe. They had a place where their hearts could remain as the companies they worked for shuffled their bodies around America. They could put down roots that could not be ripped out by forces of economic history. They had a collective stake. They had a community.

It is seven years now since I discovered the WELL. In that time, I cofounded an organization, the Electronic Frontier Foundation, dedicated to protecting its interests and those of other virtual communities like it from raids by physical government. I've spent countless hours typing away at its residents, and I've watched the larger context that contains it, the Internet, grow at such an explosive rate that, by 2004, every human on the planet will have an e-mail address unless the growth curve flattens (which it will).

15 My enthusiasm for virtuality has cooled. In fact, unless one counts interaction with the rather too large society of those with whom I exchange electronic mail, I don't spend much time engaging in virtual community at all. Many of the near-term benefits I anticipated from it seem to remain as far in the future as they did when I first logged in. Perhaps they always will.

Pinedale works, more or less, as it is, but a lot is still missing from the communities of cyberspace, whether they be places like the

WELL, the fractious newsgroups of USENET, the silent "auditoriums" of America Online, or even enclaves on the promising World Wide Web.

What is missing? Well, to quote Ranjit Makkuni of Xerox Corporation's Palo Alto Research Center, "the *prāna* is missing," *prāna* being the Hindu term for both breath and spirit. I think he is right about this and that perhaps the central question of the virtual age is whether or not *prāna* can somehow be made to fit through any disembodied medium.

Prāna is, to my mind, the literally vital element in the holy and unseen ecology of relationship, the dense mesh of invisible life, on whose surface carbon-based life floats like a thin film. It is at the heart of the fundamental and profound difference between information and experience. Jaron Lanier has said that "information is alienated experience," and, that being true, *prāna* is part of what is removed when you create such easily transmissible replicas of experience as, say, the evening news.

Obviously a great many other, less spiritual, things are also missing entirely, like body language, sex, death, tone of voice, clothing, beauty (or homeliness), weather, violence, vegetation, wildlife, pets, architecture, music, smells, sunlight, and that ol' harvest moon. In short, most of the things that make my life real to me.

Present, but in far less abundance than in the physical world, which I call "meat space," are women, children, old people, poor people, and the genuinely blind. Also mostly missing are the illiterate and the continent of Africa. There is not much human diversity in cyberspace, which is populated, as near as I can tell, by white males under 50 with plenty of computer terminal time, great typing skills, high math SATS, strongly held opinions on just about everything, and an excruciating face-to-face shyness, especially with the opposite sex.

But diversity is as essential to healthy community as it is to healthy ecosystems (which are, in my view, different from communities only in unimportant aspects).

I believe that the principal reason for the almost universal failure of the intentional communities of the '60s and '70s was a lack of diversity in their members. It was a rare commune with any old people in it, or people who were fundamentally out of philosophical agreement with the majority.

Indeed, it is the usual problem when we try to build something that can only be grown. Natural systems, such as human communities, are simply too complex to design by the engineering principles we insist on applying to them. Like Dr. Frankenstein, Western civilization is now finding its rational skills inadequate to the task of creating and caring for life. We would do better to return to a kind of agricultural mind-set in which we humbly try to re-create the conditions from which life has sprung before. And leave the rest to God.

Given that it has been built so far almost entirely by people with engineering degrees, it is not so surprising that cyberspace has the kind of overdesigned quality that leaves out all kinds of elements nature would have provided invisibly.

Also missing from both the communes of the '60s and from cyberspace are a couple of elements that I believe are very important, if not essential, to the formation and preservation of real community: an absence of alternatives and a sense of genuine adversity, generally shared. What about these?

It is hard to argue that anyone would find losing a modem literally hard to survive, while many have remained in small towns, have tolerated their intolerances and created entertainment to enliven their culturally arid lives simply because it seemed there was no choice but to stay. There are many investments—spiritual, material, and temporal—one is willing to put into a home one cannot leave. Communities are often the beneficiaries of these involuntary investments.

But when the going gets rough in cyberspace, it is even easier to move than it is in the 'burbs, where, given the fact that the average American moves some 12 times in his or her life, moving appears to be pretty easy. You can not only find another bulletin board service (BBS) or newsgroup to hang out in, you can, with very little effort, start your own.

And then there is the bond of joint suffering. Most community is a cultural stockade erected against a common enemy that can take many forms. In Pinedale, we bore together, with an understanding needing little expression, the fact that Upper Green River Valley is the coldest spot, as measured by annual mean temperature, in the lower 48 states. We knew that if somebody was stopped on the road most winter nights, he would probably die there, so the fact that we might loathe him was not sufficient reason to drive on past his broken pickup.

By the same token, the Deadheads have the Drug Enforcement Administration, which strives to give them 20-year prison terms without parole for distributing the fairly harmless sacrament of their faith. They have an additional bond in the fact that when their Microbuses die, as they often do, no one but another Deadhead is likely to stop to help them.

30 But what are the shared adversities of cyberspace? Lousy user interfaces? The flames of harsh invective? Dumb jokes? Surely these can all be survived without the sanctuary provided by fellow sufferers. 30

One is always free to yank the jack, as I have mostly done. For me, the physical world offers far more opportunity for *prāna*-rich connections with my fellow creatures. Even for someone whose body is in a state of perpetual motion, I feel I can generally find more community among the still-embodied.

Finally, there is that shyness factor. Not only are we trying to build community here among people who have never experienced any in my sense of the term, we are trying to build community among people who, in their lives, have rarely used the word *we* in a heartfelt way. It is a vast club, and many of the members—following Groucho Marx—wouldn't want to join a club that would have them.

And yet . . .

How quickly physical community continues to deteriorate. Even Pinedale, which seems to have survived the plague of ranch failures, feels increasingly cut off from itself. Many of the ranches are now owned by corporate types who fly their Gulfstreams in to fish and are rarely around during the many months when the creeks are frozen over and neighbors are needed. They have kept the ranches alive financially, but they actively discourage their managers from the interdependence my former colleagues and I require. They keep agriculture on life support, still alive but lacking a functional heart.

35 And the town has been inundated with suburbanites who flee here, bringing all their terrors and suspicions with them. They spend their evenings as they did in Orange County, watching television or socializing in hermetic little enclaves of fundamentalist Christianity that seem to separate them from us and even, given their sectarian animosities, from one another. The town remains. The community is largely a wraith of nostalgia. 35

So where else can we look for the connection we need to prevent our plunging further into the condition of separateness Nietzsche called sin? What is there to do but to dive further into the bramble bush of information that, in its broadcast forms, has done so much to tear us apart?

Cyberspace, for all its current deficiencies and failed promises, is not without some very real solace already.

Some months ago, the great love of my life, a vivid young woman with whom I intended to spend the rest of it, dropped dead of undiagnosed viral cardiomyopathy two days short of her 30th birthday. I felt as if my own heart had been as shredded as hers.

We had lived together in New York City. Except for my daughters, no one from Pinedale had met her. I needed a community to wrap around myself against colder winds than fortune had ever blown at me before. And without looking, I found I had one in the virtual world.

On the WELL, there was a topic announcing her death in one of the conferences to which I posted the eulogy I had read over her before burying her in her own small town of Nanaimo, British Columbia. It seemed to strike a chord among the disembodied living on the Net. People copied it and sent it to one another. Over the next several months I received almost a megabyte of electronic mail from all over the planet, mostly from folks whose faces I have never seen and probably never will.

They told me of their own tragedies and what they had done to survive them. As humans have since words were first uttered, we shared the second most common human experience, death, with an openheartedness that would have caused grave uneasiness in physical America, where the whole topic is so cloaked in denial as to be considered obscene. Those strangers, who had no arms to put around my shoulders, no eyes to weep with mine, nevertheless saw me through. As neighbors do.

I have no idea how far we will plunge into this strange place. Unlike previous frontiers, this one has no end. It is so dissatisfying in so many ways that I suspect we will be more restless in our search for home here than in all our previous explorations. And that is one reason why I think we may find it after all. If home is where the heart is, then there is already some part of home to be found in cyberspace.

So . . . does virtual community work or not? Should we all go off to cyberspace or should we resist it as a demonic form of symbolic abstraction? Does it supplant the real or is there, in it, reality itself?

Like so many true things, this one doesn't resolve itself to a black or a white. Nor is it gray. It is, along with the rest of life, black/white. Both/neither. I'm not being equivocal or wishy-washy here. We have to get over our Manichean sense that everything is either good or bad, and the border of cyberspace seems to me a good place to leave that old set of filters.

45 But really it doesn't matter. We are going there whether we want 45
to or not. In five years, everyone who is reading these words will have an e-mail address, other than the determined Luddites who also eschew the telephone and electricity.

When we are all together in cyberspace we will see what the human spirit, and the basic desire to connect, can create there. I am convinced that the result will be more benign if we go there open-minded, open-hearted, and excited with the adventure than if we are dragged into exile.

And we must remember that going to cyberspace, unlike previous great emigrations to the frontier, hardly requires us to leave where we have been. Many will find, as I have, a much richer appreciation of physical reality for having spent so much time in virtuality.

Despite its current (and perhaps in some areas permanent) insufficiencies, we should go to cyberspace with hope. Groundless hope, like unconditional love, may be the only kind that counts.

The Beatles: They Changed Rock, Which Changed the Culture, Which Changed US

Jeff Greenfield

Jeff Greenfield (1943–) was born in New York City. A graduate of the University of Wisconsin and Yale University School of Law, he has worked as legislative aide and speechwriter (notably for former New York City Mayor John Lindsay and for the late Senator Robert Kennedy), a television correspondent and commentator for ABC, and a syndicated columnist. His books, which frequently focus on sports, politics, and the media, include Where Have You Gone, Joe DiMaggio? *(1973),* The World's Greatest Team: A Portrait of the Boston Celtics *(1976),* Television: The First Fifty Years *(1977),* Playing to Win: An Insider's Guide to Politics *(1980),* The Real Campaign: How the Media Missed the Story of the 1980 Campaign *(1982), and* The People's Choice *(1995). He also coauthored (with Jack Newfield)* A Populist Manifesto *(1972). Greenfield contemplates the impact of the Beatles on rock, culture, and a large generation of "baby boomers" in this 1975 essay. As you read, try to identify another popular person or group that has had a similar impact on your life.*

1 They have not performed together on stage for more than eight years. They have not made a record together in five years. The formal dissolution of their partnership in a London courtroom last month was an echo of an ending that came long ago. Now each of them is seeking to overcome the shadow of a past in which

they were bound together by wealth, fame and adulation of an intensity unequaled in our culture. George Harrison scorns talk of reunion, telling us to stop living in the past. John Lennon told us years ago that "the dream is over."

He was right: When the Beatles broke up in 1970 in a welter of lawsuits and recriminations, the sixties were ending as well—in spirit as well as by the calendar. Bloodshed and bombings on campus, the harsh realities beneath the facile hopes for a "Woodstock nation," the shabby refuse of counterculture communities, all helped kill the dream.

What remains remarkable now, almost 20 years after John Lennon started playing rock 'n' roll music, more than a decade after their first worldwide conquest, is how appealing this dream was: how its vision of the world gripped so much of a generation; how that dream reshaped our recent past and affects us still. What remains remarkable is how strongly this dream was triggered, nurtured and broadened by one rock 'n' roll band of four Englishmen whose entire history as a group occurred before any of them reached the age of 30.

Their very power guarantees that an excursion into analysis cannot fully succeed. Their songs, their films, their lives formed so great a part of what we listened to and watched and talked about that everyone affected by them still sees the Beatles and hears their songs through a personal prism. And the Beatles themselves never abandoned a sense of self-parody and put-on. They were, in Richard Goldstein's phrase, "the clown-gurus of the sixties." Lennon said more than once that the Beatles sometimes put elusive references into their songs just to confuse their more solemn interpreters. "I am the egg man," they sang, not "egghead."

Still, the impact of the Beatles cannot be waved away. If the Marx they emulated was Groucho, not Karl, if their world was a playground instead of a battleground, they still changed what we listened to and how we listened to it; they helped make rock music a battering ram for the youth culture's assault on the mainstream, and that assault in turn changed our culture permanently. And if the "dream" the Beatles helped create could not sustain itself in the real world, that speaks more to our false hopes than to their promises. They wrote and sang songs. We turned it into politics and philosophy and a road map to another way of life. The Beatles grew up as children of the first generation of rock 'n' roll, listening to and imitating the music of Little

Richard, Larry Williams, Chuck Berry, Elvis Presley, and the later, more sophisticated sounds of the Shirelles and the Miracles. It was the special genius of their first mentor, Brian Epstein, to package four Liverpool working-class "rockers" as "mods," replacing their greasy hair, leather jackets, and onstage vulgarity with jackets, ties, smiles and carefully groomed, distinctive haircuts. Just as white artists filtered and softened the raw energy of black artists in the nineteen-fifties, the Beatles at first were softer, safer versions of energetic rock 'n' roll musicians. The words promised they only wanted to hold hands—the rhythm was more insistent.

By coming into prominence early in 1964, the Beatles probably saved rock 'n' roll from extinction. Rock in the early nineteen-sixties existed in name only; apart from the soul artists, it was a time of "shlock rock," with talentless media hypes like Fabian and Frankie Avalon riding the crest of the American Bandstand wave. By contrast, the Beatles provided a sense of musical energy that made successful a brilliant public-relations effort. Of course, the $50,000 used to promote the Beatles' first American appearance in February, 1964, fueled some of the early hysteria; so did the timing of their arrival.

Coming as it did less than a hundred days after the murder of John Kennedy, the advent of the Beatles caught America aching for any diversion to replace the images of a flag-draped casket and a riderless horse in the streets of Washington.

I remember a Sunday evening in early February, standing with hundreds of curious collegians in a University of Wisconsin dormitory, watching these four longhaired (!) Englishmen trying to be heard over the screams of Ed Sullivan's audience. Their music seemed to me then derivative, pleasant and bland, a mixture of hard rock and the sounds of the black groups then popular. I was convinced it would last six months, no more.

The Beatles, however, had more than hype; they had talent. Even their first hits, "I Want to Hold Your Hand," "She Loves You," "Please Please Me," "I Saw Her Standing There," had a hint of harmonies and melodies more inventive than standard rock tunes. More important, it became immediately clear that the Beatles were hipper, more complicated, than the bovine rock stars who could not seem to put four coherent words together.

In the spring of 1964, John Lennon published a book, "In His Own Write," which, instead of a ghost-written string of "groovy guides for keen teens," offered word plays, puns and black-humor satirical sketches. A few months later came the film "A Hard Day's Night," and in place of the classic let's-put-on-a-prom-and-invite-the-TeenChords plot of rock movies, the Beatles and director Richard Lester created a funny movie parodying the Beatles's own image.

I vividly recall going to that film in the midst of a National Student Association Congress: at that time, rock 'n' roll was regarded as high-school nonsense by this solemn band of student-body presidents and future C.I.A. operatives. But after the film, I sensed a feeling of goodwill and camaraderie among that handful of rock fans who had watched this movie: The Beatles were media heroes without illusion, young men glorying in their sense of play and fun, laughing at the conventions of the world. They were worth listening to and admiring.

The real surprise came at the end of 1965, with the release of the "Rubber Soul" album. Starting with that album, and continuing through "Revolver" and "Sgt. Pepper's Lonely Hearts Club Band," the Beatles began to throw away the rigid conventions of rock 'n' roll music and lyrics. The banal abstract, second-hand emotions were replaced with sharp, sometimes mordant portraits of first-hand people and experiences, linked to music that was more complicated and more compelling than rock had ever dared attempt. The Beatles were drawing on their memories and feelings, not those cut from Tin Pan Alley cloth.

"Norwegian Wood" was about an unhappy, inconclusive affair ("I once had a girl/or should I say/she once had me"). "Michelle" and "Yesterday" were haunting, sentimental ballads, and Paul McCartney dared sing part of "Michelle" in French—most rock singers regarded English as a foreign language. "Penny Lane" used cornets to evoke the suggestion of a faintly heard band concert on a long-ago summer day. Staccato strings lent urgency to the story of "Eleanor Rigby."

These songs were different from the rock music that our elders had scorned with impunity. Traditionally, rock 'n' roll was rigidly structured: 4/4 tempo, 32 bars, with a limited range of instruments. Before the Beatles, rock producer Phil Spector had revolutionized records by adding strings to the drums, bass, sax and guitar, but the chord structure was usually limited to a basic blues or ballad pattern. Now the Beatles, with the kind of visibility that made them impossible to ignore, were expanding the range of rock, musically and lyrically. A sitar—a harpsichord effect—a ragtime piano—everything was possible.

15 With the release of "Sgt. Pepper" in the spring of 1967, the era of rock as a strictly adolescent phenomenon was gone. One song, "A Day in the Life," with its recital of an ordinary day combined with a dreamlike sense of dread and anxiety, made it impossible to ignore the skills of Lennon and McCartney. A decade earlier, Steve Allen mocked the inanity of rock by reading "Hound Dog" or "Tutti-Frutti" as if they were serious attempts at poetry. Once "Sgt. Pepper" was recorded, *Partisan Review* was lauding the Beatles, Ned Rorem proclaimed that "She's Leaving Home" was "equal to any song Schubert ever wrote," and a *Newsweek* critic meant it when he wrote: " 'Strawberry Fields Forever' [is] a superb Beatleizing of hope and despair in which the four minstrels regretfully recommend a Keatsian lotus-land of withdrawal from the centrifugal stresses of the age."

"We're so well established," McCartney had said in 1966, "that we can bring fans along with us and stretch the limits of pop." By using their fame to help break through the boundaries of rock, the Beatles proved that they were not the puppets of backstage manipulation or payola or hysterical 14-year-olds. Instead, they helped make rock music *the* music of an entire international generation. Perhaps for the first time in history, it was possible to say that tens of millions of people, defined simply by age, were all doing the same thing: they were listening to rock 'n' roll. That fact changed the popular culture of the world.

Rock 'n' roll's popularity had never been accompanied by respectability, even among the young. For those of us with intellectual pretenses, rock 'n' roll was like masturbation: exciting, but shameful. The culturally alienated went in for cool jazz, and folk music was the vehicle for the politically active minority. (The growth of political interest at the start of the sixties sparked something of a folk revival.)

Along with the leap of Bob Dylan into rock music, the Beatles destroyed this division. Rock 'n' roll was now broad enough, free enough, to encompass every kind of feeling. Its strength had always been rooted in the sexual energy of its rhythms; in that sense, the outraged parents who had seen rock as a threat to their children's virtue were right. Rock 'n' roll made you want to move and shake and get physically excited. The Beatles proved that this energy could be fused with a sensibility more subtle than the "let's-go-down-to-the-gym-and-beat-up-the-Coke-machine" quality of rock music.

In 1965, Barry McGuire recorded the first "rock protest" song (excluding the teen complaints of the Coasters and Chuck Berry). In his "Eve of Destruction," we heard references to Red China, Selma, Alabama, nuclear war and middle-class hypocrisy pounded out to heavy rock rythms. That same year came a flood of "good time" rock music, with sweet, haunting melodies by groups like the Lovin' Spoonful and the Mamas and the Papas. There *were* no limits to what could be done; and the market was continually expanding.

The teenagers of the nineteen-fifties had become the young adults of the nineteen-sixties, entering the professions, bringing with them a cultural frame of reference shaped in good measure by rock 'n' roll. The "youth" market was enormous—the flood of babies born during and just after World War II made the under-25 population group abnormally large; their tastes were more influential than ever before. And because the music had won acceptability, rock 'n' roll was not judged indulgently as a "boys will be boys" fad. Rock music was expressing a sensibility about the tangible world—about sensuality, about colors and sensations, about the need to change consciousness. And this sensibility soon spilled over into other arenas.

Looking back on the last half of the last decade, it is hard to think of a cultural innovation that did not carry with it the influence of rock music, and of the Beatles in particular: the miniskirt, discothèques, the graphics of Peter Max, the birth of publications like *Rolling Stone,* the "mindbending" effects of TV commercials, the success of "Laugh-In" on television and "Easy Rider" in the movies—all of these cultural milestones owe something to the emergence of rock music as the most compelling and pervasive force in our culture.

This is especially true of the incredible spread of drugs—marijuana and the hallucinogens most particularly—among the youth culture. From "Rubber Soul" through "Sgt. Pepper," Beatle music was suffused with a sense of mystery and mysticism: odd choral progressions, mysterious instruments, dreamlike effects, and images that did not seem to yield to "straight" interpretation. Whether specific songs ("Lucy in the Sky with Diamonds," "A Little Help From My Friends") were deliberately referring to drugs is beside the point. The Beatles were publicly recounting their LSD experiences, and their music was replete with antirational sensibility. Indeed, it was a commonplace among my contemporaries that Beatle albums could not be understood fully without the use of drugs. For "Rubber Soul," marijuana; for "Sgt. Pepper," acid. When the Beatles told us to turn off our minds and float downstream, uncounted youngsters assumed that the key to this kind of mind-expansion could be found in a plant or a pill. Together with "head" groups like Jefferson Airplane and the Grateful Dead, the Beatles were, consciously or not, a major influence behind the spread of drugs.

In this sense, the Beatles are part of a chain: (1) the Beatles opened up rock; (2) rock changed the culture; (3) the culture changed us. Even limited to their impact as musicians, however, the Beatles were as powerful an influence as any group or individual; only Bob Dylan stands as their equal. They never stayed with a successful formula; they were always moving. By virtue of their fame, the Beatles were a giant amplifier, spreading "the word" on virtually every trend and mood of the last decade.

They were never pure forerunners. The Yardbirds used the sitar before the Beatles; the Beach Boys were experimenting with studio enhancement first; the Four Seasons were using elaborate harmonies before the Beatles. They were never as contemptuously antimiddle-class or decadent as the Kinks or the Rolling Stones; never as lyrically compelling as Dylan; never as musically brilliant as the Band; never as hallucinogenic as the San Francisco groups. John Gabree, one of the most perceptive of the early rock writers, said that "their job, and they have done it well, has been to travel a few miles behind the avant-garde, consolidating gains and popularizing new ideas."

Yet this very willingness meant that new ideas did not struggle and die in obscurity; instead, they touched a hundred million minds. Their songs reflected the widest range of mood of any group of their time. Their openness created a kind of salon for a whole generation of people, idea exchange into which the youth of the world was wired. It was almost inevitable that, even against their will, their listeners shaped a dream of politics and lifestyle from the substance of popular music. It is testament both to the power of rock music, and to the illusions which can be spun out of impulses.

The Beatles were not political animals. Whatever they have done since going their separate ways, their behavior as a group reflected cheerful anarchy more than political rebellion. Indeed, as editorialists, they were closer to *The Wall Street Journal* than to *Ramparts.* "Taxman" assaults the heavy progressive income tax ("one for you, 19 for me"), and "Revolution" warned that "if you go carrying pictures of Chairman Mao/you ain't gonna make it with anyone anyhow."

The real political impact of the Beatles was not in any four-point program or in an attack on injustice or the war in Vietnam. It was instead in the counterculture they had helped to create. Somewhere in the nineteen-sixties, millions of people began to regard themselves as a class separate from mainstream society *by virtue of their youth and the sensibility that youth produced.*

The nineteen-fifties had produced the faintest hint of such an attitude in the defensive love of rock 'n' roll; if our parents hated it, it had to be good. The sixties had expanded this vague idea into a battle cry. "Don't trust anyone over 30!"—shouted from a police car in the first massive student protest of the decade at Berkeley—suggested an outlook in which the mere aging process was an act of betrayal in which youth itself was a moral value. *Time* magazine made the "under-25 generation" its Man of the Year in 1967, and politicians saw in the steadily escalating rebellion among the middle-class young a constituency and a scapegoat.

The core value of this "class" was not peace or social injustice; it was instead a more elusive value, reflected by much of the music and by the Beatles' own portrait of themselves. It is expressed best by a scene from their movie "Help!" in which John, Paul, George and Ringo enter four adjoining row houses. The doors open—and suddenly the scene shifts inside, and we see that these "houses" are in fact one huge house; the four Beatles instantly reunite.

It is this sense of commonality that was at the heart of the youth culture. It is what we wished to believe about the Beatles, and about the possibilities in our own lives. If there is one sweeping statement that makes sense about the children of the last decade, it is that the generation born of World War II was saying "no" to the atomized lives their parents had so feverishly sought. The most cherished value of the counterculture—preached if not always practiced—was its insistence on sharing, communality, a rejection of the retreat into private satisfaction. Rock 'n' roll was the magnet, the driving force, of a shared celebration. From Alan Freed's first mammoth dance parties in Cleveland in 1951, to the Avalon Ballroom in San Francisco, to the be-ins in our big cities, to Woodstock itself. Spontaneous gathering was the ethic: Don't plan it, don't think about it, *do* it—you'll get by with a little help from your friends.

In their music, their films, their sense of play, the Beatles reflected this dream of a ceaseless celebration. If there *was* any real "message" in their songs, it was the message of Charles Reich: that the world would be changed by changing the consciousness of the new generation. "All you need is love," they sang. "Say the word [love] and you'll be free." "Let it be." "Everything's gonna be all right."

As a state of mind, it was a pleasant fantasy. As a way of life, it was doomed to disaster. The thousands of young people who flocked to California or to New York's Lower East Side to join the love generation found the world filled with people who did not share the ethic of mutual trust. The politicization of youth as a class helped to divide natural political allies and make politics more vulnerable to demagogues. As the Beatles found in their own personal and professional lives, the practical outside world has a merciless habit of intruding into fantasies; somebody has to pay the bills and somebody has to do the dishes in the commune and somebody has to protect us from the worst instincts of other human beings. John Lennon was expressing some very painful lessons when he told *Rolling Stone* shortly after the group's breakup that "nothing happened except we all dressed up . . . the same bastards are in control, the same people are runnin' everything."

On the Fear of Death

Elisabeth Kübler-Ross

Elisabeth Kübler-Ross (1926–2004) was born in Zurich, Switzerland. She received an M.D. from the University of Zurich (1957); served residencies in psychiatry at Manhattan State, Montefiore, and Colorado General hospitals; taught at the University of Chicago; and directed a center for terminal patients in rural Virginia. Her pivotal book, On Death and Dying *(1969), changed the manner in which the medical profession views terminally ill patients and prompted medical schools to add courses on death. Other books by Kübler-Ross include* Questions and Answers on Death and Dying *(1974),* Death: The Final Stage of Growth *(1975),* To Live Until We Say Goodbye *(1978),* Working it Through *(1982),* On Childhood and Death *(1985),* AIDS: The Ultimate Challenge *(1987), and* Death Is of Vital Importance: On Life, Death, and Life After Death *(1995). Kübler-Ross has been a leader in the hospice movement. In this essay, she argues that advances in science and the mindset of today's civilized society combine to make natural death something to be shunned and feared.*

Let me not pray to be sheltered from dangers but to be fearless in facing them.

Let me not beg for the stilling of my pain but for the heart to conquer it.

Let me not look for allies in life's battlefield but to my own strength.

Let me not crave in anxious fear to be saved but hope for the patience to win my freedom.

Grant me that I may not be a coward, feeling your mercy in my success alone; but let me find the grasp of your hand in my failure.

Rabindranath Tagore,
Fruit-Gathering

1 Epidemics have taken a great toll of lives in past generations. Death 1
in infancy and early childhood was frequent and there were few families who didn't lose a member of the family at an early age. Medicine has changed greatly in the last decades. Widespread vaccinations have practically eradicated many illnesses, at least in western Europe and the United States. The use of chemotherapy, especially the antibiotics, has contributed to an ever decreasing number of fatalities in infectious diseases. Better child care and education have effected a low morbidity and mortality among children. The many diseases that have taken an impressive toll among the young and middle-aged have been conquered. The number of old people is on the rise, and with this fact come the number of people with malignancies and chronic diseases associated more with old age.

Pediatricians have less work with acute and life-threatening situations as they have an ever increasing number of patients with psychosomatic disturbances and adjustment and behavior problems. Physicians have more people in their waiting rooms with emotional problems than they have ever had before, but they also have more elderly patients who not only try to live with their decreased physical abilities and limitations but who also face loneliness and isolation with all its pains and anguish. The majority of these people are not seen by a psychiatrist. Their needs have to be elicited and gratified by other professional people, for instance, chaplains and social workers. It is for them that I am trying to outline the changes that have taken place in the last few decades, changes that are ultimately responsible for the increased fear of death, the rising number of emotional problems, and the greater need for understanding of and coping with the problems of death and dying.

When we look back in time and study old cultures and people, we are impressed that death has always been distasteful to man and will probably always be. From a psychiatrist's point of view this is very understandable and can perhaps best be explained by our basic knowledge that, in our unconscious, death is never possible in regard to ourselves. It is inconceivable for our unconscious to imagine an actual ending of our own life here on earth, and if this life of ours had to end, the ending is always attributed to a malicious intervention from the outside by someone else. In simple terms, in our unconscious mind we can only be killed; it is inconceivable to die of a natural cause or of old age. Therefore death in itself is associated with a bad act, a frightening happening, something that in itself calls for retribution and punishment.

One is wise to remember these fundamental facts as they are essential in understanding some of the most important, otherwise unintelligible communications of our patients.

The second fact that we have to comprehend is that in our unconscious mind we cannot distinguish between a wish and a deed. We are all aware of some of our illogical dreams in which two completely opposite statements can exist side by side—very acceptable in our dreams but unthinkable and illogical in our wakening state. Just as our unconscious mind cannot differentiate between the wish to kill somebody in anger and the act of having done so, the young child is unable to make this distinction. The child who angrily wishes his mother to drop dead for not having gratified his needs will be traumatized greatly by the actual death of his mother—even if this event is not linked closely in time with his destructive wishes. He will always take part or the whole blame for the loss of his mother. He will always say to himself—rarely to others—"I did it, I am responsible, I was bad, therefore Mommy left me." It is well to remember that the child will react in the same manner if he loses a parent by divorce, separation, or desertion. Death is often seen by a child as an impermanent thing and has therefore little distinction from a divorce in which he may have an opportunity to see a parent again.

Many a parent will remember remarks of their children such as, "I will bury my doggy now and next spring when the flowers come up again, he will get up." Maybe it was the same wish that motivated the ancient Egyptians to supply their dead with food and goods to keep them happy and the old American Indians to bury their relatives with their belongings.

When we grow older and begin to realize that our omnipotence is really not so omnipotent, that our strongest wishes are not powerful enough to make the impossible possible, the fear that we have contributed to the death of a loved one diminishes—and with it the guilt.

The fear remains diminished, however, only so long as it is not challenged too strongly. Its vestiges can be seen daily in hospital corridors and in people associated with the bereaved.

A husband and wife may have been fighting for years, but when the partner dies, the survivor will pull his hair, whine and cry louder and beat his chest in regret, fear and anguish, and will hence fear his own death more than before, still believing in the law of talion—an eye for an eye, a tooth for a tooth—"I am responsible for her death, I will have to die a pitiful death in retribution."

Maybe this knowledge will help us understand many of the old customs and rituals which have lasted over the centuries and whose purpose is to diminish the anger of the gods or the people as the case may be, thus decreasing the anticipated punishment. I am thinking of the ashes, the torn clothes, the veil, the *Klage Weiber* of the old days—they are all means to ask you to take pity on them, the mourners, and are expressions of sorrow, grief, and shame. If someone grieves, beats his chest, tears his hair, or refuses to eat, it is an attempt at self-punishment to avoid or reduce the anticipated punishment for the blame that he takes on the death of a loved one.

10 This grief, shame, and guilt are not very far removed from feelings of anger and rage. The process of grief always includes some qualities of anger. Since none of us likes to admit anger at a deceased person, these emotions are often disguised or repressed and prolong the period of grief or show up in other ways. It is well to remember that it is not up to us to judge such feelings as bad or shameful but to understand their true meaning and origin as something very human. In order to illustrate this I will again use the example of the child—and the child in us. The five-year-old who loses his mother is both blaming himself for her disappearance and being angry at her for having deserted him and for no longer gratifying his needs. The dead person then turns into something the child loves and wants very much but also hates with equal intensity for this severe deprivation.

The ancient Hebrews regarded the body of a dead person as something unclean and not to be touched. The early American Indians talked about the evil spirits and shot arrows in the air to drive the spirits away. Many other cultures have rituals to take care of the "bad" dead person, and they all originate in this feeling of anger which still exists in all of us, though we dislike admitting it. The tradition of the tombstone may originate in this wish to keep the bad spirits deep down in the ground, and the pebbles that many mourners put on the grave are left-over symbols of the same wish. Though we call the firing of guns at military funerals a last salute, it is the same symbolic ritual as the Indian used when he shot his spears and arrows into the skies.

I give these examples to emphasize that man has not basically changed. Death is still a fearful, frightening happening, and the fear of death is a universal fear even if we think we have mastered it on many levels.

What has changed is our way of coping and dealing with death and dying and our dying patients.

Having been raised in a country in Europe where science is not so advanced, where modern techniques have just started to find their way into medicine, and where people still live as they did in this country half a century ago, I may have had an opportunity to study a part of the evolution of mankind in a shorter period.

I remember as a child the death of a farmer. He fell from a tree and was not expected to live. He asked simply to die at home, a wish that was granted without questioning. He called his daughters into the bedroom and spoke with each one of them alone for a few moments. He arranged his affairs quietly, though he was in great pain, and distributed his belongings and his land, none of which was to be split until his wife should follow him in death. He also asked each of his children to share in the work, duties, and tasks that he had carried on until the time of the accident. He asked his friends to visit him once more, to bid good-bye to them. Although I was a small child at the time, he did not exclude me or my siblings. We were allowed to share in the preparations of the family just as we were permitted to grieve with them until he died. When he did die, he was left at home, in his own beloved home which he had built, and among his friends and neighbors who went to take a last look at him where he lay in the midst of flowers in the place he had lived in and loved so much. In that country today there is still no make-believe slumber room, no embalming, no false makeup to pretend sleep. Only the signs of very disfiguring illnesses are covered up with bandages and only infectious cases are removed from the home prior to the burial.

Why do I describe such "old-fashioned" customs? I think they are an indication of our acceptance of a fatal outcome, and they help the dying patient as well as his family to accept the loss of a loved one. If a patient is allowed to terminate his life in the familiar and beloved environment, it requires less adjustment for him. His own family knows him well enough to replace a sedative with a glass of his favorite wine; or the smell of a home-cooked soup may give him the appetite to sip a few spoons of fluid which, I think, is still more enjoyable than an infusion. I will not minimize the need for sedatives and infusions and realize full well from my own experience as a country doctor that they are sometimes life-saving and often unavoidable. But I also know that patience and familiar people and foods could replace many a bottle of intravenous fluids given for the simple reason that it fulfills the physiological need without involving too many people and/or individual nursing care.

The fact that children are allowed to stay at home where a fatality has stricken and are included in the talk, discussions, and fears gives them the feeling that they are not alone in the grief and gives them the comfort of shared responsibility and shared mourning. It prepares them gradually and helps them view death as part of life, an experience which may help them grow and mature.

This is in great contrast to a society in which death is viewed as taboo, discussion of it is regarded as morbid, and children are excluded with the presumption and pretext that it would be "too much" for them. They are then sent off to relatives, often accompanied with some unconvincing lies of "Mother has gone on a long trip" or other unbelievable stories. The child senses that something is wrong, and his distrust in adults will only multiply if other relatives add new variations of the story, avoid his questions or suspicions, shower him with gifts as a meager substitute for a loss he is not permitted to deal with. Sooner or later the child will become aware of the changed family situation and, depending on the age and personality of the child, will have an unresolved grief and regard this incident as a frightening, mysterious, in any case very traumatic experience with untrustworthy grownups, which he has no way to cope with.

It is equally unwise to tell a little child who lost her brother that God loved little boys so much that he took little Johnny to heaven. When this little girl grew up to be a woman she never solved her anger at God, which resulted in a psychotic depression when she lost her own little son three decades later.

We would think that our great emancipation, our knowledge of science and of man, has given us better ways and means to prepare ourselves and our families for this inevitable happening. Instead the days are gone when a man was allowed to die in peace and dignity in his own home.

The more we are making advancements in science, the more we seem to fear and deny the reality of death. How is this possible?

We use euphemisms, we make the dead look as if they were asleep, we ship the children off to protect them from the anxiety and turmoil around the house if the patient is fortunate enough to die at home, we don't allow children to visit their dying parents in the hospitals, we have long and controversial discussions about whether patients should be told the truth—a question that rarely arises when the dying person is tended by the family physician who has known him from delivery to death and who knows the weaknesses and strengths of each member of the family.

I think there are many reasons for this flight away from facing death calmly. One of the most important facts is that dying nowadays is more gruesome in many ways, namely, more lonely, mechanical, and dehumanized; at times it is even difficult to determine technically when the time of death has occurred.

Dying becomes lonely and impersonal because the patient is often taken out of his familiar environment and rushed to an emergency room. Whoever has been very sick and has required rest and comfort especially may recall his experience of being put on a stretcher and enduring the noise of the ambulance siren and hectic rush until the hospital gates open. Only those who have lived through this may appreciate the discomfort and cold necessity of such transportation which is only the beginning of a long order—hard to endure when you are well, difficult to express in words when noise, light, pumps, and voices are all too much to put up with. It may well be that we might consider more the patient under the sheets and blankets and perhaps stop our well-meant efficiency and rush in order to hold the patient's hand, to smile, or to listen to a question. I include the trip to the hospital as the first episode in dying, as it is for many. I am putting it exaggeratedly in contrast to the sick man who is left at home—not to say that lives should not be saved if they can be saved by a hospitalization but to keep the focus on the patient's experience, his needs and his reactions.

When a patient is severely ill, he is often treated like a person with no right to an opinion. It is often someone else who makes the decision if and when and where a patient should be hospitalized. It would take so little to remember that the sick person too has feelings, has wishes and opinions, and has—most important of all—the right to be heard.

Well, our presumed patient has now reached the emergency room. He will be surrounded by busy nurses, orderlies, interns, residents, a lab technician perhaps who will take some blood, an electrocardiogram technician who takes the cardiogram. He may be moved to X-ray and he will overhear opinions of his condition and discussions and questions to members of the family. He slowly but surely is beginning to be treated like a thing. He is no longer a person. Decisions are made often without his opinion. If he tries to rebel he will be sedated and after hours of waiting and wondering whether he has the strength, he will be wheeled into the operating room or intensive treatment unit and become an object of great concern and great financial investment.

He may cry for rest, peace, and dignity, but he will get infusions, transfusions, a heart machine, or tracheotomy if necessary. He may want one single person to stop for one single minute so that he can ask one single question—but he will get a dozen people around the clock, all busily preoccupied with his heart rate, pulse, electrocardiogram or pulmonary functions, his secretions or excretions but not with him as a human being. He may wish to fight it all but it is going to be a useless fight since all this is done in the fight for his life, and if they can save his life they can consider the person afterwards. Those who consider the person first may lose precious time to save his life! At least this seems to be the rationale or justification behind all this—or is it? Is the reason for this increasingly mechanical, depersonalized approach our own defensiveness? Is this approach our own way to cope with and repress the anxieties that a terminally or critically ill patient evokes in us? Is our concentration on equipment, on blood pressure, our desperate attempt to deny the impending death which is so frightening and discomforting to us that we displace all our knowledge onto machines, since they are less close to us than the suffering face of another human being which would remind us once more of our lack of omnipotence, our own limits and failures, and last but not least perhaps our own mortality?

Maybe the question has to be raised: Are we becoming less human or more human? . . . [I]t is clear that whatever the answer may be, the patient is suffering more—not physically, perhaps, but emotionally. And his needs have not changed over the centuries, only our ability to gratify them.